British Library Occasional Papers 1

Canadian Studies

Papers presented at a colloquium
at the British Library
17–19 August 1983

Edited by Patricia McLaren-Turner

The British Library 1984

© 1984 The Contributors

Published by
The British Library
Reference Division Publications
Great Russell Street
London WC1B 3DG

British Library Cataloguing in Publication Data

Canadian studies: papers presented at a
 colloquium at the British Library 17–19
 August 1983.–(British Library occasional papers; 1)
 1. Information services—Canada 2. Canada
 —Study and teaching—Bibliography
 I. McLaren-Turner, Patricia II. Series
 971'.007 AG531.C3

ISBN 0-7123-0039-2

Designed by Alan Bartram
Typeset by Herts Typesetting Services Ltd.
Printed in England by Adlard & Son Ltd., Dorking

British Library Occasional Papers 1

Canadian Studies

Contents

Editor's Preface	Patricia McLaren-Turner	vii
List of participants		viii
List of abbreviations		xii
Introduction	Alex Wilson	xiii
The British Library Collections and Canadian Studies	Ian R Willison	1
Discussion		10
A Canadian perspective on Canadian Studies: 1	Thomas H B Symons	11
A Canadian perspective on Canadian Studies: 2	James E Page	19
A perspective on advanced research in Canadian Studies in the United Kingdom	Cedric May	27
Observations on the Case for Canadian Studies in the United Kingdom	Ged Martin	41
The British Copying and Acquisition Programme of the Public Archives of Canada	Bruce G Wilson	45
Resources for advanced research in Canadian Studies in the British Library Reference Division: archival materials	Daniel P Waley	55
Resources for advanced research in Canadian Studies in the British Library Reference Division: maps	Helen Wallis	59
Resources for advanced research in Canadian Studies in the British Library Reference Division: official publications	Geoffrey Hamilton	67
Resources for advanced research in Canadian Studies in the British Library Reference Division: Quebec and French Canadian printed materials	Lawrence Le R Dethan	73
Resources for advanced research in Canadian Studies in the British Library Reference Division: newspapers (A summary)	Stephen P Green	81

Canadiana deposited in the British Museum Library between 1895 and 1924	Patrick B O'Neill	83
Checklist of Canadian copyright deposits 1895 to 1924 in the British Museum Library: a note on format	John R T Ettlinger	91
The British Library Lending Division and Canadian Studies	Keith Barr	93
A Guide to Resources for Canadian Studies in Britain	Valerie Bloomfield	97
Material on Canada in the Foreign and Commonwealth Office Library	Martin Callow	101
Note on the National Sound Archive		107
Discussion		109
Bibliographic access for Canadian Studies: overview of current developments in Canada	Anne B Piternick	111
The Dictionary of Canadian Biography/ Dictionnaire biographique du Canada	Francess G Halpenny	133
Canada's Retrospective National Bibliography	Hope E A Clement	145
La Bibliographie du Québec, 1764–1967	Louise Filion	155
A Descriptive Bibliography of Upper Canada Imprints, 1801–1841	Patricia L Fleming	165
Canada's printed heritage – a microfiche collection and preservation project; the work of the Canadian Institute for Historical Microreproductions	Ernest B Ingles	171
Note on the Eighteenth-Century Short-Title Catalogue		181
The Centre for Editing Early Canadian Texts and other projects, actual and ideal	John M Robson	183
The history of the book in Canada and British research resources	Richard Landon	187
Concluding remarks and proposals for future cooperation	Guy Sylvestre	189
List of British Library items exhibited: books		195
List of British Library items exhibited: maps		199
List of British Library items exhibited: philatelic material		203
List of British Library items exhibited: photographs		205

Editor's Preface
Patricia McLaren-Turner

This Colloquium was held in the British Library in London on 17–19 August 1983. The first two days encompassed a full programme of papers and discussions and concluded with a reception at Canada House, kindly arranged by the Canadian High Commission and attended by Mr John Graham, Minister, Cultural and Public Affairs. On the third day, participants were given the opportunity to visit various areas of the Reference Division, to meet the staff and discuss matters of mutual interest on an informal basis and to view a display of Canadian items in the British Library Collections, including books, maps, philatelic material and photographs.

The papers are set out in these *Proceedings* in the order in which they were presented. In some cases, the speakers summarised their papers at the Colloquium itself; in some other cases, revised versions of the papers were subsequently submitted for publication. Notes on the discussions and for the linking summaries were taken by Messrs James Egles and Ron Ramdin and by myself. The details given in the List of Participants are those current at the time of the Colloquium.

I would like to thank all my colleagues who assisted with the Colloquium, particularly those who presented papers and those who took part in the visits and meetings on the final day. I am especially grateful to Messrs Derek Sawyer, James Egles, S N Lal and Ron Ramdin of the North American Section for their help before, during and after the event, to Mr David Way, BL Publications Editor, for his advice on the *Proceedings* and to Mr Alex Wilson, Director General, for his active interest and support.

List of Participants

Dr Robin Alston	Editor-in-Chief, Eighteenth-Century Short-Title Catalogue, British Library Reference Division
Dr Keith Barr	Executive Director, British Library Lending Division
Mr Alan Bell	Librarian, Rhodes House Library, Oxford
Miss E C Blayney	Head, Library and Records Department, Foreign and Commonwealth Office
Mrs Valerie Bloomfield	c/o Institute of Commonwealth Studies, University of London
Professor Geoffrey Bolton	Director, Australian Studies Centre, University of London
M Jean-Rémi Brault	Conservateur en Chef, Bibliothèque nationale du Québec
Mrs Anita Burdett	Archivist, London Office, Public Archives of Canada
Mr Martin Callow	Library and Records Department, Foreign and Commonwealth Office
Mr David Cameron	Assistant Under-Secretary of State (Education), Canada
Mme Monique Charbonneau	La directrice, Bibliothèque administrative, Gouvernement du Québec
Mr Derek Clarke	Librarian, British Library of Political and Economic Science
Miss Hope E A Clement	Associate National Librarian of Canada
Ms Judy Collingwood	Academic Relations Division, Canadian High Commission
Mrs Margaret Cooter	London, (researcher: British Library Canadian copyright project)
Mr Dennis Cox	Librarian, University of Leeds
Mr Lawrence Le R Dethan	Head, French Section, British Library Reference Division
Professor David N Dilks	School of History, University of Leeds
Mr James D Egles	North American Section, British Library Reference Division

Professor John R T Ettlinger	School of Library Service, University of Dalhousie
Mme Louise Filion	Responsable du Bureau de la bibliographie rétrospective, Bibliothèque nationale du Québec
Professor Patricia Fleming	Faculty of Library and Information Science, University of Toronto
Mrs Audrey Forster	Secretary, Social Sciences and Humanities Research Council of Canada
Mr Robert J Fulford	Keeper, Department of Printed Books, British Library Reference Division
Mr Stephen Green	Head, Newspaper Library, British Library Reference Division
Professor Francess Halpenny	General Editor, Dictionary of Canadian Biography/Dictionnaire biographique du Canada
Mr Geoffrey Hamilton	Head, Official Publications Library, British Library Reference Division
Mr Harry Hannam	Librarian, Foreign and Commonwealth Office
Mr Michael Hellyer	Academic Relations Officer, Canadian High Commission
Mlle Heuzey	Gouvernement du Québec Délégation Générale de Londres
Mrs Ann House	Librarian, Canadian High Commission
Mrs Alexia Howe	Assistant Keeper, National Library of Scotland
Mr Ernest B Ingles	Director, Canadian Institute for Historical Microreproductions
Rev Dr Frederick Jones	Treasurer BACS; Dorset Institute of Higher Education
Miss Margaret Julian	Library, Royal Institute of International Affairs, London
Mr S N Lal	North American Section, British Library Reference Division

Mr Richard Landon	Head, Thomas Fisher Rare Books Library, University of Toronto
Mrs Patricia M Larby	Librarian, Institute of Commonwealth Studies, University of London
M Levigueur	Public Affairs Adviser, Gouvernement du Québec Délégation Générale de Londres
Dr Peter Lyon	Secretary, Institute of Commonwealth Studies, University of London
Mrs Patricia McLaren-Turner	Head, North American Section, British Library Reference Division
Dr Ged Martin	Director-Designate, Centre of Canadian Studies, University of Edinburgh
Mr Cedric R P May	President BACS; Department of French, University of Birmingham
Mr Peter Meade	Head, Modern British Section, British Library Reference Division
Dr Robert Montague	Bibliographer, Canadian Institute for Historical Microreproductions
Mr O W Neighbour	Music Librarian, British Library Reference Division
Mr William A Noblett	Head, Official Publications Department, Cambridge University Library
Dr Patrick B O'Neill	Mount Saint Vincent University, Halifax
Mr James E Page	Special Advisor on Canadian Studies, Department of the Secretary of State, Canada
Professor Anne B Piternick	School of Librarianship, University of British Columbia
Mr David Prichard-Jones	London
Mrs Alison Quinn	Liverpool
Professor David B Quinn	Liverpool and St Mary's College of Maryland
Mr Ron Ramdin	North American Section, British Library Reference Division
Professor John M Robson	Department of English, Victoria College, University of Toronto

Mr Derek A Sawyer	North American Section, British Library Reference Division
Miss Marilyn J Sharrow	Chief Librarian, University of Toronto Library
Mr Donald H Simpson	Vice-President BACS; Librarian, Royal Commonwealth Society
Mr Murray C T Simpson	Assistant Librarian, Edinburgh University Library
Dr Guy Sylvestre	National Librarian of Canada
Professor Thomas H B Symons	Chairman of the Commission on Canadian Studies; Vice-President, Social Sciences and Humanities Research Council of Canada
Mrs Hazel D Talbot	Libraries Department, The British Council
Mr Jonathan Vickers	National Sound Archive, British Library
Dr Daniel Waley	Keeper, Department of Manuscripts, British Library Reference Division
Dr Helen Wallis	Map Librarian, British Library Reference Division
Professor Germaine Warkentin	Department of English, Victoria College, University of Toronto
Mr Ian R Willison	Head, English Language Branch, British Library Reference Division
Mr Alex Wilson	Director General, British Library Reference Division
Dr Bruce G Wilson	Chief, London Office, Public Archives of Canada
Mr Peter Winkworth	London and Montreal

List of abbreviations

AACR 1/2	Anglo-American Cataloguing Rules 1/2
ACQL	Association for Canadian and Quebec Literatures
ACSI	Association for Canadian Studies in Ireland
ACSUS	Association for Canadian Studies in the United States
ANZACS	Australian and New Zealand Association for Canadian Studies
BACS	British Association for Canadian Studies
BBC	British Broadcasting Corporation
BL	British Library
BLAISE	British Library automated information service
BLLD	British Library Lending Division
BLRD	British Library Reference Division
BNQ	Bibliothèque nationale du Québec
CANMARC	Canadian MAchine Readable Catalogue
CBC	Canadian Broadcasting Corporation
CBISSSH	Committee on Bibliography and Information Services for the Social Sciences and the Humanities
CEECT	Centre for the Editing of Early Canadian Texts
CIHM	Canadian Institute for Historical Microreproductions
CISTI	Canadian Institute for Scientific and Technical Information
CLA	Canadian Library Association
CONSER	Conversion of Serials Project
CRIAW	Canadian Research Institute for the Advancement of Women
CTA	Canadian Telebook Agency
DCB/DBC	Dictionary of Canadian Biography/Dictionnaire biographique du Canada
ESTC	Eighteenth-Century Short-Title Catalogue
FCO	Foreign and Commonwealth Office
HMSO	Her Majesty's Stationery Office
ICCS	International Council for Canadian Studies
IFLA	International Federation of Library Associations
ISBD(M)	International Standard Bibliographic Description for Monographic Publications
MARC	MAchine Readable Catalogue
NAIP	North American Imprints Program
NMC	National Map Collection
OCLC	Ohio College Library Center
ODA	Overseas Development Administration
OPL	Official Publications Library (British Library)
PAC	Public Archives of Canada
PRO	Public Record Office
RETRO	Retrospective National Bibliography of Canada
SSHRCC	Social Sciences and Humanities Research Council of Canada
UTLAS	University of Toronto Library Automation Systems

Alex Wilson

Introduction

The British Library is currently reviewing its collection and service policies in key areas. One question is to define the role of the 'National Printed Archive' in relation to Britain's historical position as an imperial power and the associated development of English as the principal world language.

Following a successful one-day meeting on American Studies, Canada seemed the obvious successor, not least because of the strong support which the Canadian Government has provided to Canadian Studies, both at home and overseas. Conscious of the excellent conferences which have been held in Vancouver 1974, Dalhousie 1981, and Edinburgh 1981, we were somewhat diffident about engaging the attendance of academics, bibliographers, librarians and archivists from both countries, and yet this was essential to create a context for our discussion of Library policy. Yet we were aware of the extent to which scholars of Canadian history and culture must depend on the Library and were convinced that national and international cooperation of librarians and archivists is essential for the undertaking of major retrospective cataloguing, microfilming and preservation programmes.

Informal discussions at IFLA in Montreal, in August 1982, succeeded by a flying visit to Ottawa in December, when the good offices of the National Librarian opened all doors, made it clear that the greatest enthusiasm existed among Canadian colleagues for the idea. This was a view confirmed in Toronto and echoed by discussions held in Quebec and London.

As it turned out the problem was to confine the Colloquium to manageable bounds within our objectives. There were indeed approaches from interested people in other European countries which had regretfully to be declined. It is hoped that the publication of these *Proceedings* may make some amends to them and will show to a wider audience the range and quality of the papers and formal discussions; they cannot tell of the many useful contacts made on the 'free' day when many delegates followed up their special interests in various parts of the Reference Division, nor of the happy atmosphere which prevailed despite a London heatwave.

Our grateful thanks are due to all the speakers and delegates, and especially to Dr Guy Sylvestre, Professor Tom Symons, and Professor Anne Piternick for their great help in shaping up the programme and supporting it so generously. Thanks are also offered to Mr Michael Hellyer, Canadian High

Commission in London, and to the Officers of the British Association for Canadian Studies. To those of my own colleagues, led by Mrs Patricia McLaren-Turner, who organised the event, my personal gratitude is expressed.

Ian R Willison

The British Library Collections and Canadian Studies

Let me begin by attempting to put this Colloquium and its proceedings into context.

The Colloquium is one of a series of meetings and reports that explore the consequences, for scholarship, bibliography and library administration, of Canada's cultural coming of age in the world: a process which by and large began in 1951 with the work of the Massey Royal Commission on National Development in the Arts, Letters and Sciences, and involved *inter alia* the creation of the Canada Council, the National Library of Canada and the Bibliothèque nationale du Québec.

In Canada itself, among the main events in recent years have been the following. In 1974 Professor Piternick organised a 'National Conference on the State of Canadian Bibliography', held in Vancouver. Two of the effects of the Vancouver Conference were to encourage work on the Canadian retrospective national bibliographies and, at the policy level, to stimulate the Advisory Board of the National Library of Canada into forming a Committee on Bibliography and Information Services for the Social Sciences and the Humanities (CBISSSH), now under Professor Piternick's chairmanship. Then on the scholarly side, in 1976 the Commission on Canadian Studies of the Association of Universities and Colleges of Canada, under the chairmanship of Professor Symons, published its report and recommendations on the state of Canadian studies, *To know ourselves*. Picking up the Vancouver recommendations on retrospective national bibliography, the Symons Report encouraged the Canada Council to establish in 1978 the Canadian Institute for Historical Microreproductions (CIHM, which Mr Ingles will be discussing later). In addition – and of more particular relevance to us here in the United Kingdom – the Symons Report, through its interaction with the post-Massey cultural programme of the Canadian Department of External Affairs (both before and after publication), was connected with the setting-up of the British Association for Canadian Studies (BACS) in 1975 and the appointment of an Academic Relations Officer at the Canadian High Commission in London in 1977 (the details can be found in Mr Page's *Reflections on the Symons Report*, 1980). Pursuing this concern with Canadian studies abroad, the Conference on 'Bibliography for Canadian Studies: present trends and future needs', held at Dalhousie University, Halifax and sponsored by CBISSSH and the Canadian

Association for Canadian Studies, included a session on 'Canadian resource collections abroad' principally in the United States and the United Kingdom (the latter being the subject of a paper by Mr Simpson, representing BACS). Indeed the essentially decentralised location, nationally and internationally, of research material relating to Canadian studies has become a major preoccupation (it will be one of our main concerns here), and the latest development in Canada concentrates on this and related issues. This is the overview presented in 1982 by Miss Clement to the first joint meeting of two other Canadian National Library Advisory Board Committees (the Bibliographic and Communications Network Committee; the Resource Network Committee) and entitled *The Resource Network: major issues facing Canadian Libraries*.

Here in the United Kingdom the present Colloquium is one in a similar series of conferences and reports arising largely in consequence of the setting up of BACS and the publication of the Symons Report. The most recent of these conferences was the 1981 Edinburgh University Library seminar on *Canadian Resources in Scottish Libraries* which – significantly now in the light of the Clement overview – saw these resources as 'part of an ... emerging ... network spanning the country' (in the words of the university librarian, Brenda Moon – one of our ablest network promoters). In this perspective the most substantial achievement has been Mrs Bloomfield's *Guide to Resources for Canadian Studies in Britain*, first published by the Canadian Department of External Affairs in 1979 (and now about to be reissued in revised form), and undertaken 'in order to assist systematic further acquisitions without the risk of over-duplication'.

I come to the British Library's interest in the Colloquium, and to the subject of my paper. In 1981 the British Library Reference Division created an English Language Branch in recognition (somewhat belated) of the cultural independence which not only Canada but other former British dominions, colonies and dependencies had achieved, largely in the wake of the United States, and in recognition of the effect this has had and will continue to have on the United Kingdom. The Branch consists of a domestic section, the national printed archive – and an Overseas English Section which deals with the United States, Canada and so on, and which may be seen as an extension of the national printed archive since much of its material is acquired by legal deposit – as a result of the predominance of transnational publishing in the English-speaking world. (Responsibility for current science and technological material lies more outside the Branch, in the Science Reference Library, as does responsibility for 'special materials' – newspapers, maps, music and stamps: newspapers and maps being the subject of separate papers in the Colloquium by Mr Green and Dr Wallis. The national manuscript archive, the national sound archive and the national loan collections will be discussed by Dr Waley, Mr Vickers and Dr Barr.) From the Library's point of view the present Colloquium is the second in a series that began last year with an experimental round-table discussion on the Library's role in United States Studies. This series is designed, firstly, to identify the features that are common to the various overseas English-language communities which as fields of study have gone or are about to go through what we might call the Massey-Symons process of systematization. With this as a basis our staff can, in properly coordinated fashion, build the cores of material acquired by transnational legal deposit up to the level acquired by present and projected future demand. Given the necessity of resource networking, the second aim of the colloquia is to define how the English Language Branch, and indeed the British Library, can best participate in the networks that are emerging internationally as well as nationally. A Colloquium on Australian and New Zealand Studies in February 1984 will complete our survey of what Professor Bolton has called the former 'Colonies of Settlement'. Further colloquia will then consider some of the remaining major distinctive English language areas (Bolton's 'Colonies of Alien Rule'): South Asia and Africa.

Within this general framework, let me first outline the Library's understanding of the nature of Canadian studies. Let me then outline the configuration of our Canadian collections and some aspects of their future development. I feel it particularly appropriate to the present occasion that much of what I have to say is influenced by the writings of two of Canada's major scholars and critics: Harold Adams Innis and Northrop Frye.

* * *

It might be said that the histories of North America and Australasia have had at least nine major features in common. The first common feature is, of course, the universally revolutionary matrix of European exploration, discovery, trade and initial settlement – the colonies being to begin with little differentiated from the colonies of alien rule in so far as all were part of the old mercantile empires that lasted from Cartier, say, to Cook and Botany Bay. The second feature is the emergence from this mercantilism, and the predominance in the later colonial and ex-colonial economies, of staple exports to Europe – cod, fur (both the subject of classic analyses by Innis), tobacco, timber, wool, wheat and so on – and, so far as manufacture was concerned, imports largely from the mother country: a colonial dependency sooner or later overcome by import substitution on American lines. The third common feature is the creation of a basic ethos for the increasingly independent colonies by mass-immigration from the rapidly industrialising British Isles (and Europe) from the early nineteenth-century onwards: an immigration made creative, and not, as later, confusing, by the safety-valve effect of a more or less open internal frontier (the celebrated thesis of Frederick Jackson Turner), though at the same time achieved only at the cost of hegemony over the ethos of the pre-colonial inhabitants. The fourth feature is the more strictly political effect of immigration and the open frontier, shown by the significance of the section (the region, the province) in the structure of the new republics and dominions – Turner's second thesis. The structure of politics in Canada, in Australia, in New Zealand (until the twentieth century), and even in the United States, is essentially confederal; and there is a palpable contrast between this confederalism and the 'high politics' characteristic of England and France (though not perhaps of the rest of Europe: 1815 was the year of the birth not only of Sir John A Macdonald – but also of the master of confederal politics in another continental heartland, Bismarck).

The fifth common feature is the importance of the various modes of communication and business, from railway to print and the newspaper (the subjects of Innis's first and last monographs), which attempted, never entirely successfully, to hold together such extended territories. The sixth common feature, then, is the continuing search for genuine and effective national identity through the pursuit of literature, in the broadest sense of the word. For here 'literature' means not only the exploration and discovery of national identity by creative writers using symbol and myth – the Whitmans, the E J Pratts, the Henry Lawsons, the Frank Sargesons – but also the retrospective ordering according to international standards, the 'canonising' we might say, of these necessarily local discoveries by what Emerson in *The American Scholar* called 'the delegated intellect' and Frye in the *Anatomy* 'criticism', so that the citizenry might see their new, but local, identity – their complex fate – in perspective. Moreover, unlike the more socially integrated traditional European man of letters, the delegated intellect in the ex-colonies has tended to be 'garrisoned' (another term of Frye's) in a sequence of militantly high cultural institutions: church – university and library – government agency. A classic example of the delegated intellect is the Reverend Herman Northrop Frye himself and the hard-won harmony between, on the one hand, his neo-Aristotelian, universalising *Anatomy of Criticism* and, on the other, his impressively normative conclusions to the canonising of the Canadian literary experience in the collaborative *Literary History of Canada: Canadian Literature in English*. Even so, despite such homogenisation, the seventh common feature is the fact that the former 'fragments of Europe' have been re-entering the world arena as pluralist, multi-cultural entities, built up from the original pre-colonial inhabitants – American Indians, Aborigines, Maoris – as well as subsequent immigrant groups, whose self-articulation has broken the 'WASP' hegemony. In the words of Glazer and Moynihan's now famous study of contemporary New York City, it is a case of 'beyond the melting pot'.

Indeed, the eighth common feature is the fact that this re-entry on to the world scene has been largely occasioned by and mediated through another universally revolutionary matrix: twentieth-century world war. The effect of the same revolutionary matrix of world war on the mother country is in part responsible for the ninth (and final?) common feature. This is the growing effect on the identity of the demoralised mother country of 'backtrailers' from the former ex-colonies, finding their true vocation as either promoters, or critics, of the post-war suburbia that is, in many ways, the unexpected, ironic consummation of the frontier experience. One thinks of F W Woolworth, or T S Eliot; of Roy Thomson, or (*in absentia*) Marshall McLuhan; and now, perhaps, of Rupert Murdoch, or Germaine Greer. It is this last feature that has been (as I have said) the proximate cause of the setting up of the Library's English Language Branch.

Briefly, in the Library we find it important to regard all these common features (and their descriptions) as cognate with the grand, geo-political frontier and section theses of F J Turner that I have mentioned, which counterpointed Sir John Seeley's doctrine of the homogenous expansion of England as the key to the history of the English-speaking world; helped launch American studies as an independent discipline; and were developed (even if antithetically) by Innis and others into a world-picture of pluralistic intercommunication and interaction. Indeed we note how powerful still is the influence of Turner-style theses, ninety years on, in major initial attempts at self-identification in our other overseas English areas: to take the case of Australia, we find a Turnerian point of departure in the two recent seminal works of Russel Ward, *The Australian Legend*, and Geoffrey Blainey, *The Tyranny of Distance*. One might say, then, that the Library tries to construe the development of its overseas English collections in relation to the detailed examination, and potential revision, of such theses by successive generations of scholars working at various levels of 'canonisation', among the pre-eminent being the compilation not only of a collaborative literary or general history but also a dictionary of national biography (in much the same way as *our* first generation of professional historians at the end of the nineteenth century used our DNB to examine the grand equations of Macaulay, and Green and Lecky). Professor Halpenny will be speaking to us about the *Dictionary of Canadian Biography*; and we plan to have presentations about the *Dictionary of Australian Biography* and the forthcoming revision of the *Dictionary of New Zealand Biography* in our third colloquium. Supporting this progressive solidification of Canadian (and other) studies – and a process with which the British Library must be an active collaborator – will be the consolidating of the relevant bibliographic infrastructure. This includes the completion of the retrospective national bibliographies and the making universally available of the national printed archive which Miss Clement, Madame Filion, Professor Fleming and Mr Ingles will be discussing. It also involves the authoritative editing of the texts of the country's authors, together with other applications of the history of the book, both of which require a secure and accessible bibliographic infrastructure (I have asked Professor Robson and Mr Landon to elaborate on this).

* * *

Let me now introduce the survey of the Canadian collections in the Department of Printed Books – which is to be the main theme of the first session tomorrow – and also comment on the small display of items we have chosen to help dramatise the range of the collections.

The particular configuration of our Canadian collections can perhaps be best understood in the light of our history. Like other European national research libraries, for example the Bibliothèque Nationale, the Department has passed through four major and contrasting phases. First, there were the great semi-private collections – Sloane, Harley, Banks, George III, and (as a glorious epilogue) Grenville: the so-called foundation collections and their like that came into the Library during the *ancien régime* and its aftermath. This was followed in the mid-nineteenth century by the classic period of systematic, encyclopedic collecting inaugurated by Panizzi and inspired largely by the German concept of nationalised *Wissenschaft* that emerged from the French Revolution. The system was meant to be self-sufficient – autarchic – and was based on the effective enforcement of legal deposit (and the extension of it to hitherto neglected ephemera such as newspapers) complemented by a greatly increased annual purchase grant, and by international exchange arrangements to deal with the new mode of bureaucratic, official publication *hors de commerce* with which Mr Hamilton will be dealing later. (This period also marks the beginning of the Canadian collections as such, symbolised by the publication of the first – and so far only – catalogue of the collections as of 1856 by Henry Stevens, which is on display). The third phase was characterised by the contraction of this encyclopedism, as part of the general passing of the zenith of European power in the world at the end of the nineteenth century, and the greater reliance on legal deposit alone. Fourthly and currently, we have the reconstruction of the Library's acquisition strategy, beginning with the post-war expansion of higher education and research in the 1950s (the period of Massey and, in this country, the Robbins and other related reports): a strategy which was no longer autarchic but interdependent with the other major research collections in each particular area of scholarship.

Thus – to take in turn various aspects of Canadian Studies – firstly: the mercantilist thrust of our foundation collections means that for the age of European discovery the Library has not only one of the two best collections of travel books, with 45% of all known European Americana (the other collection being at the Bibliothèque Nationale), but also has a similarly pre-eminent collection of maps – the 1508 Egerton, the 1537 Harleian and so on. In our display we show the Grenville copies of the Cartier *Brief recit* of 1545, Champlain's *Des Sauvages* published in 1603, and Daniel Claus' Mohawk Primer of 1781 (the Bibliothèque Nationale appears to have no copy of the Cartier).

Secondly: the importance of the map collection also coincides with that of our nineteenth-century newspaper and official publication collections as printed primary source material for the subsequent immigration into, and highly regionalised settlement of, Canada. Of the major official publications and newspapers listed in the latest volume of the *Dictionary of Canadian Biography*, the Library has 31 of the 40 official publications and 52 of the 64 newspapers. (As examples of the range of this material we show in our display the first issues of *Le Canadien*, the *Cariboo Sentinel* – a newspaper from the mining town of Barkerville, British Columbia – and the Winnipeg *Canadian Sitch*, a Ukrainian monarchist newspaper. For official publications relating to frontier settlement, we show, for the early period, Claus' Mohawk Book of Common Prayer, and, for the closing of the frontier, the first Census of the Northwest Territories under the 1885 Census Act. For the rise of confederal politics we show the first volume of the Journal of the Legislative Assembly of the Province of Canada formed in 1841.)

Thirdly: literature exploring the Canadian experience emerged from travel books and reminiscences of immigration and settlement, though from the end of the nineteenth century onwards there was an increasing amount of autonomous fiction, poetry and criticism. So far as our collections of this category of material are concerned, legal deposit operated more or less effectively, since until after Confederation most of the books were published in the United Kingdom. Moreover, the purchase grant enlarged by Panizzi and channelled through hand-picked agents such as Henry Stevens accounted for a significant proportion of items which early legal deposit had failed to capture, or which had been published in North America – in the United States as well as the Canadas. (As an example of this retrospective purchasing we show our copy of *The History of Emily Montague* by Frances Brooke which the *Literary History of Canada* calls 'the earliest Canadian novel' and which was published in London by Dodsley in 1769 but not acquired by the Library till a century later in 1876.) Although our purchase grant declined in the late 1880s, the extension of the Library's legal deposit rights in 1895 to include Canada – as Dr O'Neill and Professor Ettlinger will elaborate later in the Colloquium – together with the growth of United States publishing agencies in the United Kingdom, meant that effective current acquisition continued until the end of the Library's Canadian legal deposit in 1924 (which, admittedly, coincides with the arrival of the modern Canadian novel in the work of Frederick Philip Grove and Morley Callaghan). Thus, of the fiction listed in Watters' *Checklist of Canadian Literature* (and only half of the authors concerned are thought worthy of canonisation in the *Literary History of Canada*), our preliminary investigation suggests that the Library holds about two-thirds. As an example of occasional 'double legal deposit' (that is, where there were both British and Canadian publishers of the same book), and as an example of the value of this for the textual criticism of Canadian authors, we show our copies of the London and Toronto editions of Sara Jeannette Duncan's *His honour and a lady*, which reveal differing numbers of illustrations as well as minor textual variants. Moreover the legal deposit of books published within the North Atlantic Triangle continued to operate even after 1924. Callaghan, for example, like his literary associates Hemingway and Fitzgerald, was published by Max Perkins at Scribners' in New York, with the result that some of his books continued to be deposited in the Library by Scribners' London agency. (As an illustration of North Atlantic Triangle publishing we show our copies of the first five of Pratt's commercially published books of verse, originating mainly from the Macmillan offices in Toronto, London and New York.)

Fourthly and finally: turning to the multi-cultural aspect of Canadian Studies, an important item in the reconstruction of the Library's acquisition strategy commencing in the 1950s was the agreement negotiated in 1964 with the Quebec government, whereby notable current Quebec publications were donated via the Délégation Générale du Québec in Paris. (We show our copy of the first edition of Gabrielle Roy's first novel, *Bonheur d'occasion*, which was received under this agreement.) In 1980 economic pressures forced the discontinuance of the donation, and it was replaced by an intensive purchasing drive for earlier as well as current Quebec material (which is in part the cause of the recent increase in our Canadian budget from £6,000 to over £20,000 in the past four years). The effect of all this, and of pre-1924 legal deposit, is shown by Mr Dethan's estimate in his paper that the British Library holds very nearly 50% of the titles in Barbeau and Fortier's *Dictionaire bibliographique du Canada Français*.

★ ★ ★

I conclude with a brief review of the current and possible future activities of the Canadian Section of the English Language Branch. As I have just said, the Branch has an annual purchase grant for Canadian imprints of upwards of £20,000; and in the last financial year nearly 2,000 monographs were purchased and over 400 serials received (to which must be added, of course, material received by transnational legal deposit). Our international exchange agreements involving Canadian provincial as well as federal publications have been re-negotiated and our accessions of Canadian newspapers are currently under examination. In general, our Canadian collection development policy requires us to select (primarily from the current national bibliography *Canadiana*) material of research potential by taking our line from the various attempts of canonising the Canadian experience already referred to, such as the *Literary History of Canada* and the related bibliographies of Watters, Barbeau and Fortier and so on. (In much the same way, in the case of our United States or Australian or New Zealand collections, we take our line from the exposition and the bibliographical sections of Spiller's *Literary History of the United States* or Leonie Kramer's *Oxford History of Australian Literature* or W H Oliver's *Oxford History of New Zealand*, as we would expect major research libraries in the English speaking world abroad to take their lines from the Cambridge and Oxford Histories of English Literature and the related *Cambridge Bibliography of English Literature*). Even so, I repeat that our Canadian collections are no longer intended to be autarchic; and they depend on a collaborative, resource-sharing network in at least two important aspects.

In the first place our collections are unlikely by themselves to satisfy the demand of those researchers who are mavericks within the scholarly consensus, and whose research material will be outside our scope. However, their requests can now usually be satisfied, in reactive fashion, by the national and international lending system based on the British Library Lending Division which Dr Barr will be discussing.

The second aspect is more susceptible to systematic forward collaboration. The same historical factors that have made our existing Canadian collections pre-eminent in Europe are also responsible for their considerable imperfection when judged 'canonically'. Sloane, Banks, and Grenville and the rest may have assembled 45% of early European Americana, but what about the other 55%? The thirty items of the over 1,200 in the Tremaine period, including two not in Tremaine, that we have acquired since the Stevens survey of 1856 may be representative of contemporary publications – treaties, proclamations, sermons, episcopal charges, primers in English and Mohawk, and so on – but their substantive contribution to the actual pre-1801 corpus of texts is minuscule. The Reference Division's holdings of nineteenth-century newspapers and official publications, though wide in range, are noticeably incomplete. Pre-Confederation 'imperial' legal deposit was practically never enforced in Canada and even after Confederation the deposit of official publications did not include certain provinces, such as Manitoba and New Brunswick. In the first half of the twentieth century, when the Library's annual Canadian purchase grant sank so low as to be negligible, North Atlantic Triangle legal deposit was by no means equally effective for all canonical authors, particularly following the end of direct legal deposit from Canada in 1924. In the case of Frederick Philip Grove we have his first two books of non-fiction published before 1924 but only three of his eight novels. In the case of Bliss Carman, a writer publishing within our Canadian legal deposit period 1895–1924 (though admittedly publishing more in the United States than in Canada), we lack 29 of the 53 titles listed in Watters. The sense of a world literature in the English language – as opposed to English literature, or American literature, or Canadian literature – had not reached a sufficient degree of cohesion in the minds of publishers and readers (let alone critics and scholars) to support a fully effective North Atlantic Triangle legal deposit system. Indeed, it is still in process of so doing.

These gaps are being filled by acquiring desiderata as they appear in the book trade. Nevertheless the scale of the task, and recent relevant developments in national research library objectives and technology, make a three-part forward resource-sharing strategy both desirable and feasible. The first element is to complete the bibliographical infrastructure of the canon of Canadian Studies by adding to RETRO items unique to the Reference Division (and to other extra-Canadian libraries): for example those not in Tremaine but in the ESTC, those in the proposed Nineteenth-Century Short-Title Catalogue, and those in the Library's 1895–1924 Canadian legal deposit. (Dr O'Neill, Professor Ettlinger, Miss Clement and Dr Alston will be touching on those matters.) The second element is for us to acquire Mr Ingles' CIHM corpus:

already the first five units which we have just purchased have reduced our Bliss Carman gaps by nine. Thirdly – what should be a merely automatic consequence of the other two but is likely to cause many tears – libraries must collaborate in making each national database record smoothly interchangeable. In this way the 50,000 items proposed in the CIHM project can be made available at speed to users in the same general array of collateral records held in Panizzi's soon-to-be-converted General Catalogue. This would be a not insignificant part of the 'Grand Design' to bring the capabilities of the emerging world information order to bear on the advancement of learning: the fundamental *raison d'être* of major research libraries throughout the ages.

Discussion

In the subsequent discussion, a number of points were raised: the selection of current printed material in the English Language Branch presented difficulties but the basic aim was to provide for future generations a research collection embracing the total spectrum of works relating to Canada; regarding retrospective acquisition, it was mentioned that nothing from Newfoundland had been received by the BL despite the 1887 Copyright Act; the need for practical action on acquisition was stressed; it was stated that the collections at BLLD were largely based on demand and that BLLD and BLRD cooperated over major acquisitions; gifts were received by BLLD and by BLRD Department of Manuscripts; libraries should take into consideration the importance of collecting ephemeral material which could provide a resource of significance to individual scholars; the BACS Library and Resources Group was looking into areas of cooperation and was trying to use the BACS Newsletter as a means of disseminating knowledge about potential needs as well as about material acquired; staff cut-backs due to public expenditure cuts led inevitably to a lack of efficiency; Canadian scholarship had not yet developed to a position of complete bibliographical control of Canadian Studies.

The following people took part in this discussion: Dr Barr (BLLD); Mr Cox (Leeds University Library): Professor Ettlinger (Dalhousie University): Mr Fulford (BLRD); Professor Halpenny (DCB/DBC); Mr Landon (Toronto University Library); Dr O'Neill (Mount St Vincent University); Mr D Simpson (Royal Commonwealth Society); Mr M Simpson (Edinburgh University Library); Dr Sylvestre (National Library of Canada); Dr Waley (BLRD); Mr Willison (BLRD); Mr Wilson (BLRD).

Thomas H B Symons

A Canadian perspective on Canadian Studies: 1

I have been invited to speak, from a Canadian perspective, about the current state of Canadian Studies. If I may, I will do so rather informally and frankly, looking at some of the recent developments and also at some of the new or continuing problems in this area. It may also be helpful to our discussions over the next few days to put the topic into a brief historical context, and perhaps the best way to do that is to review briefly the work of the Commission on Canadian Studies, and a number of related events.

You may recall that there were increasing concerns in Canada in the late 1960s, and early 1970s, about whether adequate attention was being paid to the Canadian dimensions of Canadian education. In particular, there was a growing unease about the extent to which the curriculum and research orientation had become Americanised. But the movement to have more attention given to the Canadian content and context of our educational programmes was not just a reaction to these concerns. It was also the result of a long-standing, if somewhat quiescent, interest in teaching and research about Canada that had been developing slowly and steadily over the years. This interest had been expressed, for example, in the development of strong programmes in Canadian history at many universities in the first half of this century, in the establishment of the Institute for Canadian Studies at Carleton University in 1957, in the launching of the Dictionary of Canadian Biography in 1959, and in the establishment of Mount Allison University's programme in Canadian Studies in 1969. The fostering of teaching and research about Canada was one of the declared objectives of Trent University at the time of its founding in 1962 and this led to its sponsorship of a new quarterly, *The Journal of Canadian Studies*, in 1965.

Thus, there was considerable activity in the field of Canadian Studies prior to 1970. But such activity was low-key, scattered, and on a very small scale. It was far from being sufficient to allay the fears of those who thought that Canadian interests and subject matter were still being neglected.

In the absence of firm data, however, it was difficult to assess the state of teaching and research about Canada. No one had the facts or really knew what was going on. The need for hard data on which to base any judgement about the state of Canadian Studies should perhaps be stressed. Without such information, aggregated on a national and regional basis and by discipline, statements about the condition of Canadian Studies could only be expressions of opinion or subjective impressions. While there has been substantial progress in gathering information about what is, and what is not, being taught or researched in the field of Canadian studies at institutions across the country, there is still a long way to go before a full and reliable inventory is available. It continues to be difficult to learn what attention is being given in many disciplines to Canadian content and context. Gathering such information on a discipline or national basis is still a trail-breaking exercise and this continues to be a major problem for those working in the field.

It may be appropriate, at a colloquium at the British Library, to wonder if my Commonwealth colleagues in Australia, New Zealand, India, and the other forty-three countries of the Commonwealth may not discover that the absence of such data, and the difficulty of gathering it, is for them, too, a major problem as they move to strengthen programmes of teaching and research about their own societies. On recent visits, for example, to Australia, India, New Zealand, Nigeria, Ghana, Malaysia, Hong Kong, and the West Indies I sensed the same lack of firm knowledge about what was and was not being taught and researched about these countries in their own universities and in many academic areas.

Here, too, in the United Kingdom, where there are so many important resources for Canadian Studies, it has been one of the great challenges simply to find and identify these resources and then to make their existence and availability properly known to interested scholars. In this regard, I must pay tribute to the work done by a growing number of British scholars and institutions and by the British Association for Canadian Studies, often with encouragement and assistance from Canada House. The *Guide to Resources for Canadian Studies in Britain* and its supplements prepared for the Department of External Affairs by Valerie Bloomfield has already been of invaluable assistance to Canadian researchers, who are also frequently indebted to Michael Hellyer, the Academic Relations Officer at Canada House, for help in many forms. Warm thanks, and congratulations, must also be expressed to the British Library and to Alex Wilson, the Director General of its Reference Division, for organising this colloquium.

The result of all this activity has been a substantial increase in the amount of attention being devoted to Canadian Studies in both teaching and research in the United Kingdom. Various surveys have documented this development which is also demonstrated in impressionistic ways. Earlier this week, for example, I found that a notice board beside which I was standing quite by chance at the University of Birmingham was entirely devoted to Canadian Studies.

Much, of course, remains to be done in locating all the resources of potential interest to Canadian scholars in Britain. For example, on a visit yesterday to Cardinal Newman's remarkable library at the Oratory in Birmingham I noticed a number of volumes, papers, and artifacts of significance for students of Canada. I rather doubt that the existence of these materials has been noted in any inventory of the library resources for Canadian Studies. Indeed, the answers to my inquiries suggested that no Canadian scholar had made use of these materials within the memory of those entrusted with their care. Thus, the first task for those interested in Canadian Studies, in Britain as elsewhere, still largely continues to be one of finding out the facts: what is the full range of resources available for such studies and what is being done? This is the essential first step to any informed opinion about the state of Canadian Studies, in Canada or in other countries.

It was in recognition of this need that the Commission on Canadian Studies was established in 1972 by the Association of Universities and Colleges of Canada 'to study, report, and make recommendations upon the state of teaching and research in various fields of study relating to Canada'. Such a Commission is in itself a fitting subject for a Canadian study because of the curious, round-about way in which it must be set up. Because of the responsibility given to the provinces for education, it is not easy to make arrangements for a national study of educational questions in Canada. Yet such national studies are needed from time to time, and they must be paid for. In the best of possible worlds, the provinces would no doubt cooperate amongst themselves to establish a Commission, or some other review mechanism, and to pay for it. But in practice this rarely happens. In this situation, a variety of strategems have been evolved that enable the country to get on with what must be done, despite the fragmentation of educational responsibilities. The Commission on Canadian Studies was the not untypical product of one such strategem, being appointed to undertake a national study in the field of education by neither the federal government nor the provinces, but by a national voluntary organisation, and then being partially funded from federal sources by means of a grant negotiated for this purpose with an arms-length federal granting agency, in this case the Canada Council. It is a complex way to launch a national study but it works. It even has its advantages in the distancing of such commissions from possible government control or influence.

The Commission proceeded in the customary manner to research its subject, and to invite briefs and participation in public hearings which were held in all provinces. There was a remarkable response to this invitation. Over 1,000 briefs and some 30,000 letters were received. More than 2,500 people attended the public hearings. Additional meetings were requested by representatives of some 200 academic societies, educational associations, community organisations, and government departments and agencies. All this was immensely helpful. But it was also a large task and enormously time-consuming.

The Commission released the first two volumes of its Report, entitled *To Know Ourselves*, in 1976. In these volumes, it examined some fifty academic areas and suggested that in each of these areas, in both teaching and research, there was need and opportunity for greater attention to be paid to Canadian content and to the Canadian context. It found this to be true in science and technology, and in the professions, as well as in the humanities and social sciences. These volumes also reported on the state of Canadian Studies abroad and on the Canadian Studies dimensions of archives, community colleges, audio-visual resources, and some questions of funding – examining in particular the potential key role of the private donor in supporting such studies.

As it set about its work, the Commission had found that it was necessary to deal with even the most basic questions assumed in its mandate, including the development of definitions. There was, for example, no agreed definition for Canadian Studies. Indeed, in so far as there was any definition for Canadian Studies it might best be described as a 'definition in progress.' The Commission proposed as its definition for working purposes 'teaching or research in any field that, as one of its major purposes, promotes knowledge about Canada by dealing with some aspect of the country's culture, social conditions, physical setting, or place in the world.' However, the Commission was also concerned, more broadly, with the adequacy of attention given to the Canadian content and to the Canadian context of teaching and research in all appropriate fields, whether or not the promotion of knowledge about Canada was one of the specific and major objectives. This definition, and its broader corollary, appear now to have found a general acceptance.

Similarly, there was no agreed rationale for Canadian Studies, even amongst those engaged in such studies. For some, it was an exercise in patriotism or nationalism. For others, it was a means of fighting the Americanisation of Canada. For still others, it was a way to promote Canadian unity and identity. The Commission did not accept any of these quasi-political rationales for Canadian Studies. It argued, instead, that the only appropriate rationale for teaching and research about Canada is the importance of knowledge for its own sake, and the unwisdom of neglecting any area of knowledge in the way in which knowledge about Canada had been neglected in so many fields. For Canadians, this rationale for Canadian Studies can be extended and amplified because of the further and particular importance of self-knowledge. A society, like an individual, needs to know itself, its history, institutions, cultures, geography, and physical terrain.

Such knowledge is valid in itself. It is part of the legitimate response to the challenge of knowing and understanding that confronts all mankind. But knowledge about Canada and about the Canadian experience is also one of the special contributions that Canadians should be making to the international pool of knowledge. Canadian Studies is often, in addition, a very practical area of study for Canadians because the knowledge it generates is needed to help foster a better understanding of our own circumstances, and it may help us to address more effectively some of our problems and opportunities. In this sense, adequate attention to Canadian Studies is a matter of prudent housekeeping and of responsible stewardship.

The development of this rationale may have been one of the most useful contributions made by the Commission. But neither the rationale nor the Commission's findings were uniformly popular when *To Know Ourselves* was published. The report was fiercely attacked from two sides. On the one hand, some of the more extreme anti-American nationalists saw it as a bland document that obscured the roots of our academic problems which they believed were primarily the result of American influence and American faculty members. This group would have been happy with nothing less than a violent denunciation of the United States, followed by the ceremonial burning of the Stars and Stripes on the steps of the Parliament Buildings in Ottawa.

At the other end of the spectrum were some senior Canadian university leaders (in fact, quite a few, and many of them originally from the United States), both teachers and administrators, who regarded Canadian Studies as provincial, parochial, peripheral, inconsequential – in fact, as unscholarly.

The Commission heard, of course, a good deal from both these ends of the spectrum. But it heard, also, from literally thousands of others who seemed to welcome the report and to find it helpful. The seven years since the publication of the report have been a rather interesting, and demanding, personal experience. Briefs and letters have continued to arrive in astonishing numbers. There have been, indeed, another 30,000 letters. There have also been more than 300 reports on the report, prepared by universities, colleges, faculties, academic departments, learned societies, educational associations, school boards, foundations, voluntary organisations, and by many departments and agencies of both the federal and provincial governments. In such reports, the organisations concerned were usually examining and reporting on those aspects of the Commission's report that related to their own situation.

Many of these reports were prepared in consultation with the Commission. The Commission was also frequently called upon to advise and assist with the development of appropriate new programmes and policies, and with the implementation of various of its recommendations. The report had put forward 275 specific numbered recommendations and another thousand recommendations or suggestions were made, *en passant*, in the text. About one-half of these recommendations have now been implemented or at least acted upon to some measurable degree. Indeed, as Ian Willison, the Head of the English Language Branch of the British Library Reference Division, was kind enough to point out in his opening remarks, this Colloquium and our meeting here today was set in train by the section of the Commission's report that drew attention to the importance of Canadian Studies abroad.

There has been, on the whole, a very positive and extensive response to the Commission's report, including a remarkable number of specific innovations and reforms. But perhaps the most important response has been the change in the academic climate, from one of indifference and frequent hostility to Canadian Studies to one more inclined to recognise the academic legitimacy of this new area and to perceive the value of and need for teaching and research in studies relating to Canada. All these developments have been very welcome, but they occupied a great deal of time and entailed a substantial on-going service function for which the Commission had neither staff nor budget.

None the less, a further, third, volume has now been prepared by the Commission which will be published this fall. Entitled *Some Questions of Balance: Human Resources, Higher Education, and Canadian Studies*, this volume continues and extends the theme of meeting Canadian needs, examining a wide range of questions about the current state of Canadian higher education and about the current and future supply of human resources required to support Canadian teaching and research. As in the first two volumes, the Commission calls for a reasonable balance in higher education, in this case in order to meet the country's present and future needs for highly qualified graduates. From its research, the Commission concludes in this volume that few areas of teaching and research about Canada have been more neglected than the study of Canadian higher education itself. I hope that my colleague and co-author, James Page, may say a little more in his paper about some of the other issues discussed in *Some Questions of Balance*.

Despite the considerable progress of recent years in the development of Canadian Studies, some large problems continue to challenge those interested in this field. I am confident that these problems can be overcome; but they need, first, to be recognised in order that they can then be properly handled. May I draw your attention to just two? The first of these is the problem of resources and financial support. This problem becomes all the more acute in a period of economic recession such as we have seen in recent years. A time of cut-backs or, at best, of little growth is especially hard on a comparatively new academic area like Canadian Studies. Canadian Studies are new in a double sense. First, because of past neglect, the content of these studies often constitutes a new field. Second, Canadian Studies are also new in the methodological sense, in that those engaged in such studies are frequently pursuing a pioneer approach to transdisciplinary studies, cutting across old academic boundaries and synthesising knowledge from many fields into one.

The second problem to which I must draw your attention concerns the academic standing of Canadian Studies and, as a corollary, of those engaged in these studies. Despite a notable improvement in recent years, there is still need for a more welcoming recognition on the part of many individuals and institutions of the academic value – indeed, the academic legitimacy – of Canadian Studies. There continues to be a good deal of indifference towards teaching and research in this area, an indifference that is sometimes not far removed from disapproval. While it is true that most of the open hostility that was once shown to Canadian Studies by many senior scholars and administrators has disappeared, at least some of this sentiment has simply gone underground. It is still there, and it is often more difficult to deal with it now than when it was more overt.

Canadian Studies must, of course, honestly merit academic respect. Fortunately, there is a substantial and growing body of scholarship in this field that commands such respect. But there are also signs that a few people are treating the field as a convenient and fashionable growth industry that lends itself to exploitation in the cause of personal advancement rather than of the advancement of scholarship. It may be timely to underscore the importance of genuinely good scholarship by genuinely good scholars in this field as in every other.

May I close on a note of emphasis of the importance of Canadian Studies outside of Canada. Such studies have a legitimate place in teaching and research in other countries simply as a part of the challenge of knowledge. Moreover, a better knowledge and understanding of Canada may often prove helpful to the countries in which the studies are conducted. But the pursuit of teaching and research about Canada in other countries is particularly important for Canada and for Canadians, and for the whole enterprise of Canadian scholarship. Such academic work in other countries helps Canadians to know themselves, and to see and understand their place and problems and opportunities through the eyes of others and in a wider context.

This point was made by the Royal Commission on National Development in the Arts, Letters and Sciences (the Massey-Lévesque Commission) in Canada, in 1951, in its chapter on 'The Projection of Canada Abroad'. You may recall the view it expressed, that 'the promotion abroad of a knowledge of Canada is not a luxury but an obligation, and a more generous policy in this field would have important results, both concrete and intangible.' It was well said, but there was little action in response. The Massey-Lévesque Commission's view of the importance of Canadian Studies abroad was underlined and elaborated a quarter of a century later by the Commission on Canadian Studies in 1976. In fact, the point emerged as a major theme in *To Know Ourselves*. I am happy to note that it has been further re-inforced recently by the strong statement made on this subject by the Federal Cultural Policy Review Committee in the Applebaum-Hébert Report.

The Report of the Commission on Canadian Studies not only stressed the value of promoting a wider knowledge and understanding of Canada abroad. It placed a strong emphasis on the need to research, to study, and to teach more about Canada's roots, origins, and context, including, for example, studies about the exploration and opening up of the country, about immigration, and about the origins of our institutions and their subsequent inter-action with institutions elsewhere. Other contextual studies are needed in such fields as diplomacy and defence, trade and economics, and education and culture. There is tremendous scope for, and need for, co-operative and comparative programmes of teaching and research that will associate Canadian scholars, and universities and other appropriate institutions, with those of other countries.

There should, of course, be nothing xenophobic or inward-looking about

Canadian Studies. On the contrary, to know ourselves we must know others. Every national community needs to look out, and to reach out. We owe that to ourselves, and we owe it to others.

James E Page

A Canadian perspective on Canadian Studies: 2

When preparing for the topic 'Canadian Perspectives on Canadian Studies', adopted for this session of the colloquium, I was reminded of a charming story told to me by my guide during a visit to Trinity College, Dublin. It concerns three priests who were arguing amongst themselves about which order of clerics was closest to God. The first, a Jesuit, claimed that the Society of Jesus, as defenders of the true faith, as teachers, missionaries and philosophers, had to be closest to God's heart. The next, a Franciscan, said that the simplicity and humility of the followers of St Francis made them the apple of God's eye. The third, a Dominican, explained why, in his view, his order, contemplative and self-sacrificing, had a special place in heaven. They could not agree, so to settle the argument they decided to pray for a sign, each in his own way. The next morning they approached the altar to concelebrate mass. This story is of a recent event, and my tour guide was up on his liturgy. The three Fathers found, as they arrived at the altar, the following words burned into the altar cloth – it was the sign they had prayed for. 'All religious orders and all priests are close to my heart equally', the words said. It was signed 'God – S.J.'.

My perspective on Canadian studies is not based on the kind of certainty that the Jesuit Father of this story had of the place of the Society in the heavenly order of things. My comments are based more on the humble uncertainty of the Franciscan.

The reason for this is that whenever one talks about Canadian studies these days, references are inevitably made to the Symons Report, *To Know Ourselves*, and to the words of the Canadian Studies oracle, Tom Symons. In this context and given the liturgical tone my talk seems to be adopting, I am reminded of some comments by Ron Baker, then president of the University of Prince Edward Island, at the beginning of a short observation he made on the Commission's study. He said that most Canadian faculty treat the Symons *Report* as they treat the Bible; they have heard of it but have not read it. A few are fundamentalist believers, accepting every word literally; some think it too kind to sinners; and some think it too optimistic about the millenium. Fortunately, as with most other holy books, it can accommodate a wide variety of faiths. He mused about which chapter might be called Genesis, which Judges, Numbers, Kings, Chronicles, Proverbs, and of course, Job. I must confess that I was tempted to begin this talk with an appropriate quotation from the Epistle to the Collection builders where, if I remember correctly, there is a passage which dealt with some aspects of resource needs for Canadian studies.

To carry Ron Baker's comment just a bit further, I suspect that *Reflections on the Symons Report*, a subsequent study, which I was commissioned to prepare for the Department of the Secretary of State, might be considered a kind of 'Pilgrim's Progress'. In that sense, and generally speaking, I reported in *Reflections* that there had been some remarkable reactions to the biblical admonitions of the Commissioner and his colleagues: that there had been a number of governmental, agency, university and college responses to the Commission's recommendations. However, as far as Canadian Studies are concerned as a distinct area of academic endeavour, I concluded that there is much to be done in Canada, that some colleges and universities have responded to Canadian studies matters with not much more than window dressing.

I would like to spend a few moments clarifying that general point before making some comments about Canadian perspectives on Canadian studies abroad.

The key to any perspective on the state of Canadian studies is, not surprisingly, a clear view of what is being examined. The Commission on Canadian studies adopted, as its basic premise, that Canadian studies were those studies which would advance Canadians' knowledge of themselves, who they are, where they are in time and place, where they have been, where they are going, what they possess, what their responsibilities are to themselves and of course to others. The Commission's definition of Canadian studies was equally broad:

Canadian studies consist of teaching and research in any field that promotes knowledge about Canada by dealing with aspects of Canada's culture, social conditions, physical setting or place in the world.

The Commission's document demonstrates that this approach to the field is not at all limiting and the first two volumes of the Commission's study can only be described as enormous. With over 1,000 general and about 295 specific recommendations, the task of writing the 'Pilgrim's Progress' was not only daunting but virtually impossible to handle with anything approximating completeness.

Using the original formulations in Dr Symons' version of Genesis, I have isolated three different 'generic approaches' to Canadian studies, and in *Reflections on the Symons Report* I dealt, principally, with one of them. These approaches could be labelled in any number of ways. Here I have elected to call them 'Canadian content Canadian Studies (or Canadian Studies in the Social Sciences and Humanities)'; 'Integrative (or interdisciplinary) Canadian Studies' and 'Applied Canadian Studies (or Canadian Studies in the pure and applied sciences)'. These are not surgically neat distinctions, but hopefully they are useful. An important part of a perspective on Canadian Studies is to note that the first approach is much more highly developed than the second and much more advanced than the third.

Canadian studies seen as attention to Canada in the various disciplines appeared as the central pre-occupation of the Commission's curriculum chapter and some other sections of the first two volumes of that *Report*. Canadian studies, defined as Canadian content in the disciplines, is based on the simple notion that if Canada is the focus of study then Canadian Studies are taking place.

In terms of the health of Canadian studies defined this way, I think that some considerable strides have been taken. Nonetheless, there are some disciplinary areas and some specialties in which much research remains to be done, fields like industrial archeology come to mind, and areas like the history of science and technology in Canada need considerable work. With regard to teaching there are still too many areas that are underdeveloped. Canadian literature is still not given its due in the undergraduate curriculum, to cite but one example.

The Commission on Canadian Studies also dealt with Canadian studies as a special field, in and of itself, as an 'integrative' national study. In this sense, Canadian studies are only now in the process of being developed. When Symons published his volumes, there were twenty-two formally designated Canadian studies programmes in Canada, now there are thirty-three. These programmes are defined both in terms of the focus of study, Canada, and by their methodologies. The concern is to introduce students to the study of Canada through the examination of a major issues or themes using a number of disciplinary perspectives. The language used to describe these approaches is getting increasingly arcane: from interdisciplinary and multidisciplinary through to crossdisciplinary, transdisciplinary, collaborative and cooperative studies. These programmes operate, usually, with the cooperation of a number of departments, some of them built on a series of disciplinary subjects with several core 'integrative' courses required as well.

This approach to Canadian studies is at the heart of the work done by the Canadian Association for Canadian Studies. It is the approach that I selected to emphasise in *Reflections on the Symons Report*. My reasons for so doing were many and varied. They include the fact that, in these times of fiscal constraint, non-departmental programmes often are made to suffer. That is the case, I believe, if the correspondence that I have received from a number of Canadian studies programme co-ordinators is any indication. Most of these programmes presently have little, if any, administrative support. The co-ordinators are typically junior appointments, and a number of them have expressed concern that their academic careers may be jeopardised by being too visibly connected with non-departmental activities, especially of an interdisciplinary nature. Another reason for my interest in these programmes is that it appears clear that a number of universities, in order to be able to claim that they had taken the

Symons document into account, gave token acknowledgement to the field by relabelling some courses into an informal Canadian studies package, the kind of window-dressing referred to earlier and noted in some detail in my report.

The third 'generic approach' to Canadian studies, also found in the Symons volume, is what is often styled 'applied' Canadian studies. As indicated, this term means work on Canadian questions done in the applied arts and the applied sciences as well as in some of the professions. Symons dealt with these in the final two chapters in his first volume which were entitled 'Science, Technology and Canadian Studies' and 'The Canadian Component in Education for the Professions'. Examples of applied Canadian studies might include some engineering work on specifically Canadian problems, or architectural responses to Canadian climatic or building conditions. An example of one of the dimensions of this approach is a current Science Council of Canada study of the Canadian context of science education.

Despite the different degrees of development of these approaches there are some common problems to note:

• financial constraints affect the ability of university and research libraries to continue aspects of collection building;

• the Canadian archival system could be said to be in serious ill-health – gaps in archival collections and standards are serious – as well, there is pressing need for trained archivists and appropriate archival science teaching programmes;

• financial problems facing projects like CIHM and scholarly publishers in Canada, *eg* the McGill-Queens and University of Toronto presses;

• problems of Canadian publishers generally and, in particular, the distribution of Canadian materials abroad.

There are growing numbers of students, teachers, researchers and scholars in countries around the world studying Canada. Associations to promote Canadian studies have been established in Australia, Britain, France, Ireland, Italy, Germany, Japan and the United States. There are centres for such studies in Austria, Belgium, Denmark, Holland, India, Israel, Norway, Sweden, the Soviet Union, Thailand and elsewhere.

These centres and programmes explain some of the basic notions about Canadian society, its structures and culture, as well as using some sophisticated methodological approaches to Canadian studies. In many cases students are learning one or both of our official languages as a prerequisite to explorations of our literature, history and traditions.

Reasons for foreign interest are as many and varied as the list of countries might suggest. Some of them are federal states and comparative studies intrigue scholars in them. Others have become students of Canada because they, as anglophones or francophones themselves, have stumbled onto what is for them a new promising literary lode to mine. Still others have been attracted because of Canada's particular place in the world as part of the

Commonwealth, or as part of the developed world, or as part of the 'North–South' dialogue. Whatever their reasons, they are interested and their numbers are increasing.

Many Canadians find foreign interest remarkable. Some express surprise and delight, others mild amusement, and still others disbelief. For their part, those from abroad are often astonished by the fact that Canadians appear to show relatively scant interest in themselves.

The fact that our society in general and that our educational system in particular have undervalued or ignored Canadian issues and concerns has been amply documented in a number of major studies. The most important of them is *To Know Ourselves: The Report of the Commission on Canadian Studies*. I doubt that a similar document could be written about any other developed nation although some Australian colleagues tell me otherwise. Symons wrote that:

. . . there are few other countries in the world with a developed post-secondary educational system that pay so little attention to the study of their own culture, problems and circumstances in the university curriculum.[1]

Not surprisingly, the Commissioner encouraged Canadians to learn more about Canada themselves.

The parallels between non-Canadians and Canadians in respect to the development of Canadian studies are not all that far-fetched. In order to learn about their country, many Canadian colleges and universities need to develop new resources and to push forward, often from fairly undeveloped premises, research into Canada's history, literature, sociology, cultural studies, and so on.

It is dangerous to generalise about Canadian studies abroad, but I would like to hazard a few observations. In doing so I would like to draw attention, where possible, to the areas or disciplines in which work on Canada is being pursued in some detail.

First of all, there are a number of nations in which Canadian studies have developed sufficiently that organisations or societies have been established to aid in the sharing of scholarly or curricular work. And there are a few other countries in which associations have been established as catalysts to encourage the development of Canadian studies. Without attempting to explore which situation is chicken and which egg, I think that it is safe to say that in most instances the interest in Canadian studies has predated the development of the organisations, although there are a few instances where scholars, sometimes expatriates, sometimes not, have felt impelled to draw attention to Canadian studies as an area of potential value to non-Canadian colleagues.

In addition to Britain and Canada, and as I have noted, there are associations or societies for Canadian studies in Australia and New Zealand, Ireland, Germany, France, Italy, Japan, and the United States. The oldest and most established of these is the Association for Canadian Studies in the United States, ACSUS. Richard Preston has recently completed an examination of Canadian studies in the United States called *The Squat Pyramid*; the report demonstrates that there is considerable interest in Canadian studies in the United States but that the field is not free of problems and needs. One problem is generating student interest in undergraduate programmes. Another is the difficulty American students, professors and librarians encounter trying to purchase Canadian books. Both of those problems, especially the latter, may be problems shared here in the United Kingdom.

Generally speaking, European interest in Canadian studies is focussed on work in the disciplines, principally geography, literature and history. Interest in French Canada is widespread and there are courses being taught on French Canada's literature and history in most of the countries I have mentioned. In the United Kingdom there appears to be considerable interest in literature, geography and in history, Atlantic Canadian history in particular. There are a host of reasons for the latter, and the availability of source materials of various kinds on the early settlement of Maritime Canada means that there is much to attract scholarly interest. We will learn much more about Canadian studies in the United Kingdom from Cedric May.

The associations in Europe vary in size and in vigour. The British association numbers about 150 members, the German about 200, the Italian about the same, and the French about 250 scholars and researchers. One of the most vigorous associations, in terms of conference and publishing activity is, perhaps, l'Association française des études canadiennes, although one would have a hard time finding elsewhere the level of enthusiasm for Canadian studies that there appears to exist in the Gesellschaft für Kanada-Studien. The annual conferences of the German society are quickly becoming legendary, both for the quality and intensity of discussion, and for cultural events and a splendid table.

The Japanese Association for Canadian Studies evidences interest primarily in economics, literature, history and sociology. There is particular interest in trade and resources management matters as well, for obvious reasons. Japanese students seem attracted to Canadian studies courses in preparation for careers in business, finance and tourism. There is also interest in the history of the Japanese in Canada.

The newest associations are the Australian/New Zealand organisation and the Irish association. ANZACS, the acronym for the Australian and New Zealand Association for Canadian Studies held its inaugural conference on the theme 'Comparative Theory and Practice' in Australian and Canadian studies. This raises an important point. Increasingly interest in Canada abroad is taking on a comparative edge. For example, the newly established centre for Canadian studies at the Free University of Brussels, in Belgium, is planning its first conference on the topic 'Great Neighbours', and plans to compare the Canadian-American experience with the Belgian-French one. Canadian studies in Ireland, it seems to me, could quite easily and advantageously take on a comparative aspect as well. Work on Irish immigration to Canada is, of course, a cornerstone of interest there.

All of the Associations for Canadian Studies have agreed to establish an International Council for Canadian Studies. I would like to conclude with a few very brief observations about the Council and its work.

The ICCS was established in June 1981, during the Learned Societies Conference at Dalhousie University. The Council has nine member associations and a number of non-Canadian centres or programmes of Canadian studies outside of those nine nations have become affiliates. The Council acts as a clearing-house for information on Canadian studies developments in this international network. A regular, rather extensive, newsletter is published. The Council held a major international symposium on Canada in June 1983 during the Learned Societies meetings at the University of British Columbia. The next full meeting and conference of the Council will be in Montreal in 1985 under the chairmanship of Pierre Savard, the new ICCS president.

The Council is also interested in drawing attention to Canadian studies in appropriate ways, and in encouraging developments in the field. To that end, the Council has joined with a major Canadian corporation in announcing the Northern Telecom International Award in Canadian Studies. This Award is designed to honour scholars, teachers, or researchers who have made outstanding contributions to the development of Canadian studies, or to the study of Canada. The Award, which will be presented annually, is to be administered by the International Council for Canadian Studies. Northern Telecom, the sponsor of the Award, will present a medal made of one-half a pound of gold and $10,000 to the winner. The first award winner, chosen by an internationally constituted panel of five chaired by Donald Simpson of the Royal Commonwealth Society, was Richard Preston of Duke University.

Reference

1. T H B Symons, *To Know Ourselves: The Report of the Commission on Canadian Studies*, AUCC (Ottawa: 1976), Vol.1, p.128.

Cedric May

A perspective on advanced research in Canadian Studies in the United Kingdom

I am very grateful to the colleagues and friends who have answered a questionnaire which the High Commission kindly circulated for me earlier this year. Without the information they provided, I would not presume to pronounce on this vast and rather daunting topic.

The subject to which I am asked to address myself seems couched in too ambitious terms. Few of my informants would consider that they were involved in 'higher' research in 'Canadian Studies'. 'Higher' research, perhaps, but then their subject would be Canadian *history* or Canadian *government* for example. Research in 'Canadian Studies', perhaps, but this would be at a very humble level, preparing interdisciplinary material for undergraduate survey courses. Most agree that the academic study of Canada in the United Kingdom is either rigorously based in a single specialism or exploring in a tentative way what the concept of 'Canadian Studies' might mean for the United Kingdom academic working within the British University system. There does, however, appear to me to be a great deal of support and even enthusiasm for the interdisciplinary approach, if not necessarily in teaching and research, at least in symposia and seminars where the cross-fertilisation made possible is considered highly beneficial.

The need for or the justification for research in Canadian subjects goes without question on two grounds. First, it is necessary to counter the appalling ignorance of Canada in this country. The coverage of Canadian affairs in the British press and through radio and television is abysmal. Canada is too familiar to be interesting, too commonplace to be important, and the public turns away, relieved that Canada can be taken for granted. Despite that, the average British undergraduate cannot give reliable answers to simple questions about the principal cities, the salient dates of Canadian history or about something vaguer such as the size of Canada. The second reason for studying Canada is that it provides excellent material for the specialist in a number of fields. Canada's unique legal system, its political solutions, its constitutional debate, its geography, its history, its patterns of settlement and of urban development, its social and ethnic diversity, its adaptation to problems of climate, scale and terrain, the forms its culture gives to its self-affirmation, all these and much more provide rich pickings for the scholar whether they are treated singly or comparatively.

The immense variety of material and approach just hinted at creates immediate problems of credibility for Canadian Studies, though not more so than in the case of US or Australian Studies and rather less than in the case of African or Latin American Studies. Few generalists can claim to be competent in more than a fraction of the subjects covered by the 'Studies' concept. However, on the plus side, Canadian Studies can usefully challenge the narrowness of British academic studies, their jealous guarding of disciplinary frontiers. They can continue patiently to point to the reasonableness and the benefits of the inter-disciplinary approach, even at the undergraduate level, and I make that last remark somewhat guardedly. Canadian Studies is more than just a product of the Ottawa dream-factory, more than just a gleam in the eye of Mr Michael Hellyer. But it can never have in this country the urgency or the sense of intuitive coherence that it has for a Canadian, an urgency and coherence of which Professor Tom Symons is the eloquent exponent. Canada will long remain for the British academic an interesting working hypothesis. Like molecular theory, it is verifiable to a large degree but also requires quite a dose of faith and imagination. It works as a hypothesis as long as the exceptions it throws up do not invalidate the paradigm.

The consequences of what I have very briefly sketched out so far seem to me to be the following:

1. Canadian Studies risks being for an indefinite time to come a low order generalisation which calls for qualities of erudition, versatility and imaginative grasp of a rare and exceptional kind if it is to become 'higher' anything, let alone 'higher research'.

2. Those who venture into Canadian Studies (as distinct from Canadian history or literature or some other specialism) must beware of getting bogged down in the basics – the fate of, say, teachers of Russian. Introductory surveys, broad overviews, however sophisticated and perceptive, can never pass for higher research.

3. We must beware, too, and I am indebted to Professor Shepperson for the helpful formulation of this idea, of importing the mystique of Canadian Studies. Canadian Studies must not become a cult, a concept worshipped, promoted, defended irrationally by devotees who are always mortally offended by coolness, lack of fervour in others. We owe it to ourselves, to our profession and to our subject, to be generously imaginative and eternally sceptical. Canada remains for us no more than a working hypothesis.

4. The *sine qua non* of the 'studies' approach and of the academic generalist, and here lies the justification of this colloquium and others like it, is a good library.

This leads me to a topic implicit in many of the comments I received from my correspondents. Where is higher Canadian research best pursued? I have always sent my graduate students to Canada. My correspondents stress time and again the importance of frequent contact with Canadian colleagues, access to Canadian resources, facilities for student and faculty exchanges and the opportunity to study and also teach in Canada. Two comments only on the foregoing which seems self-evident: there is a certain amount of work to be done here: Professor Roy Parker's study of child immigration or Dr Margaret McKay's work on migration from Tiree. The scope here is limited. Much more valuable to British researchers on Canada in this regard is the advantage of distance and detachment from the object of study. Once we have amassed our material, we gain appreciably from being able to consider it in isolation, away from vested interests, ideological, political, economic, which motivate and perhaps distort research in Canada on Canada. I have always been struck by the surprise I could provoke amongst Québec literature scholars in Québec by asking questions they had stopped asking, by mentioning texts that were unfashionable. It is naturally frustrating not to have one's materials readily to hand, and this is a real drawback we have to face when working at this distance, but the values of detachment are not to be sniffed at.

One curious phenomenon intrigues me and I invite your reflexions on it. Why has the British learned community not produced an Auguste Viatte, a Mason Wade, a Howard Miner, an E C Hughes or an André Siegfried? We seem not to breed the kind of academic prepared to chance his arm at the ambitious synthesis which spans the entire spread of his subject and hits the right balance between erudition and popularisation. Many detached, objective observers of Canada have come from outside, few from Britain. Is it that we lack the de Tocqueville mentality, that we are good at the fine detail, at the mechanics of a subject, but suspect, or lack the power to produce, the broad imaginative synthesis as Matthew Arnold claimed a century ago? The over-specialisation, the scorn for the inter-disciplinary approach, the tradition of strong discipline-based university departments have much to answer for here. We may care to note, however, that this year's Northern Telecom award for service to Canadian Studies went to British-born Dick Preston who, like our other distinguished Canadianist, Professor James Wreford Watson, pursued his career very largely outside Britain and devoted his energies to popularisation as well as scholarship, to creating enthusiasm in others and to undergraduate teaching. Perhaps our British genius lies in these directions. We may wonder, too, whether, to judge from the achievements of Wreford Watson, Scotland is not particularly receptive to Canada as an academic subject.

The issue of British academic attitudes is neatly summed up by a lawyer, though his comment applies in other disciplines too:

Most law schools and learned legal associations are still very narrow-minded; they play down the inter-disciplinary aspects of law; connections with sociology, economics and politics are therefore often missed.

What is the state of Canadian Studies in the UK today? Who is equipped to give an answer? I still smart when I think of an article which appeared in Canadian colour supplements in June 1978, by Ross Henderson.

Scholars all over Europe are signing up in droves for courses in a fashionable new subject – Canada . . . Canadian Studies are a hot academic growth industry all the way from Birmingham to Bologna.

This was maybe telling the Canadians what they wanted to hear but it was neither what Mr Henderson was told nor what he could observe. No purpose is served by exaggeration or by hyperbole which is not matched by the facts. The Canadian High Commission is occasionally guilty of oversell of this kind. Its recent Canadian Academic Newsheet no. 14, Spring 1983, paints a picture of 'a developing network of Regional Canadian Study Centres' and of 'a network of Canadian Studies in Britain'. The term 'network' suggests a degree of strategy, of inter-communication and of collaboration which is not matched on the ground. It suggests a consensus about Canadian Studies which frankly does not exist and which has hardly ever been considered. We must be scrupulously honest about these things and very careful not to create expectations which we cannot fulfil. The reality was well illustrated at the concluding session of the BACS Annual Conference at Leeds in April 1983. Professors and lecturers from Law, Sociology, Politics, English Literature and Russian outlined what he or she was doing related to Canada in his or her department. Canadians present were up in arms at what emerged. Why no undergraduate survey course on Canada? Why no concerted effort to promote an inter-disciplinary approach? Why must Canadian literature suffer the indignity of being studied only as a component of a comparative Commonwealth literature course? Why only one or two Canadian novels when it is Canadian theatre which is most impressive and most accessible to students? And so on. And yet the Leeds approach, cool, fragmentary, discipline-based, highly selective, is not untypical of what goes on in British universities. There is some undergraduate teaching. There are undergraduate survey courses. My strong impression is that, with perhaps the exception of the excellent work done in Edinburgh, undergraduate teaching on Canada does not provide a stream of postgraduate students keen to work on Canadian topics. We can ask why as a number of my informants do. The career prospects for graduates who have specialised on Canada are not obvious. The lack of library resources and basic research data deter some postgraduates. Then again, is the SSRC, for example, more likely to fund relevant projects researching British or European problems rather than research on North America?

I attempt to describe here what I see, and what I see, very largely, is a considerable body of higher research on Canadian subjects pursued in relative isolation by academics who see themselves in terms of their subject-discipline and who are not immediately aware of the advantages of greater coordination under a Canadian Studies umbrella. The list of topics is lengthy but worth hearing:

Canadian history including federalism, Commonwealth relations, the Governor-generals and Canada Africa links; planning in Canada, glacial geology, Indian map-making, Canada as an element in a geography of the Pacific rim, regional problems and policies, oil revenues and migration; comparative perspectives on the capitalist state, international economic relations; Romance linguistics, sociolinguistics and bilingualism; Canadian literature in English and in French; International justice, Canadian jurisprudence, UN peace-keeping, Canadian private international law; world-wide terrorist violence, the politics of health, party politics and regionalism, questions of national identity, futurology; media policies and cultural sovereignty.

One of my informants commenting on the very fragmented nature of Canadian subjects in her university concluded as follows:

As these *separate* areas become better established, more inter-disciplinary studies should be possible – but that's still very much in the future for us here.

This seems to me a healthy situation. British academics will not welcome attempts to impose foreign concepts on their work. The growth of the BACS, the provision of resources for Canadian Studies, the future of the book market, the funding of research, must all proceed from an honest and realistic appraisal of the situation as it can be observed to exist.

I want to turn now to research on Canada in the UK and to ask how it can be furthered and supported and by whom. I will range rather widely here because a subject such as sixth-form curriculum development may not appear to impinge on higher research but might clearly be seen as part of a long-term strategy for giving academic legitimacy to a subject area. I will discuss the facilitating of research under the following heads:

1. Academic relations at the High Commission and the role of the Provinces.
2. Travel.
3. Libraries.
4. Teaching provision and the Centres.
5. The British Association for Canadian Studies, the Foundation for Canadian Studies in the UK and the International Council.

1. Canadian Government Academic Relations

One of my informants, in particular, praises the centralised information service provided by Michael Hellyer through his Academic Newsheets and in other ways. I would add to that my own whole-hearted endorsement of the work done by Michael Hellyer. I have criticised a bit of over-enthusiastic window-dressing by the High Commission and I wonder to what extent this is a response to pressure from Ottawa to promote Canadian Studies in the UK on a certain model and at a certain pace. In my experience, External Affairs in Ottawa has shown some insensitivity to the reality of Canadian Studies in this country and this has not been helped by a rapid turn-over of staff in Academic Relations in Ottawa and frequent changes of policy made worse by a communications problem. Let me stress that this is very much the surmise of an outsider and may be wide of the mark. In view of the spectacular success of Michael Hellyer in his job, I hope he is allowed to carry it out without too much pressure from across the Atlantic. He pursues his objectives intelligently, tactfully, cheerfully, listens patiently, learns fast and responds constructively and is of enormous help and encouragement to all who work with him.

Several of the Canadian Provinces have delegations in London and, in theory at least, have an officer one of whose duties is academic relations. Lack of funds, lack of staff, lack of a clear strategy no doubt hamper them in anything they might contemplate doing. My contacts with Ontario House have been friendly and useful and my Department of French has had a steady and fruitful relationship with Québec House for the past twenty years. The Québec government for several years gave my Department a postgraduate scholarship, and a second reciprocal scholarship with Birmingham was negotiated and ran for a few years. These have now gone and the Québec government has replaced them with a scheme to send us up to five Québec academics or writers each year. This involves us in a great deal of administration arranging visits and setting up tours with other universities. There is also the constant worry over finding audiences but the scheme has had a reasonably successful first year. I would encourage the Provinces to give serious thought to the ways in which they can contribute to the British academic programme, perhaps by making their official publications readily available. Their best course, without any doubt, is to collaborate closely with Mr Michael Hellyer but they do not need me to tell them this.

2. Travel

Financial aid to facilitate travel to Canada for the purposes of research comes through the High Commission's Faculty enrichment programme, from the Foundation for Canadian Studies in the UK and from the Canadian Government through the BACS. All my informants stress the importance of this assistance and attest the value of regular contacts with Canadian colleagues, access to Canadian materials, the possibility of field research and the stimulus of attending Canadian conferences. I hope that Canadian spending on Canadian Studies is constantly reviewed so that any finance which seems to be being used unproductively can be redirected into support for research visits.

3. Libraries and book-purchase

My informants frequently refer to the difficulties of obtaining Canadian books and other materials. One person found the Lending Division of the BL slow in obtaining recent material and would like to see improved Canadian official publications holdings at the BL, but does not specify whether he means provincial or federal publications. Many colleagues requiring Canadian publications use friends in Canada and one, like me, has friends in publishing and book-selling. Given the small size of the market and the almost total absence of any bulk demand, I am surprised at the patience and enthusiasm of the Canadian publishers who have been very good friends of the BACS. I keep wondering when the honeymoon will be over. One of my correspondents comments that naturally the trade thinks in terms of teaching-based research and must find the kind of single-copy trade we give them costly and time-consuming. On this front, I see lots of goodwill but poor prospects for improvement to a frustrating situation.

To my question: 'Is the concentration of research facilities in one or two centres (London and Edinburgh, for example) desirable or do you favour a greater proliferation?' the response was almost unanimous: concentration every time. The best comment spoke of 'critical mass'. Until a research library reaches this 'critical mass', it will disappoint its customers. The wide dissemination of scarce resources makes research impossible. The High Commission has been inclined to pursue a 'seed-corn' and 'token presence' approach. Times are against such an approach paying off. The development of Canadian Studies in Wales, Northern Ireland and London must not be carried out at the cost of neglecting the one or two centres of excellence which exist and are conspicuously successful. Three things impress me on the Canadian scene in the UK, the example set by Academic Relations in London, the library collection of the British Library and the Centre of Canadian Studies in Edinburgh. I applaud the appointment of the new director there, I see there signs of growth, the buiding of a reputation which attracts scholars of repute and I personally would see that these three centres of excellence were not starved of funds.

Since I first contributed to the discussion on Canadian Studies at Magdalen College in 1977, I have argued consistently against proliferation and you may be interested to know that I was opposed to the creation of a Centre for Canadian Studies in Birmingham when the idea was first floated.

Voices in favour of concentration are naturally more muted when they come from Belfast or Durham. The simple answer to the problem, an acute one, of the rising cost of travel, is to make travel funds available to allow researchers from the provinces to work on the material available in London or Edinburgh. One good point that emerges from my survey is a plea for a research library open to all, not just to readers at the BL or to those with access to a university library. What, I wonder, are the chances of expanding and publicising the research potential of Canada House?

Modified forms of the proposal for concentration suggest more centres, perhaps six: Edinburgh, Leeds, Birmingham, London, Wales and Northern Ireland. University Librarians here may like to comment on the implications of such a proposal for them, their staff and their book-stock.

Together with these proposals, can I mention another which I have been making regularly since I first outlined it in a letter of 2 May 1977, to Richard Noyes Roberts, namely the creating of specialist research collections based on existing collections in university libraries? For the sake of argument, in addition to maintaining a basic reference collection and an appropriate undergraduate collection, Edinburgh might specialise in Geography and History, Leeds in English Canadian literature and Sociology, Birmingham in French Canada and Fine Arts, London in Political Science. Collections in other specialist areas such as Church history might be sited in Dorset, and so on. I can appreciate that it might be difficult to reach agreement on the detail of such a scheme but I feel it makes sense, it attempts to do something about the wastage involved in the random dissemination of scarce resources and it is a practical step towards creating the 'critical mass' already referred to without which research at any level is impossible.

4. Teaching provision in the UK

I have serious doubts about the value of teaching Canada at the undergraduate level. Students find survey courses exciting and enjoyable but they retain little of what they learn and rarely go on to specialise on Canada. A graduate student thoroughly grounded in a discipline such as Geography, History or Literature, soundly trained through the medium of orthodox course-work, will very rapidly acquire a knowledge of Canada adequate at least for the specialist research he will be conducting. I say this after twenty years of undergraduate teaching on the literature of Québec.

Prospects for postgraduate study are not good but this is where our efforts should be concentrated. Research money is increasingly difficult to obtain and good students, given the climate, opt automatically for safe, mainstream subjects and fields of research. As more than one of my respondents comment, it is hard to attract good graduate students into research on Canada.

Rather than seeking to create teaching posts in British universities, posts to which enthusiasts cannot get their colleagues to give any kind of priority, or temporary, fixed-contract posts with the accompanying human tragedy which follows from lack of tenure, we should be directing available finance into funding collective research projects. I am sure that proposals would be forthcoming from British academics. Our Birmingham Centre for Urban and Regional Studies is working out a collaborative project with a University in Alberta to study legislation for leisure pursuits and the administration of tourism. I can imagine them coming forward with a carefully budgeted proposal involving some expense for travel and materials but providing a place for a graduate student who would do the bulk of the work under direction and come out of it with the basis for his or her graduate thesis. This appears to me to be the way to give validity and academic standing to our subject.

5. The BACS

Founded in 1975, the British Association for Canadian Studies is a small learned body with a *Bulletin*, a *Newsletter*, an Annual Conference and several subject Committees, fulfilling a valuable role, if I am to believe my informants, in promoting the serious study of Canada in Britain. It is readily admitted that its scope for fostering higher research is limited. It is rather a fellowship of scholars and others with an interest in Canada who benefit from the stimulus of being occasionally together in inter-disciplinary gatherings. Where BACS can help research is by coordinating and publicising the availability of resources for Canadian Studies (I refer to the work of Donald Simpson, Valerie Bloomfield and Michael Hellyer) and by acting as an informed channel for the distribution of research money: understandably, British academics working on Canada often prefer to attend the meetings of their appropriate learned society. Others, who feel that their learned society ignores their personal interests, naturally see the value of a body such as BACS. Of course, some of my informants see BACS as dominated by certain sectional interests but, by and large, the formula finds favour. I have enjoyed and profited immensely from my work with BACS since I convened the first annual conference in Birmingham in 1976 and later as Secretary, Vice-President and President, and have never resented the considerable demands it makes on my time or been sceptical about the point of it all. We need members. The annual subscription is tiny and I encourage everyone even marginally interested to give us their support. One of my informants said that the BACS was not for him as he was not a mainstream Canadianist. The BACS is, on the contrary, the forum for sidestream Canadianists which is what most of us have to confess to being. The creation of the International Council for Canadian Studies does not immediately appear to have any relevance to the subject under discussion, though it has already shown skill in attracting funds for Canadian Studies and some of these may be used one day to stimulate research.

I conclude with a list of recommendations and discussion points and one plea – that we will not idly pursue Canadian Studies but rather discover it as the happy, accidental by-product of our devotion to our own unique involvement with some branch of the study of Canada. Canadian Studies is like the 'feu follet' that lured pioneers onto the marshes and of which Québec folklore, superstition and literature is full. It is not an end in itself but a place of meeting and as such it has already established itself sufficiently not to need to justify its existence or its 'raison d'être'.

Summary, recommendations and discussion points

1.0 The academic study of Canada has a valuable contribution to make to the world of learning.

1.1 It automatically challenges our assumptions, offering us an alternative America.

1.2 It provides interesting comparisons with the major Western cultures against which it asserts itself – British, French and United States.

1.3 It permits us to study an emerging culture, developing rapidly because of its vast resources.

1.4 It lends itself readily to the interdisciplinary approach, so calling into question the narrowness of traditional discipline-based research.

1.5 It can help to dispel ignorance of Canada in Britain.

1.6 We need to demonstrate the evident value of Canadian Studies by involving those with a latent interest: in teaching projects, in seminars and colloquia, in the BACS and in collaborative research.

1.7 Those of us with a voice in the main learned societies should take the opportunities which undoubtedly exist for proposing Canadian speakers or subjects. With the help of the Government of Québec, I recently had Marie-Claire Blais invited to the gathering of the SFS (Society for French Studies) in Birmingham; this session was very well received.

1.8 Britain has not produced the grand, comprehensive synthesis on Canada and the inter-disciplinary approach still seems premature. We are clearly involved in a long-term exercise.

1.9 There are distinct rewards for the academic studying Canada. It is an uncluttered field and the detachment, the cool perspective, provide a proper critical distance permitting original insights.

2.0 The consequences of the foregoing call for very serious attention:

2.1 For some time to come, Canadian Studies as an organising principle is likely to remain a low order generalisation in the UK. It is best seen as a happy by-product of our involvement with some branch of Canadian subjects.

2.2 We must avoid making a mystique of Canadian Studies.

2.3 We must be aware of the dangers of alienating colleagues by oversell.

2.4 Our Canadian counterparts must not expect and must not try to impose Canadian approaches to Canadian Studies here.

2.5 Those involved in Canadian Studies in the UK, as officers of the BACS, as members of Centres or of other teaching and research teams, as contact persons with the Canadian High Commission, as co-ordinators of programmes for visiting Canadian academics and writers, must keep a sharp eye on the demands made on them and on their priorities. It is far too easy to get bogged down in basics and to make bad decisions in allocating one's time and energy amongst the conflicting aims of research, teaching, administration and public relations. These individuals must be protected where they are in danger of sacrificing their research potential.

3.0 Canadian government and other agencies make an important contribution in facilitating research, the acquisition of resources and academic travel and exchanges.

3.1 Mr Michael Hellyer is doing a splendid job as Academic Relations Officer and should be given as much autonomy as possible to develop his programme in response to the particular situation which obtains in the British academic world.

3.2 The Agents General for the Provinces should think out their role in consultation with the academics and with Mr Hellyer. It may seem churlish not to be grateful for the symbolical gift (single volumes in luxury bindings, etc) but this kind of tokenism and publicity-seeking is an embarrassment which can involve wasted expense and does nothing for academic studies.

3.3 Visiting Canadians can stimulate interest in Canada at every level. The following regularly arrange visits: the High Commission Cultural Affairs Section, the Québec Delegation, the Union des Ecrivains du Québec. In addition, the Edinburgh Centre regularly has academic visitors whom other universities wish to invite. To these must be added the single visit, the visit of Margaret Atwood, for example, arranged by the Welsh Arts Council. The work involved in arranging visits and audiences is considerable. Sponsors must see there are no bad apples in this basket and it is imperative that generous lead-time is given in every case to those welcoming visitors.

3.4 The Foundation for Canadian Studies in the UK has a good record. It should aim in any new initiatives at providing research monies rather than at funding temporary teaching posts. To see that it is fully advised on the effectiveness of its programme, it might consider taking on additional academic members to its board.

3.5 The facilities for travel provided by the Canadian High Commission Faculty Enrichment Awards, the Foundation for Canadian Studies in the UK Travel Grants and through the BACS are the greatest incentive to research and should be given high priority. Such funds are no doubt open to abuse but there is now sufficient competition to ensure that only worthwhile projects are supported and the scrutiny of the applications should rule out any scepticism about the returns on this kind of investment. It is, however, worth noting that the Québec scholarship given annually to the Birmingham French Department was withdrawn because the returns did not justify the outlay.

4.0 Book-acquisition, the location of resources and questions of Canadian bibiliography are rightly seen as fundamental in any higher research programme.

4.1 The High Commission's Book Donation programme is of considerable benefit and a model of its kind.

4.2 The BACS Library and Resources Committee with which the work of Mrs Valerie Bloomfield is associated, has already attacked a number of the questions raised in this area in a very intelligent and effective manner. The work of their chairman and committee is warmly commended.

4.3 The following matters could well receive their attention:
4.3.1 Vigorous liaison with our friends and contacts amongst Canadian publishers to retain their goodwill.
4.3.2 The urgent need to rationalise book acquisition on Canadian subjects in UK libraries to minimise duplication and to create research collections with the necessary 'critical mass'.
4.3.3 The preparation of a listing, possibly for publication in the BACS *Newsletter*, of second-hand booksellers in Canada, listed by specialism where appropriate. Co-operation from booksellers would, I presume, be readily forthcoming.
4.3.4 Making proposals for the creation of a very small number of reference collections of Canadiana, or for strengthening existing collections. These proposals to include one for a collection open to all (which is not strictly the case with the BL or university libraries).
4.3.5 Making proposals for financial aid to permit researchers to consult such research collections in the UK or even in Europe if necessary.

5.0 Whilst maintaining our long-term investment in teaching at the secondary and tertiary levels, we should concentrate any new initiatives that become possible on postgraduate research.

5.1 Consideration should be given to the possibility of responding to requests from universities for support for collaborative research projects, either between Canadian and British institutions or involving two or more colleagues in a British institution. Such projects should normally involve postgraduate students who would carry out the bulk of the research under guidance.

5.2 BACS should follow the lead given by the Association for Canadian Studies in Ireland and incorporate into their Annual Conference a session at which postgraduate students would have the opportunity briefly to present their research.

6.0 The British Association for Canadian Studies is run by overworked academics. Its flaws can all be attributed to this factor. Despite a certain inefficiency which it is constantly trying to correct, it appears to fulfil its function of acting as a fellowship of specialists with an interest, often a very secondary one, in Canada. It plays a useful role in providing interdisciplinary stimulation and cross-fertilisation.

6.1 The ICCS (International Council) makes sense in North American terms, but the much younger, smaller European associations are inclined to see it as a very costly luxury. It is successful in attracting funds and it is to be hoped that these could be used to promote rather than to reward research.

6.2 I can personally attest to the considerable value of interchange between the various European associations, having in the past year read papers at the conferences of the French and Irish Associations. We share a common perspective with our European colleagues. The differences are negligible but are largely beneficial.

6.3 Such interchange should be encouraged and even institutionalised.

6.4 Particularly close links must be maintained between the BACS and the ACSI (Ireland).

Cedric May wishes to thank the following who responded to his questionnaire for their valuable assistance:

Dr R Allison, College of St Mark and St John, Exeter
Miss J M Balchin, University of Leeds
Dr J W Cairns, The Queen's University, Belfast
Mr I Campbell, University of Edinburgh
Dr C Carter, College of Art, Dundee
Mr D Clough, North East Surrey College of Technology
Mr R Collins, Polytechnic of Central London
Dr A J Crosbie, Centre for Canadian Studies, Edinburgh
Ms M Davis, The Queen's University, Belfast
Mr B Dickson, The Queen's University, Belfast
Mr D V Donnison, University of Glasgow
Mr K A Goddard, The Queen's University, Belfast
Professor T E Hope, University of Leeds
Dr C A Howells, University of Reading
Dr L Hunter, University of Wales Institute of Science and Technology
Professor A James, University of Keele
Dr J G Kellas, University of Glasgow
Mr A H M Kirk-Greene, Oxford University
Mr G M Lewis, University of Sheffield

Ms L Lloyd, Keele University
Dr M Lynn, The Queen's University, Belfast
Dr P Lyon, University of London
Mr A Macdonald, University of Leeds
Dr A F Madden, Nuffield College, Oxford
Mr P Madgwick, Oxford Polytechnic
Mr G Mercer, University of Leeds
Professor R Moore, University of Aberdeen
Mr P S Noble, University of Reading
Mr J Othick, The Queen's University, Belfast
Professor R A Parker, University of Bristol
Mr R M Punnett, University of Strathclyde
Mr D J Ratcliffe, University of Durham
Dr P A Russell, University of Birmingham
Mr L J Sharpe, Nuffield College, Oxford
Professor G A Shepperson, University of Edinburgh
Dr B C Smith, University of Bath
Professor A Straw, University of Exeter
Professor P Wilkinson, University of Aberdeen
Dr A F Williams, University of Birmingham
Mr M J Winterburn, Ealing College of Further Education

Ged Martin

Observations on the Case for Canadian Studies in the United Kingdom

I am most grateful to Cedric May for his kind comment on my appointment as Director of the Centre of Canadian Studies at Edinburgh, and, as one in the process of moving from the Irish Republic, I can also pay tribute to his work in encouraging close links with the Irish Association. My job at Edinburgh will involve working with many people already active in the study and teaching of Canada, and so at this stage I am obviously speaking only for myself, but I think it is fair to say that the intention is to move from Canadian studies with a small s, to use the distinction employed by Professor Symons this morning, towards Canadian Studies with a capital S, a more consciously interdisciplinary or cross-disciplinary teaching approach.

In doing so, it seems to me that we on this side of the ocean must have a conscious and independent intellectual reason for our involvement in Canadian Studies, not least so that we may make the contribution to Canadians' understanding of themselves which Jim Page sees as one of the benefits of the international movement. The danger is not, as Cedric May fears, that Canadians will impose their own approach upon us, because Canadians are not people who impose, but rather that we may feel, without further enquiry, that we can adopt their definition of Canadian Studies and so slip inside a garment which cannot fit us.

The rationale for Canadian Studies in Canada is – I quote Tom Symons from his remarks this morning – 'very simply, the need for self-knowledge'. Clearly, that cannot apply in anything like the same way here. 'To know ourselves', the Canadian motto for Canadian Studies, is of relevance to us at best marginally and obliquely. We must seek some other basis on which to found Canadian Studies in Britain.

But if we apply the need 'to know ourselves' to the perhaps disparate group of people engaged in the study and teaching of Canada in this country, the membership of BACS, I suspect that we shall find common origins to our own enthusiasms in an identification with Canada – perhaps because we matured at a time when Commonwealth associations were taken more seriously, perhaps because of family links with Canada – or from living or working there, which also suggests prior identification with the country. My fear is that these associations no longer mean very much to the eighteen-to-twenty year-olds whom we wish to draw into our classes. Thanks to the work of organisations like the Commonwealth Institute and the Royal Commonwealth Society, the retreat from the Commonwealth identity has been stemmed, but I doubt if it will ever again have the pull it possessed twenty years ago. Similarly, and contrary to what Professor Bolton has said of Australia, the migration links with Canada will become weaker.

Thus it would seem that we must recognise that our interests in Canada originate in an identification which will tend to mean less to students nowadays. Consequently, we must reverse our approach – work not outwards from our identification with Canada, but seek to define needs within higher education and show how these can be met by Canadian Studies. There can be no doubt that we need an independent British rationale for what we are doing. Such a rationale would, for instance, recognise openly that over here we have to distinguish between the importance of the French fact and the French language, that we cannot place the emphasis upon bilingualism which Jim Page, among others, regards as essential for Canadian Studies in Canada, but rather we must rely on translation – an area in which Cedric May is obviously so well qualified. It would also enable the British Library to see its Canadian holdings in a wider perspective, recognising for instance that a scholar interested in social patterns in Newfoundland may need a local history of Teignmouth or Poole not available anywhere in Canada.

One need which is widely felt to exist in British higher education is the development of cross-disciplinary studies. I take Cedric May's point that literature does not immediately relate to a whole range of subjects, but I think the obstacles are not as great in other areas. As a historian, for instance, I can present an introduction to Canadian Studies only around the theme: 'Canada: history versus geography or history plus geography' – has the country been created in spite of its geography or because of it? Yet a historian taking into account geographical elements – distance, climate, terrain, resources – is not in the same position as a geographer analysing the same questions, any more than a geographer acknowledging Canada's inheritance from the past will necessarily discuss the significance of the material in historical terms. Thus a geographer and a historian may collaborate in teaching a cross-disciplinary course on a subject which can hardly be accused – as is sometimes the case with the 'Studies' approach – of having an artificial and contrived focus. I was very glad to hear Tom Symons confront the issue of scholarly rigour in Canadian Studies. It is an essential challenge for any cross-disciplinary study, and I believe that by drawing upon well-established scholarly disciplines, we can demonstrate that Canada is a field of study in which the highest standards may be maintained – by drawing upon the work of those studying some aspect of the country within individual subjects. Thus, although, as Cedric May says, the standard practice in British higher education of taking in a Canadian topic within a departmental degree can be seen as a step to the future, it can also be seen as a guarantee of standards, a foundation in two respects. My own approach starts from the overlap of the historical and geographical ways of thinking about Canada, but I believe that this can easily be broadened to include economics and economic history, sociology and indeed literature. Our first line of argument for Canadian Studies in Britain, then, should be a response to the need for cross-disciplinary degree programmes which focus on a real and defined experience and draw upon established and respectable published work – rather than some cobbled-together notion of a collective experience which has a coherence only in terms of the boundaries imposed upon it by its progenitors and lacks any depth of recognised scholarship upon which to draw.

I believe also that a second line of justification for Canadian Studies – indeed for any study of the Canadian experience – can be found by asking what have been the basic purposes behind degree courses in the humanities and social sciences since they were established in our universities in the nineteenth century. I suggest that they have two basic functions: the first, to transmit cultural values and attachment to institutions, and the second, to train people in the solution of problems. Arts faculties over the past century have attempted to educate, first, statesmen, then administrators, teachers and – more recently and perhaps with less striking success – social workers. Behind these tacit motives lay still more latent assumptions – that our values and institutions could be indefinitely passed on, and that problems were invariably susceptible of solution. Since the optimistic 'sixties, we have come to realise that the latter at least is not true, that some problems are permanent and intractable, and that their prolonged existence threatens our institutions and values. How do we uphold democracy and individual freedom, and co-exist with the Russians? How can we fight evil in Northern Ireland and at the same time maintain the principles of our legal system?

It is with reference to this troubled world of the 'eighties that I believe we can advance a case for the study of Canada as a problem-accommodating society. One of Canada's distinctive features, in political terms, is that it is not a problem-solving country, in the sense of ultimately resolving and writing *finis* to the conflicts and strains between regions and cultures, and still less to the challenge of maintaining identity and independence alongside the American giant. Essentially Canadian symbols of leadership are not to be found in Lincoln and Roosevelt, but in Macdonald and Mackenzie King, men who maintained and built while seeming only to evade and manipulate. If we wish to prepare students to live in a twenty-first century world, we can do worse than introduce them to a society whose political ABCs are adjustment, balance and compromise, a society which defends and transmits its values – and ours – while accommodating the insoluble. Approached from this angle, Canadian Studies can be presented not as a luxury or an exotic in British higher education, but as the embodiment of the greatest challenge of our civilisation: *survivance*.

These two approaches – the validity of Canada as a focus for cross-disciplinary study and the importance of the Canadian experience in combining conservatism of principle with compromise of practice – represent a personal view of the case for Canadian Studies in British higher education. Others may doubt the value of these arguments, and prefer to make the case from alternative premises. What is important is that we on this side of the ocean should formulate our own independent intellectual basis for what we are doing. Only by so doing can we make the contribution to the Canadians' own understanding of themselves for which Jim Page has called.

Bruce G Wilson

The British Copying and Acquisition Programme of the Public Archives of Canada

It is a maxim long accepted by Canadian scholars that the development of Canada cannot be adequately studied without access to British archival resources.

Perhaps the most adequate way I have of summarising British documentation available for the study of Canada is through the acquisitions and copying programme which my institution, the Public Archives of Canada (PAC), has conducted over the past century in Great Britain and Ireland. I am not claiming that the programme is anything like a perfect mirror of available manuscripts relating to Canada, but its efforts and results are well worth considering if one wishes to develop some sort of overview of available archival resources.

I should first tell you something about the PAC and the history of its British programme. The collecting mandate of the PAC is much wider than that of most national government archives and extends well beyond the acquisition and conservation of national public records. We collect public records, private manuscripts, maps, photographs, watercolours, prints and drawings, sound recordings and radio broadcast tapes, films and machine-readable data. Most of our collections are quite large and from our beginnings, collecting in Great Britain has been a major interest of the PAC. The first Dominion Archivist, Douglas Brymner, was appointed in 1872 and felt strongly that the new nation should be searching for its past among the papers, both official and private, of its former imperial administrator. Brymner, therefore, visited London in 1873 to begin preparing lists of pertinent documents. In 1880, transcribing was begun in the British Museum and, in 1883, in the Public Record Office. By 1902, Brymner's archives consisted of 3,300 volumes, all but about 500 of British origin.

Brymner's successor, Sir Arthur Doughty, is something of a legend among Canadian archivists and historians. A man of considerable charm and tenacity with a fierce dedication to acquisition for his institution, Doughty transformed the Public Archives from a fledgling institution into a major cultural force. He continued the transcription programme, but for him transcripts did not have the glamour and prestige of originals, and so he concentrated with much success upon collecting the papers of colonial administrators, British governors and governors-general. Doughty also put a heavy emphasis upon the collecting of documentary art, especially military topographical art, and maps, and built a collection of documentary prints and watercolours within the PAC which will never be challenged in its extent.

After Doughty's administration, the PAC's overseas programme languished, until Dr Kaye Lamb introduced microfilm to the copying operation in the early 1950s, with one camera in the Public Record Office and the other in our London office. In the next decade and a half, microfilm allowed us to copy much more than we had in the preceeding seventy years. Lamb expanded somewhat the scope of acquisition both in public records and private papers by encouraging copying relating to religious and commercial matters. The main focus of collecting, however, remained political and the prime emphasis was still upon the papers of colonial officials. This, then, has been the broad pattern of our collecting to the time of the present Dominion Archivist, Dr Wilfred Smith.

The Dominion Archivists prior to Dr Smith had taken a personal hand in the runnings of the PAC's British acquisition programme, an indication of the importance the institution attached to the programme. Under Dr Smith, that has changed. There has been in his period of office enormous growth in the PAC at home, and a development of specialisation, especially among archivists working in manuscripts. Heavy emphasis is being placed on collecting in Canada in such subject areas as science and technology, business history, sport and women's history. With the more intense concentration on Canadian resources, the London office has been increasingly left to go its own way and in the last few years, it has been questioned whether the office's continued operation would be useful. I will return at the end of this paper to the question of what might remain to be copied in order to encompass the entire spectrum of archival resources for the study of Canada in Great Britain.

At present, the PAC's manuscript collection from the British Isles and Ireland consists of 7,000 reels of microfilm and 1.3 million pages of originals and transcripts. Using a calculation of 600 frames per reel, if all paper, our collection would amount to 5.5 million pages or about 2,000 shelf feet. To that one might wish to add 2,000 volumes of the records of the British army in Canada, which, with the permission of the War Office in the 1880s, were allowed to stay in Canada and the official papers of the governors-general – about 2,500 volumes – which are the property of the Crown, but again have been allowed to stay. Of the collection acquired in Great Britain, three-quarters is film and about one-quarter is paper. By anyone's standard, the collection is large and a few statistics are necessary to encompass it.

Where has it come from? Only about 5% of the total are originals, either purchased or donated, so that there is an overwhelming predominance of copy. That means, of course, that most of the material I will discuss is still here in Great Britain or Ireland, for the use of researchers. Again, 91.5% of the material we have has been copied from repositories, leaving only 8.5% which was copied or acquired from individuals.

Far and away the most important source for our project is the Public Record Office. The government records stored within that repository and records still in government departments under its general supervision have accounted for 78% of our copying. We started our work there in 1883 and in theory, at least, could probably go on copying its material *ad infinitum*. For a long period, through the PRO's generosity, we had our office in the Chancery Lane premises and through the 1950s to the mid-1960s we employed our own camera there and paid for an operator.

Within the PRO classes, those of greatest interest to us were naturally the Colonial Office classes. These classes encompass 56% of our copying in the PRO and, indeed, 44% of our total collection. We began very early to hand-transcribe this material and to prepare full calendars of it. Even today, one often runs across references in Canadian scholarly publications to our old 'Q' Series covering Ontario and Quebec, the 'A' Series covering Nova Scotia and others.

The introduction of microfilm greatly speeded up the pace of copying and the PAC now holds virtually a total coverage of the classes relating to each Canadian colony. In addition, we have copied a substantial portion of CO 5, which covers military and naval matters for all of British North America before the Revolution and the correspondence on what were to become the lost American colonies. The PAC has copied as well from CO 6, a class which deals with North America in general and includes material on US-Canadian boundary disputes and Arctic exploration. Copying has been carried out in classes relating to emigration, patronage, relevant Confidential Prints and relevant registers.

Seven percent of our PRO copying has come from Admiralty classes, mainly in letters from Canada and station records with a scattering of logs and navy board records concerning the building and running of Canadian yards. The War Office constitutes 10% of our PRO copying and includes in- and out-letters, monthly returns and regimental enlistment registers. There is a heavy representation of ordnance classes concerning canals, fortifications and other structures in Canada. The papers of William Amherst, Commander-in-Chief of British North America, and Sir George Murray, a governor of Quebec, have been copied. The Audit Office holds 3.5% of our PRO copying, mainly accounts for various military works and the individual claims of Loyalists after the American Revolution. The Treasury is only 0.6% of the copying and there, scattered documents relating to financing or policy on a wide variety of government projects have been copied. The Foreign Office accounts for 7% of the copying, mainly FO 5 which deals with the USA and perforce US-Canadian relations. More limited copying has been done from the Courts of Bankruptcy, Board of Trade, Chancery, Cabinet Office, Board of Customs and Excise, Privy Council, State Papers Office, Treasury Solicitor and others. We are presently copying at the General Post Office Archives and have completed more than 200 reels relating to the postal service to Canada.

If the PRO dominates our copying, then London in general also predominates. In addition to the PRO, 9.3% of our copy comes from other London repositories and 3.6% from private hands in London to give a grand total of 91% of our collection. Repositories outside London have contributed only 4% and of that, 2.8% came from outside England, in Wales, Scotland or Ireland. Material in private hands contributed 2.5% for a total of 6.5% outside London. The percentage may not seem high, but it is well to keep in mind that 6.5% of 5.5 million pages is still a substantial amount of material – about 357,500 pages. A further 2.5% in private hands is not now identifiable by location.

Most of our copying is of fairly recent origin, 76% being since the initiation of microfilming in 1950 so that three times as much has been copied in the past 25 years as in the previous 70 years. Only 6% was done from 1880 to 1920, with the 1920s and 1930s contributing 8% and 6% respectively. Despite the fact that most of the material has been recently copied, there is a predominance in the collection of rather traditional sources. If one were to exclude the PRO, where it is virtually impossible to pigeon-hole the classes by subject, roughly 55% of the rest of the collection concerns political or military affairs, political being 33% and military, 22%. General social material makes up 28% and economic, 16%.

Political papers have remained a high priority throughout the programme and there has been a conscious drive to copy the papers of British administrators of Canada in the eighteenth and nineteenth centuries. The private papers of British-born governors-general have been a priority and an area where the programme has had a great deal of success. The PAC holds copies or originals for all the British-born governors-general from Confederation with the exceptions of two between 1926 and 1935, Willingdon and Bessborough. The PAC has also copied extensively in the papers of British political figures heavily involved in Imperial and Canadian affairs. For example, Bathurst, Dartmouth, Shelburne, the 3rd Earl Grey, Cardwell, Curzon and Joseph Chamberlain. Special emphasis has been placed on secretaries of state for the colonies. Material has been copied from papers of diplomats involved in the negotiations of treaties significant to Canada, boundary commissioners, radical politicians like William Roebuck who had links with Canadian radicals, papers of the British Labour Party and even of Canadian politicians like George Brown and Sir Allan McNabb, portions of whose papers are in Great Britain.

On the military side, the PAC has concentrated on the papers of soldier-administrators like Amherst, Carleton, and George Murray as well as Haldimand and Bouquet, both of whose papers are in the British Library. It has also copied papers of those more strictly involved in military matters – Wolfe, in the Seven Years' War, and Prévost for the War of 1812–14. British training of Canadian troops and militia is covered in the Hutton Papers which are in the British Library. The PAC has assembled a substantial collection of diaries and journals of various British soldiers involved in Canadian campaigns, as well as correspondence discussing military actions and military life. There are papers or copies of papers of engineers, surveyors and hydrographers involved in military construction and a smattering of material relating to military medicine. Military men are heavily represented as well in material relating to exploration and social history in general.

Social history as I am using the term is quite a broad and general category. Of the 28% it constitutes, about 5% deals with exploration mainly in the Arctic so that we have done fairly extensive copying from the Royal Geographical Society, the Scott Polar Research Institute at Cambridge and the National Maritime Museum. Another 5% deals with religious history, a subject area in which the PAC has collected fairly systematically so that we do hold material from the Society for the Propagation of the Gospel, the Church Missionary Society, the New England Company, the Colonial and Continental Church Society, the Moravian Brethren, Fulham Palace and the Church of Scotland: Colonial Committee.

Travel journals and general comments on lifestyle and social conditions constitute another large category which as well links closely to collections dealing with emigration. Emigration constitutes both collections of diaries and letters of those who actually emigrated as well as those societies and individuals involved in aiding emigration. The massive transcripts of the papers of Thomas Douglas, 5th Earl of Selkirk, who sponsored projects in the Canadian Maritimes, central Canada and the Red River Colony in the Canadian West are a good example. We have a good deal of material on assisted emigration and have, for instance, filmed close to 170 reels of Barnardo's Children's Homes records as an on-going project. A few collections deal with education, such as the Rhodes Scholarship Trust or societies and clubs such as the Canada Club. There is proportionately little dealing with literary matters, music, science, sport or medicine that we have filmed in Great Britain.

Economics is a category which is somewhat deceptive. As you undoubtedly know, much emphasis in the writing of Canadian history has been placed on the fur trade which, it can be argued, has as much to do with exploration and social history in general as with economics. Many of the collections listed under economics concern the fur trade and none more so than the papers of the Hudson's Bay Company. The PAC holds 1,650 reels, mostly copied in London before the papers were transferred to the Provincial Archives of Manitoba. The reels cover virtually all the HBC records up to 1870 and an on-going exchange programme will permit the PAC to acquire on film the material beyond that date. The HBC papers are the primary source for the study of the early Canadian West and they have been extensively used not only by economic historians, but also by anthropologists, archaeologists, students of architecture and many others. A study of Canadian weather and climatic changes over two centuries has been done from them and a study of the speed at which information was disseminated in the seventeenth century as well as studies of epidemics among the native populations. Material in the papers has also provided the necessary background for the restoration of various forts.

In addition to the fur trade material, there are a substantial number of collections dealing with commerce and shipping, the involvement, for instance, of firms on the English west coast in the Newfoundland fisheries. The PAC holds copies of the relevant papers of the Allan Line and the Canadian Steamship Line. Much of the economic material concerns investment and development, notably the papers of mercantile banks such as Baring Brothers of which the PAC holds 32 feet of originals and Glyn Mills and Company. Both banks were heavily involved with Canadian firms, railways and governments at various levels. There is, on the other hand, very little British material in our collection relating to manufacturing or mining. There is virtually nothing on the twentieth century.

The percentages of the total collection that these subject areas constitute has remained fairly static until the last decade. In the 1970s, the proportion of political and military material declined sharply, while economic material also underwent a slight decline. Material dealing with social history, however, rose sharply to 49% of the total. If one were to look at the proportion of original material as opposed to copy acquired in Great Britain, it has varied from one-quarter to one-half by numbers of collections per decade and there is no discernible pattern. Although I have stressed that originals constitute only a small proportion of our total collection – about 5% – I do not wish to imply that they are unimportant. I have already mentioned the 32 feet of Baring Brothers papers we hold – to this would be added various deposits of the private papers of governors-general. Lord Charles Stanley Monck, Canada's first governor-general, can stand as an example. Perhaps the most important collection of originals of British origin held by the PAC is the Northcliffe Collection, presented in 1923 by Sir Leicester Harmsworth as a memorial to his brother, Viscount Northcliffe. The collection contains manuscripts and rare printed works relating to the Seven Years' War in British North America, including papers of Robert Monckton, George Townsend and James Wolfe. We still acquire some original material in Great Britain and much of it comes as unsolicited donations. In the past few months I have received a journal of an Aberdeen merchant touring Canada, the letters of a member of the Canadian Expeditionary Force in the First World War, a phonograph record of a speech by Governor-General Vincent Massey and the papers of an exiled Polish general who lived in Canada. We also buy from members of the public, from dealers and at auction.

There is good reason to suspect that there is still much material relating particularly to nineteenth- and twentieth-century Canada in private hands in Great Britain. We are, I think, fairly careful in our purchases to limit ourselves to items of specifically Canadian interest and to avoid competition with British institutions who may also have an interest in a collection.

One field in which the PAC has consistently purchased originals is that of topographical art. The PAC came very early into the field at a time when the

National Gallery of Canada was still concerned with establishing a collection of 'international' status which in effect meant the purchasing of European works of art. The PAC began to collect documentary art about 1900 and between the wars, when material was still plentiful and cheap, it purchased on the London market almost literally by the caseload. It now possesses about 90,000 watercolours, oils and prints, the largest such collection in Canada and one which cannot now be duplicated. We do continue to buy on the London market and documentary art, at the moment, is the area in which the majority of our purchases are made.

Cartography is another area in which we purchase in Great Britain and the PAC has stressed not only the purchase of maps of Canada, but also globes and atlases which would show the increasing perceptions of North America by Europeans. As a result the PAC holds, for instance, the most extensive collection of French and Italian atlases in North America. Copying has also been carried out in Britain for the National Map Collection, at one time by draftsman and later through contact prints. The NMC maintains a large reference collection of reproductions, many of them drawn from the British Library or the Public Record Office. We do occasionally buy photographs in Great Britain for our National Photography Collection but that has not yet become a major sector of our activities.

It is easier to point out individual areas of strength within the PAC's British holdings than to address the more general question: to what extent can the British collection of the PAC be considered a true mirror of Canada's past, an accurate reflection of our complex relationship with our imperial progenitor?

It behoves me first to stress the strengths of the copying and acquisition programme. Its most obvious one is its continuity. In over a century of effort, the PAC has built up a substantial knowledge of archival resources in Great Britain relevant to Canada. The scope of the programme has always been fairly wide – social and economic material as well as political and military have been consistently copied. Media other than manuscript have received attention. It is certainly an indication of the importance the institution has placed on its British programme that it received the personal direction of three of the PAC's most dynamic Dominion Archivists and it is an indication of the significance of the PAC's British collection that the work of at least the first two generations of Canadian historians was largely based upon it and could not have been accomplished without it.

If one were to look at the weaknesses of the programme, one would have to take into account the overwhelming dominance of London and the PRO. English County Record Offices and related repositories such as university and public libraries account for less than 2% of our total copying. In Wales, Scotland and Ireland, we have acquired less than 3% of our total collection. The libraries of Oxford and Cambridge, generally conceded to form with London the golden triangle of archival resources, account for less than 1% of our collection. Even in London, many large and small institutions remain largely untapped. I can find no evidence, for instance, that the PAC has done any major work in the British Library since the 1930s. And, although it is not quantifiable, I suspect there is a good deal of material in private hands relating especially to the British middle class and its activities vis-à-vis Canada. Moreover, the nature of material collected is altering, but not quickly enough to satisfy the demands of a new clientele of archivists consisting not only of historians working in new areas but a significant group of social scientists who are beginning to realise the importance of archives to their disciplines.

To rectify this situation, the PAC has undertaken a general survey of manuscripts relevant to Canada in British repositories. Outside London, my office is attempting a systematic coverage of record offices and related institutions by personal visit. Smaller repositories are being contacted by letter. Within London, we are not only reviewing institutions from which we have previously copied, but are also approaching institutions which in the past might not have been touched – the Wellcome Institute for the Study of Medicine, the Royal Botanic Garden, the libraries of the British Museum (Natural History) and of the Institution of Electrical Engineers can stand as examples. Sufficient to say that we are finding little in the way of major collections of administrators or politicians of interest. The PAC has done its job well in those areas. We are finding that much still remains of interest in the papers of religious organisations – we had not previously touched the archives of the Roman Catholic Church or of the Quakers, for instance, and that in many cases where we have previously filmed in religious repositories, there is further material. Specialist repositories are proving a very fruitful field and we have come up with many collections dealing, for example, with medicine, botany and zoology in Canada as well as engineering, architecture and a host of other fields.

Business records, particularly those of the twentieth century, remain a nut which we are unable to crack. Business records are usually described by the category – board minutes, sales books and the like – rather than by the geographical areas in which business was done. Even where business records relating to Canada can be discovered, a simple filming of specific Canadian content may take such material out of context, while the filming of all of a company's records would often be too bulky to consider. For these reasons and because of the sheer magnitude of the task of approaching British companies, this is an area we have left largely untouched.

Finally, the Public Record Office continues to offer challenges despite our extensive copying in the past. We have done relatively little with the classes there which deal with economic matters – Customs, Audit Office and Treasury. Twentieth-century government records dealing with Canada have hardly been touched, although the discovery of twentieth-century material relevant to Canada is much more difficult because of the lack of clearly defined geographical classes – nevertheless, material is still there: in examining the records of the British Atomic Energy Commission, for example, I came across

2,000 volumes of material relating to the Canadian Chalk River project in the Second World War to provide heavy water for the production of an atomic bomb.

Our project has so far left material in private hands largely alone and searches for it could well constitute a separate project after the completion of the present one.

Although the PAC has discovered and copied many collections in Great Britain of relevance to Canada, there is still much left to be done and Great Britain remains a vast and complex storehouse for material for the study of Canada.

Daniel P Waley

Resources for advanced research in Canadian Studies in the British Library Reference Division: archival materials

As a preliminary I should explain that I will take the word 'archival' in my title as referring to all manuscript material and that the papers to be discussed here are much less voluminous than those relating to Canadian history in the Public Record Office. Another preliminary word: any visitor to the Department should have armed himself with the following volume: M A E Nickson, *The British Library: Guide to the catalogues and indexes of the Department of Manuscripts*.

Full catalogues of the Department's holdings have been published for material acquired up to 1955. For subsequent acquisitions readers must turn to the 'Rough Register' held *in situ*. The rough registers for the 1960s and 1970s have been published by the List and Index Society. The annual lists published in the Historical Manuscripts Commission's 'Accessions to Repositories' are also useful. Students should not omit to consult the list of photocopies held in the Department, of which one volume has been published by the List and Index Society, though more recent material is only listed *in situ*. The copies are mainly of manuscript material which has been exported. It is also advisable to look at the register of material on loan. This is not voluminous, but some of it is important and it is not recorded in the published catalogues. Readers should also make use of the 'Amalgamated Index' which brings together in convenient form the index entries from the numerous published catalogues.

The Public Archives of Canada has published a *General Inventory of Manuscripts*, 1974, in which pages 310–372 list transcripts of English material in the Department. Particularly important are the Haldimand Papers. Sir Frederick Haldimand was a Swiss who held positions of command during the Seven Years' War and the American War of Independence. There is also a multi-volume calendar to the Haldimand Papers on the open shelves in the Students' Room. Such aids and a good deal else are of course mentioned by Mrs Valerie Bloomfield in her *Guide to resources*, 1979. Mrs Bloomfield also emphasises the importance of the Royal United Services Institution maps (Additional MSS 57701–57710). About 100 of these maps are of Canadian interest, mostly dating from the period of the Seven Years' War, though a few are earlier and some later. Before proceeding to offer a little information about Canadian material which has slipped through the net of the PAC or is too recent to have achieved publicity as yet, one should refer to the existence of items of topographical interest in the Department of Prints and Drawings of the British Museum.

I shall now turn to describe a few historical sources which may have escaped Canadian scholars. The papers of Sir Charles Dilke, once thought a future Prime Minister, bear on many colonial and imperial matters. Dilke, the author of *Greater Britain*, wrote a number of articles on Canada. The main items of Canadian interest in our collections are in Additional MS 43877, which contains letters from Laurier (1899) about a possible Canadian export duty on nickel and from Sir William Vallance Whiteway, Prime Minister of Newfoundland, (1897–98), about training fishermen for the Naval Reserve.

The papers of H O Arnold-Forster, who was Parliamentary Secretary to the Admiralty, 1900–1903, and Secretary of State for War, 1903–5, have a certain amount to offer. Among the information on imperial defence should be noted correspondence in Additional MS 50304 (1904) about the controversial appointment of a Chief of Staff in Canada.

The Dropmore (Grenville) Papers constitute a vast collection (Additional MSS 58855–59494: 610 volumes). They are mainly papers of William, Lord Grenville, Prime Minister in 1806–7. Additional MSS 59230–59239 contain much that is of Canadian interest, mostly dating from 1785–1790. Grenville was Vice-President of the Board of Trade, 1786–9. There are also some copies of earlier material and some interesting papers for the period after 1790.

Sir Evelyn Wrench (1882–1966) was the founder of the Royal Overseas League and of the English-Speaking Union. Sir Evelyn presented his diaries and much correspondence in 1950, though access to them was reserved until 1975. The diaries describe visits made to Canada in 1906 (Additional MS 59563), in 1912 (Additional MS 59570) and in 1937 (Additional MSS 59582–3).

We come to a very significant recent acquisition, the Carnarvon papers. The 4th Earl of Carnarvon was Under-Secretary for the Colonies, 1858–9, Colonial Secretary in 1866–7 and again in 1874–78. The Earl's 'official' papers were presented to the Public Record Office, but the descendants of his second marriage sold a very large collection which had become separated from what was believed to be the main one, and this was purchased by the British Library at Sotheby's auction in 1978. It has been arranged in 365 volumes. It contains much of Canadian interest, both in the correspondence and the travel diaries and elsewhere. In the correspondence the main Canadian volumes are Additional MSS 60781 and 60803. Additional MS 60781, which is mainly of 1858–9, has letters about the Newfoundland fisheries and some from Governor Douglas of British Columbia. The possibility is mooted of Queen Victoria opening the St Lawrence Bridge, there is material on Nova Scotia and one enquiry: 'Whether I can obtain permission for myself and a few friends to see Buckingham Palace tomorrow'. Additional MS 60803 covers the period 1862–1890; again there is a good deal on Nova Scotia, also information about the fire of 1890 at Toronto University Library. A poem of 1883 is worthy to be recorded:

Earl much-beloved! Permit a bard obscure
A word or two to waft thee on thy tour.

Additional MS 60804 contains notes made before the Earl's tour, in 1882. These mainly chronicled information from various sources about Canada ('Social Separation of French and English,' etc). There is also some speculation, for example, on an 'Anglo-Saxon Alliance'. Thus 'it would be possible to establish an offensive and defensive alliance between England, US, Canada and Australia – all the fragments of the English-speaking race – it would be in some respects like the old German Bund'. Additional MS 60921 is a travel diary (31 August to 20 September 1883). It records interesting talk with Macdonald, the Prime Minister. Macdonald gave the Earl his own proposed solution to the problems of Ireland: 'state-aided emigration of the Celtic population and state-aided immigration of Anglo-Saxons to take their place'!

So far I have mentioned no literary item. I can offer one which bears on Frances Brooke's early novel set in Canada, *The History of Emily Montague* (1769). Additional MS 29747 contains, on folios 68–9, a letter of Frances Brooke to her publisher Robert Dodsley of 29 August 1769. The letter, which is of considerable importance for eighteenth-century publishing history, discusses the book and gives details concerning its publication and sales.

I come now to an acquisition so recent that it has not yet been incorporated into our collections. This is the archive of the Imperial Federation League, received as a gift through the British Records Association. The League was a pressure group which existed from 1884–1894, the chief protagonist being Sir George Parkin. The League did not preserve its correspondence or financial records. The material consists of the minutes of the Executive and General Committees and of the Women's Committee as well as the 'Imperial Federation League in the United Kingdom'. There is also a volume of replies (1891–2) to a questionnaire sent out about imperial federation. Printed pamphlets in the same gift are now in the Department of Printed Books. Some 30 replies were received to the questionnaire, one of the respondents being Sir James Bryce. The minutes of the committee meetings reveal that Sir Charles Tupper, who was among the doubters about federation, helped to break up the League by stating that many of its members were 'mainly interested in levying a large contribution on the revenues of the Colonies for the support of the army and navy of Great Britain'. The break-up of the League occurred partly over the question of imperial free trade, partly over fear of alienating the French-speaking population in Canada. The papers are interesting as revealing the working of a pressure group and a number of the personalities involved were men of importance, such as Bryce, Sir John Seeley, W E Forster, J E Gorst and Lord Rosebery.

Helen Wallis

Resources for advanced research in Canadian Studies in the British Library Reference Division: maps

The British Library possesses collections of early maps and charts of Canada which may claim to be among the finest in the world. We owe these collections to the British Museum's rich heritage and also to enlightened policies pursued by the Museum in collection development over the years.

The Foundation Collections of the Old Royal Library

When the British Museum was established in 1753, many maps and charts came to the Library in the three foundation collections, Cotton, Harleian and Sloane. The fourth collection, the Royal Library, presented by George III in 1757, also included cartographic materials. With the opening of the Reading Room in 1759 the importance of these holdings was quickly recognised. Among the early visitors was Captain Palliser, Governor of Newfoundland, Captain Cook's commanding officer and later friend and patron. He called on 27 April 1764 to inspect the sea charts of the Sloane collection. 'Special leave was given to see them, though the Museum was not open.' Presumably Palliser was interested in the MS maritime atlases (or Waggoners) of America by William Hack, c1680.

King George III's Topographical and Maritime Collections

Despite some notable items, the Old Royal Library was not as rich in maps and atlases as might have been expected. This is explained by the fact that the King had retained many maps as documents of state, and these were to form the nucleus of King George III's Topographical and Maritime Collections built up during the period 1760 to 1820. World-wide in compass and especially rich in areas of British interest such as Canada, they comprise perhaps the greatest geographical collection in the world for eighteenth-century North America. In this period war was a great stimulus to surveying and map-making, and the North American continent as the theatre for two wars, the Seven Years' War (the French and Indian War), 1756–63, and the American War of Independence (1766–82), was therefore a major region of surveying activity. The King's Topographical Collection contains a wealth of plans, maps and views, printed and manuscript, illustrating forts, towns, battles and military operations, and also the development of territories in the aftermath of war.

Examples of military maps and plans are: 'Carte du lac Ontario' by Pierre Labroquerie, 1757, MS K.Top.CXXI.14., showing the naval action between the British and French fleets, and plans of the siege of Quebec, 1759, K.Top.CXIX.35. etc, and the siege of Louisburg, Cape Breton Island, 1755, K.Top.CXIX.91. etc. It may be said that nearly every modern Canadian project for the reconstruction of an eighteenth-century fort requires photographs of items in the King's Topographical Collection. One of the most notable examples of a survey to implement the terms of a treaty of peace – the ceding of Canada to Great Britain in 1763 – was the surveying of the St Lawrence river, begun under the orders of Brigadier-General James Murray in 1761. Two of the five known examples of the enormous map produced are in the King's Topographical Collection, K.Top.CXIX.24–27 and K.Top.CXIX.29. Surveys by Samuel Holland, John Montresor, William Gerard de Brahm and Captain Cook which were part of the same operation for the mapping of Canada are also well represented. Later on, after the American War of Independence, the settlement of the Loyalists in Upper Canada brought about the establishment of a new province, with General John Graves Simcoe appointed governor in 1791. His wife Elizabeth Simcoe accompanied him on his travels, and depicted on birchbark thirty-one views of Upper Canada, many of which provide the earliest scenes of places in the province. She also drew a map of Upper Canada, c1795, marking Simcoe's projected new towns and proposed and existing military roads. Governor Simcoe presented the collection (K.Top.CXIX.15) to the King. Study of the maps and views side by side with Mrs Simcoe's diary provides further insight. For example, the 'Scene near Fort Erie' (K.Top.CXIX.15.i.) depicts one of Captain Cook's tents. Mrs Simcoe wrote on 4 August 1793 'After dinner we left the Mississaga and slept to-night in the canvas house'. The editor J Ross Robertson comments 'The canvas house was one of three or four large and small tents that Governor Simcoe bought in London at the sale of the effects of Captain Cook, the explorer. The original drawings of these tents are in the British Museum.' The tents were those used by Banks and Solander on Cook's first voyage, 1768–1771.

A considerable number of maps in the collection are of major political significance. 'The New Map of Nova Scotia' by John Green, 1755, which was issued in a series of revised issues between 1755 and 1794, documents the rival territorial claims to the region. Four examples of John Mitchell's map of North America (1755, with later editions to 1777) are in the King's Topographical Collection (besides others in the general collections). The most famous is the Red-lined map', also known as 'King George's map', which Richard Oswald the British Commissioner at the peace negotiations in Paris in 1782 annotated to show the lines of demarcation between the United States and Canada as well as all significant boundaries from the Treaty of Utrecht (1713) onwards. Regarded as the most important map in North American history, the Red-lined map has to be taken into account in all major territorial disputes concerning the continent.

There was one notable and deliberate exception. While the negotiations were proceeding between the British and American governments which culminated in the Ashburton Treaty, 1841, the Red-lined map was kept under lock and key in the British Museum. It was believed that the evidence of the map would run counter to the case being argued by the British contestants, for by then there was a general consensus in Great Britain that Oswald as a negotiator had been unduly favourable to the Americans.

The evidential value of the Red-lined map and other maps in the Collections can be assessed from their extensive use in the case which came before the Privy Council in 1926 on 'the matter of the Boundary between the Dominion of Canada and the Colony of Newfoundland in the Labrador Peninsula'. During the last two years our maps have been consulted by advisors for the two parties in the dispute between Canada and USA over St George's Bank, lying between Nova Scotia and Cape Cod. This case will be determined by the International Court of Justice at The Hague.

The King's Topographical Collection came to the British Museum in 1828 as part of the King's Library, but even then it was very nearly lost on account of the military significance of the materials. The Treasury had approved the transfer (June 1828) when news came that one of the Assistant Librarians of the Royal Library was authorised to retain 'the whole of the Military Plans, the Charts, Topography and Geography'. It turned out that these were to be passed to Captain Parry of the Admiralty. Through the personal application of the Prime Minister Robert Peel to the King on behalf of the British Museum the Trustees finally secured the transfer, on condition that the maps would be available to any Department of State which wished to consult them. It was agreed that 'the Nautical Charts only shall be transferred to the Admiralty'. Thus the King's Maritime Collection was passed to the Admiralty, but in 1844 the major part was offered to and accepted by the Museum with a further transfer of items in 1952. A further dispute of a similar kind, this time over the custody of the military plans, arose in 1836 when the Board of Ordnance informed William IV that the Board's plans had been 'inadvertently sent' to the British Museum; they were of significance for defence and should not be seen by the public. The dispute continued until 1838, and fortunately was settled in favour of the Museum.

The King's Topographical and Maritime Collections are held in the Map Library. Items of special significance for Canada are mainly in the numerical sequence K.Top.CXIX (Canada), and CXXI (State of New York), and in K.Mar.VII.

Development of the collections

These magnificent additions to the map collections of the British Museum inspired Antonio Panizzi, then Assistant in the Department of Printed Books, with the idea (in 1837) of forming 'a geographical collection which might be called *complete*', and he asked for a fund of £1000 for the purpose, recommending the appointment of a special bookseller to assist in the purchasing of suitable maps. The British Museum thus initiated an active policy for the acquisition of modern foreign maps, such as maps of the USA. British publications were acquired by copyright and those published in Canada came under Colonial Copyright, as I shall mention later.

The real beginning of the map collections as an administrative unit dates from 1844 when Richard Henry Major was placed in charge of them and the first catalogues appeared (see p. 65). From 1867 until his retirement in 1881 Major was in charge of a separate Department of Maps and Charts, which included both printed and manuscript material, but in 1892 the MS maps (with the exception mainly of those in King George III's Topographical and Maritime Collections) were transferred to the Department of Manuscripts. The Keepers of both Printed Books and Manuscripts were engaged alike in the work of acquisition in the map field during these years, and subsequently.

Acquisitions policy aimed not only at building up a modern collection but also in filling gaps in the antiquarian collections. Selected examples of important 'Canadiana' added to the general collection are:

1. Giovanni Matteo Contarini's world map of 1506, the only known example of the first printed map showing any part of America. South America is depicted as a separate continent, John Cabot's discoveries 1497-98 as a cape of Asia. The map was purchased by the British Museum in 1922, and a facsimile published by the British Museum in 1926. *Maps C.2.cc.*

2. Map of Canada, 1592, by the Dutch cartographer Peter Planicius, engraved by Johannes van Doetechum. A facsimile was published by the British Museum in *Six Early Printed Maps*, 1928. *Maps C.2.a.3.*

3. Map of Cabotia, compiled by J Purdy, published by J Whittle and R H Laurie in 1814, an abortive attempt to rename Canada. *Maps 70615.(18.)*

The Royal United Services Institution Sheet Map Collection

The most important purchase of Canadian material in the library's history was made in 1968 when the Trustees bought the sheet map collection of the Royal United Services Institution. This included two important collections for North America, the collection of Lord Amherst, Commander-in-Chief in North America in the Seven Years' War, and of Sir Augustus Frazer, who appears to have acquired and passed on to the Royal United Services Institution a major official topographical archive preserved at Woolwich. The maps and plans in these collections are complementary to those in the King's Topographical Collection. They include, for example, a plan of the naval battle in Lake Ontario by Pierre Labroquerie (RUSIA.27.31b) which may be compared to K.Top.CXIX.14.

One remarkable item is an Indian birchbark map found in 1841 by a Captain Bainbrigge of the Royal Engineers on 'the ridge' somewhere between the River Ottawa and Lake Huron. In addition to a drawn-out plan interpreting the markings, there is a note in a military hand:

> Forwarded to the United Services Institution in the hope that it may shew young officers how small an effort is needed to acquire that most useful art of Military Sketching since even Savages can make an intelligible plan.

(Map Library RUSI Misc I). The map was lent to the Arts Council exhibition *Sacred Circles. Two thousand years of North American Indian Art* (item 682) on display in the Hayward Gallery, London, 1976–77, and later in Kansas City, USA.

In all there are about sixty to seventy manuscript items relating to Canada. The collection as a whole is divided between the Department of Manuscripts and the Map Library. The North American items in the Department of Manuscripts have been incorporated as Additional MSS 57701–57716.

The Colonial Copyright collections

The rapid development of Canadian map publishing in the second half of the nineteenth century was comparable with that in the USA. It was inevitable that the British Museum's collections of map publications from the USA, though remarkable, are selective. For Canada, however, deposit by Colonial Copyright brought the whole range of publications in the field of cartography and topography, including photographs. These items bear the Colonial Copyright deposit number and date.

The deposited material includes a large collection of Fire Insurance Plans published in Canada from 1875 by Charles E Goad. These are the counterpart of the Sanborn-Perrin Company's publications for the USA, begun in 1869. Goad's stopped producing FIPS in Canada in 1917, and the rights were handed over to the Insurers' Advisory Association, which ceased publication in 1975. (Goad's was liquidated in Canada in 1931.) The volumes deposited in the Map Library, some 250 in number, form a remarkable record of the anatomy of Canadian towns in the later nineteenth and the twentieth centuries. A typescript list of the holdings was recently completed.

The wealth of Canadian material in the Map Library can be seen in an extract from the *Catalogue of Maps* covering Quebec, specially printed in 1908. The then Superintendent of the Map Room, Basil H Soulsby, explains in a Prefatory Note of 25 March 1908:

> The heading 'Quebec' in the British Museum Catalogue of Printed Maps was recently revised for Part XLI of the accessions, published in March 1908. The following pages, 143 to 153, are an excerpt, issued for private circulation, and may possibly be of service in connection with the proposal to purchase the Plains of Abraham for the City of Quebec.

If any recipient of this list should know of any other map, plan, or view of Quebec, he is requested to send a complete copy of the title or description to
BASIL H SOULSBY FSA
Superintendent of the Map Room

Through the vicissitudes of fortune the material received in the three Canadian deposits during the period 1895 to 1924 has been lost. The Map Library's collections are thus unique. For example, although the National Map Collections of the Public Archives of Canada obtained Canadian FIP volumes from Goad in England (whence the family had moved in 1885), the Canadian holdings in Ottawa are still not nearly as comprehensive as those in the British Library. The Goad Company in Hatfield is now cataloguing its own holdings of the plans, and should have the complete list by the end of October 1983.

Acquisitions of current mapping

As a 'partial depository' the Map Library was acquiring for some years up to 1969 the official series of Canadian topographical mapping. Since 1969 it has been a full depository, receiving maps of the National Topographic System of Canada at all scales, and in addition all thematic maps for sale to the public, all atlas maps, all 'military' city plans and indexes. Monthly lists are received, together with the map catalogue (on fiche) issued by the Survey and Mapping Branch.

Exhibitions and catalogues

In view of the wealth of the British Library's cartographic materials for North America, every opportunity has been taken to make the holdings generally known. The exhibition *Europe in Canada* held in the King's Library in 1967 contained many maps and views. These were then borrowed for the exhibition *A Pageant of Canada: Pages d'histoire du Canada. The European Contribution to the Iconography of Canadian History*, held in the National Gallery of Canada, Ottawa, 1967. In 1975 an exhibition on *The American War of Independence* was staged in the King's Library and then transferred to the Museum of Our National Heritage, Lexington, Massachusetts, for the American Bicentennial in 1976.

The catalogues of these exhibitions and the catalogues recording Canadian materials in the British Library are listed below:

CATALOGUES

1. Catalogues of Maps, Prints, Drawings, etc. forming the Geographical and Topographical Collection attached to the library of . . . King George the Third, 1829.

2. Catalogue of King George III's Maritime Collection. About 1850. (MS and printed charts. Dictionary arrangement. Reproduced by the 'carbonic process', not published. Copies in Map Room, Reading Room, and Department of Manuscripts).

3. Catalogue of the Manuscript Maps, Charts, and Plans, and of the Topographical Drawings in the British Museum, 3 vol. London, 1844–61. (Vol 1 and 2, 1844; vol 3, 1861. Reprinted 1962. Compiled by John Holmes and R H Major. Classified arrangement. Each volume includes material in the collections to the date of its publication. Manuscript material in the King's Topographical Collection is included in all 3 volumes, but that in the King's Maritime Collection only in vol 3. Accessions of maps in the Department of Manuscripts after 1861 are entered in the periodically printed Catalogue of Additions to the Manuscripts.)

4. The British Museum Catalogue of Printed Maps, Charts and Plans. Photolithographic edition up to the end of 1964. London, 1967. Ten-year Supplement 1965–1975. London, 1978. Later accessions on card catalogue in the Map Library.

EXHIBITION CATALOGUES

1. *A Pageant of Canada: Pages d'histoire du Canada. The European Contribution to the Iconography of Canadian History*. Ottawa, The National Gallery of Canada, 1967.

2. *The American War of Independence 1775–83*. A commemorative exhibition organised by the Map Library and the Department of Manuscripts of the British Library Reference Division, 4 July to 11 November 1975. London, British Museum Publications.

BIBLIOGRAPHY

The British Library. The Reference Division Collections. London, British Library Publications, 1983.
Henry Stevens, *Catalogue of American Maps in the Library of the British Museum*, London, 1859.
Helen Wallis, 'The Map Collections of the British Museum Library' in H Wallis and Sarah Tyacke *My Head is a Map*, London, 1973, pp. 2–20.
Helen Wallis, *The Royal Map Collections of England*, Centro de Estudos de Cartografia Antiga CXLI Secção de Coimbra, Coimbra, 1981.

Geoffrey Hamilton

Resources for advanced research in Canadian Studies in the British Library Reference Division: official publications

The purpose of this paper is to indicate how Canadian official publications are acquired by the Reference Division and the extent of the collection; to describe the public services for readers and remote users; and to comment on patterns of use and some problems associated with the use of official publications in Reference Division.

By far the most important method of acquisition is the official exchange which, in the case of Canadian federal government publications, celebrates its centenary in 1983. It was in January 1883 that the British Treasury acted upon the recommendation from a committee which had reported in October 1882 that 'in view of the wish of foreign governments to possess British official documents, and the need of the British Museum . . . for foreign government publications, reciprocal exchange was desirable . . .'. HM Stationery Office was instructed to implement exchanges with the United States and with a number of other countries who had made applications, among these being Canada where the Library of Parliament was to receive British parliamentary papers, in return for which Canadian official publications were deposited in the Library of the British Museum. Although this exchange has operated only during the past 100 years, pre-1883 Canadian official publications feature – albeit somewhat patchily – in Reference Division's collection, mostly acquired by legal deposit.

The British Library is now the only library in the United Kingdom with full depository status for Federal documents, though a number of other libraries – mainly in universities – have selective deposit status. British parliamentary papers continue to be sent to the Library of Parliament in Ottawa, and non-parliamentary publications published by HMSO which are selected by the National Library of Canada as having research interest for their users, are sent to that Library. Publications are dispatched by HMSO, but since 1973 the full published price of publications used in exchanges has had to be paid by the British Library.

The publications of provincial governments are acquired in various ways. An exchange of parliamentary publications has operated with Newfoundland since 1905, and more limited exchanges have been set up with Manitoba (1966), Alberta (1972) and Quebec (1983). Some official publications of other provinces are received by purchase or donation, but in general the coverage of provincial government publications is not as complete as that of Federal publications.

As some indication of the extent of Reference Division's holdings of Canadian Federal government publications, there are 130 pages of entries for them in the British Library Catalogue of Printed Books to 1975, and a further 25 pages in the 1976–1982 supplement. The arrangement of official publications on the shelves in the Department of Printed Books is by country and department, publications from each Canadian province following after Canadian Federal publications. A survey of shelf space occupied by official publications was carried out in January 1982, and this showed there were 891.5 metres (2,942 feet) of Canadian federal and provincial publications. (This figure excludes Official Gazettes, which are separately shelved.) In addition there is an unmeasured quantity of Canadian official publications concerned with scientific and technical subjects in the Science Reference Library, to which such publications are allocated when they arrive under exchange arrangements. It is interesting to compare this figure with statistics in the National Library of Canada's Official Publications Count Report, August 1982, showing 6,917 feet of provincial and 10,914 feet of Federal publications in April/May 1982. This suggests that in crude terms the Department of Printed Books collection is probably about one-sixth the size of that in the National Library of Canada, though no doubt in the case of Federal publications the British Library's holdings represent a larger fraction of the National Library's collection.

A separate Reading Room, known as the Official Publications Library, is provided in the British Museum building where government publications from all countries can be delivered for readers' use. The seating, for some 80 readers, is normally ample for the number of readers who, at any one time, wish to use official publications. The Official Publications Library has on its open shelves the various printed and microform British Library General Catalogues of printed books as well as bibliographies and guides to official publications and government organisation manuals from around the world.

The Official Publications Library (OPL) is the successor to the State Paper Room in the British Museum Library, which for several years until the mid-1960s had served as a specialised unit carrying out all the functions of acquisition, cataloguing and book storage and delivery in respect of official publications, in addition to reference and reader assistance. From 1967 onwards all functions other than the last mentioned were progressively distributed to other branches of the main library, so that as Mr Willison has explained it is now the Overseas English section of the English Language Branch which is responsible for acquiring Canadian official publications. OPL forms part of the Public Services Branch within the Department of Printed Books, and carries out reference and reader assistance work not only for official publications of all countries but also for the social sciences generally. OPL's services are being developed to attract use from a wider clientèle than had traditionally been associated with the British Museum Library's reading rooms, and there has been in recent years a particularly marked and welcome increase in enquiries, often received by telephone from 'remote users', which call for the provision of information rather than the delivery of a publication to a reader's seat. OPL supports the British Library's Business Information Service, located at the Science Reference Library, especially by answering enquiries concerning law or statistics. OPL is open six days a week, for a total of 44¼ hours, and has no more than three professional staff who are available for regular duty at the enquiry desk. The manning of this desk during evening and Saturday openings, and at other times to cover for unavoidable absences, is therefore achieved by drawing staff from rotas, who are in most cases employed in other areas of the Department of Printed Books outside Public Services Branch and therefore have relatively few opportunities to become familiar with the amazing range of enquiries which regularly arrive in OPL, or with the large numbers of bibliographies and other reference tools which have to be used in attempting to answer them. However, the experience of official publications acquisitions work and cataloguing which many of these people bring to OPL is valuable, and these arrangements help to foster links between OPL and the Language Branches. By the same token, even the regular OPL staff handle enquiries relating to the official publications of a particular country (except for Britain and to a lesser extent the United States) comparatively infrequently, and thus do not have the opportunity to develop particular expertise in the publishing practices and bibliographical tools for individual countries. Readers are (with some exceptions) notoriously ill-informed about the potential value of official publications as a resource which can be exploited in almost any area of research or study, and it is difficult to see how this can be changed, unless a gradual increase in citations to official publications in works of scholarship draws attention to the range of relatively easily accessible material which has remained largely unused. OPL is keen to take advantage of any opportunity to help spread awareness of the research value of official publications in general and of the Reference Divison's resources of this material in particular, and would welcome suggestions for activity which might help to achieve this aim.

In order to provide a picture of existing use of Canadian official publications in OPL the records of enquiries handled by OPL staff during an 18 month period (July 1981–December 1982) were examined, and 18 enquiries – an average of one per month – were identified as relevant. This reinforces the point made above about the limited opportunities for OPL staff to develop expertise in the publications of a given country. The topics covered by these enquiries were: law (6 enquiries, of which 2 concerned provinces); statistics (5 enquiries, including the Canadian retail price index in 1935); Federal departments (4 enquiries, including an enquiry about annual reports of the Parliamentary Library for 1914–1918, which it turned out were not printed); and one enquiry apiece about Canadian standards, timber in Canada in the 1850s and the Canadian Medical Service Journal. This is not a very impressive collection, and cannot be dismissed on grounds such as a general lack of interest in Canada. It may be an indication that other libraries have the resources with which to satisfy demands for Canadian information, though it seems improbable that is the full explanation.

The previous paragraph was concerned with questions which had been handled at the OPL Enquiry Desk, including those arriving by telephone or letter. A second object of scrutiny was the file of Readers' applications for books. When the reader returns a book to the Issue Desk the application form is filed in date order. This file is thus a convenient way of establishing what publications have been in use at any time. At this point it is necessary to explain that, in common with most official publications from overseas countries, Canadian official publications are housed at Woolwich Arsenal, some 8 miles east of Bloomsbury, where the British Library has the use of three storage buildings in an area which is still subject to Ministry of Defence security arrangements. A van service links Bloomsbury and Woolwich on a regular schedule several times a day, but this inevitably results in a 'next day', rather than a 'same day', delivery for most official publications. A further disadvantage of this situation is that there is no opportunity for professional library staff to become familiar with the stock on the shelves, other than by making special arrangements to visit Woolwich. However, apart from the inevitable delay in supplying items requested – which is simply a consequence of the distances involved – the OPL book delivery service works well.

Readers' applications handled at the OPL Issue Desk during January and February 1983 were examined. A total of about 1050 applications were processed in those months, of which 37 (3.5%) were for Canadian official publications. Several requests were for multi-volume works or for runs of a serial publication. In addition, there were 3 staff requests and 4 requisitions of publications by the Reference Division Photographic Services. Of the items called for by readers, 8 were Royal Commission reports, 10 were census reports, 3 were Parliamentary papers, 10 were Department of Labour publications. Other requests included a Department of National Defence publication on badges of Canadian forces and a 1913 report on fur farming. When the publication dates for requested items are analysed it can be seen that 13 requests were for nineteenth century publications, 14 for publications issued 1901–1914, one each for the 1920s and 1930s, and 3 in the post-1945 period – the most recent imprint date specified being 1969. It is only the presence in the sample of a staff request for a 1982 issue of the Newfoundland Official Gazette that provides any confirmation that this is a collection which does contain up to date material and that it covers provincial government publications as well as those from the Federal government.

It would be unwise to generalise too much on the basis of such a limited sample, in which the requests from a single reader account for over half the total. However, these results largely confirm the impressions of OPL staff, that the heaviest demand (not only in the Canadian case) is for the major and best-known series which have been in circulation for some time. Clearly there are some types of government publication – census reports and reports of Royal

Commissions are examples – which are basic tools for research in various disciplines, and will therefore be in continuing demand by readers in OPL. What is equally clear is that among the large number of other, less well known publications which flow from government bodies there are some few at least which deserve the attention of researchers, but which at present are often overlooked. This small survey shows also how difficult it is to base decisions on collection development – for instance, on the selection of provincial publications for acquisition, or on possible relocations of parts of the collection – on evidence of use when the main conclusion that can be drawn from such evidence is that the material is under used. Conversely, the evidence of under use might be adduced in support of a proposition that certain categories of lightly used material in the British Library should be given a new status, as items which can be made available either to readers in the Reference Division reading rooms or for use in other libraries by interlibrary loan arranged via the British Library Lending Division. It is worth noting that OPL is a back-up library for Lending Division, which passes on requests for official publications for which it has no other location. The OPL response, after verifying that the requested publication is in the collection, is to pass the request on to the Reference Division Photographic Services, when copying is possible and permissible. This is potentially an important contribution to making the Reference Division's official publications collection more widely available to researchers, though few of the requests which arrive are for Canadian publications.

This paper has shown that the British Library Reference Division's collection of Canadian Federal and provincial official publications is extensive and contains much that is of value to researchers. Use of the collection appears to be low, not only in the case of Canadian official publications. The reasons for this are unclear, but are probably a combination of the peculiar characteristics of official publishing which make for difficulty in using official publications, the unevenness of the bibliographical recording of official publications, and local circumstances, such as the absence of individual catalogue records for many official publications (which can therefore be located only via records which are not accessible to readers) and the outhousing of most official publications. However, the Division provides special services for readers and remote users of official publications which are aimed at making it as easy as possible for them to get the official publications or the information they need. The expertise of the Official Publications Library staff, although this is of an extensive nature rather than an intensive knowledge of the official publications of particular countries, is itself a resource which we are always happy to make available to the advanced researcher in Canadian studies.

Lawrence le R Dethan

Resources for advanced research in Canadian Studies in the British Library Reference Division: Quebec and French Canadian printed materials

Acquisition of the Collections

The history of the acquisition of material in this area is indistinguishable from that of our general Canadian acquisitions until the mid-1960s. Research into the early period is being conducted at this moment by Dr O'Neill, with reference to the period of Canadian copyright deposit 1895–1924, and by Miss Sternberg of the British Library staff, who is studying aspects of overseas acquisitions by the British Museum library during the colonial period. The French section of the British Library has begun a programme of surveys of its holdings of Canadiana and their mode of acquisition.

Preliminary results of these researches would indicate that, apart from the wealth of background material relating to the early history and exploration of Canada contained in the British Museum foundation collections – a wealth exemplified by our inability to find any items to purchase in a recent most comprehensive bookseller's catalogue devoted to this area – little more was acquired until Panizzi, having obtained a major expansion of the book fund, launched a vigorous acquisition programme in the late 1840s as part of his concept of a universal library. This drive concentrated on the purchase of material from earliest times up to within about four years of the current date, as Panizzi was determined to make use of Imperial copyright legislation in existence since 1842 to acquire recent publications. In the event, colonial copyright remained largely ineffective for the next thirty years and Canadian publications were acquired predominantly by purchase and sporadic donations. A check of the mode of acquisition of items in the *Catalogue of Canadian books in the Library of the British Museum Christmas 1856* by Henry Stevens, London, 1859, reveals that, of the 46 items whose origins can be traced, 5 were received by copyright, 6 were donated and the remaining 35 purchased from various booksellers, notably Stevens himself, Asher, Pickering and Rodd. A typical list of Canadian books purchased from Rodd on 8 December 1840 for £22.17.0 lists 75 items chiefly published in the years 1833–1937, but also items from 1774 and 1797. (See Appendix 1. p.77–78.)

In 1895 the Canadian copyright act took effect, stipulating that, of the three copies of each work deposited, one copy should be sent to the British Museum. This legislation expired in 1924 but material continued to arrive for several more years. The benefits of this period of deposit are hard to exaggerate: not only was a comprehensive collection of nearly thirty years of Canadian book production preserved from the disasters which befell its counterparts in Canada (see Dr O'Neill's paper p.83–90), but also far more material was obtained than would otherwise have been possible following the drastic cuts in the Treasury grant in 1887 and again during the First World War. The remaining inter-war years saw a general decline in British Museum acquisitions; money and staff were both in short supply and such resources as were available were often devoted to the acquisition of early European books in connexion with the programme of publication of Short-Title Catalogues. Many periodical orders were cancelled and current French-language acquisitions were limited to the purchase of major works by established authors from metropolitan France: the intake of material from Belgium, Canada and Switzerland virtually ceased. In 1927, for example, the purchase fund for all current Canadian books in any language was about £60 p.a. This unfortunate state of affairs continued until the mid-1950s: during the Second World War the British Museum acquisitions machinery only ticked over and the limited resources available in the immediate post-war years were devoted to rebuilding our acquisitions network and filling the major gaps in our holdings of serials and monographs caused by the complete loss of contact with many of our suppliers for over four years. Another major activity was the listing and partial replacement of the near quarter of a million books destroyed in the Blitz.

The expansionist period which followed the austere post-war years saw the welcome appointment of an Assistant Keeper with specific responsibility for the Canadian collections, who not only formed a core-collection of important works published after 1945, but also negotiated an agreement in 1964 whereby the Québec government most generously donated regular consignments of notable current Québec publications via the Délégation générale du Québec in Paris. Approximately 150 items per annum were received by this means until 1980 when the current international economic crisis forced retrenchments upon the Québec budget and the donations programme was discontinued. Since it was obvious that the most convenient method of acquisition would in future be purchase and since the majority of Québec publications were in French, it was decided to transfer responsibility for the acquisition of all material from Québec, in whatever language, together with works in French published in the other provinces, to the French section of the Department of Printed Books as from June 1981. Current acquisitions activity in this area can be summarised as follows:

1. *Canadiana* and the *Bibliographie du Québec* are scanned regularly and orders

for the items selected are placed with a Montreal bookseller; over 300 items were received in 1982. Each book is selected individually; there are no blanket orders. Under the previous system, where the majority of books received in this area came in by donation, considerable arrears of acquisitions inevitably accumulated as we waited to see whether books would be donated before eventually ordering them from our agents: these arrears have now been cleared up. Special catalogues, such as *Recent trends in Québec literature*, Laval University (1982) and C May *A guide to the study of Québec for teachers and students in Britain*, Birmingham University, 1982, are checked and missing works ordered.

2. Catalogues are received regularly from five antiquarian booksellers in Québec and gaps in our holdings from 1800–1950 are still being filled, although the vigorous acquisition effort in this area since 1970 means that it is increasingly difficult to find worthwhile items to buy in hard copy.

3. Our exchange of official publications with Québec having completely ceased in the early 1970s, a new agreement for the exchange of official publications to an annual value of Can.$1500 has been signed between the Québec government and the British Library with effect from April 1983 and the first requests have been despatched. All major Québec state papers are now on order, together with publications of the Bibliothèque nationale du Québec: these items are selected from the *Liste mensuelle des publications du gouvernement du Québec*.

4. Areas covered by our current acquisitions policy include: bibliography, social sciences, law, religion, economics, fine arts, history, biography and belles-lettres. Areas excluded are: children's books, science, clinical medicine, school text-books and minor local and family history.

Resources survey

Staff of the British Library are often asked how comprehensive our holdings are in a particular field; although we can usually give a fairly accurate estimate this is generally based on many years' experience of using the catalogues and checking bibliographies and booksellers' lists rather than on any hard statistical evidence. Obviously we will have to wait for greater mechanisation of our catalogue before we can attempt statistical surveys of major collections, but in smaller areas such as the present one, an empirical attempt at a collection statement is possible. For the purposes of this survey it was decided to check the Library's holdings against V Barbeau and A Fortier: *Dictionnaire bibliographique du Canada français*, Montréal, 1974. Despite the obvious drawbacks of this compilation – its omission of most official publications and anonymous headings such as Bible or Liturgies and the curious internal arrangement within the author headings – it had certain advantages which weighed heavily in its favour. Within the parameters it set itself it is complete and its size and alphabetical arrangement permitted an easy comparison with our catalogues and acquisition records. We intend to supplement the findings of this survey with further checks against other more specialised or more comprehensive bibliographies eg, RETRO, *Bibliographie du Québec, 1821–1967* and *Laurentiana parus avant 1821*. Each item in Barbeau and Fortier was checked against our records, items in our collections not mentioned in the bibliography were inserted, including many items by minor authors who chanced to have the same surname as authors in the bibliography but who had escaped the notice of its compilers. (The relative paucity of surnames in Québec worked to our advantage here and located many rare items which could only otherwise have emerged from a complete reading of the catalogue.) Of the 8194 items checked in Barbeau and Fortier the British Library had 4060 (although not always in the same edition), or very nearly 50%. This is very high when compared, for instance, with our present coverage of about 20% of the total annual book production of France and is accounted for by the 30 years of near-total copyright deposit, 1895–1924, and by the different collecting parameters in earlier years before the creation of the Science Reference Library which have tended to inflate the average percentage, although we have not yet had time to study this in detail.

Total scores for holdings of individual authors chosen for their importance or prolific output (or sometimes both) are given in Appendix II (p.79). Although the general coverage is very good, some serious gaps have come to light in our holdings of major authors and our coverage of the period 1800–1850 is far from complete. The next step will be the creation of a desiderata list, based on the results of this survey and further surveys mentioned above, and on our list of war-destroyed books (of 283 books from our area destroyed in the last war only 14 have been replaced so far). The survey has also revealed a substantial number of errors in our catalogue: wrong attributions, authors appearing under 2 or even 3 different headings and a series of minor howlers all of which have been earmarked for correction.

Future developments and projects

1. As a result of our new exchange agreement with the Québec government our holdings of Québec official publications should be adequate from 1983, but we are conscious of major gaps in earlier holdings. We intend to make a survey to identify these gaps and replace them on microform and by subscribing to retrospective publications such as the *Débats de l'Assemblée législative 1867–1963*.

2. The growth of the reprint and microform industries and our subscription to CIHM will reduce our need to purchase originals, many of which are often in a poor state of conservation. Resources can therefore be concentrated on identifying rare and bibliographically significant books of which the originals are still desirable.

3. Our holdings of serials are still very patchy, partly as a result of the inter-

war cuts and partly as a result of over-dependence on the Québec donation programme which did not always have the resources to supply us with continuous sets of serials. The gaps must be identified and runs completed by the acquisition of microform.

4. Dr O'Neill's work on the 1895–1924 copyright deposits has revealed substantial holdings of Québec items which are almost certainly not held anywhere else. The French section's survey has revealed a possible desiderata list of some 1000 items needed to complete our collections. The situation seems ripe for an international exchange of microfiche or microfilm of these items. An energetic programme of consolidation of our holdings over the next two or three years, combined with the riches of our earlier holdings and unique foundation collections will guarantee the British Library's status as the principal resource centre for Québec studies outside Canada.

Appendix I

Items purchased from Rodd, 8 December 1840, for £22.17.0

Edits, Ordonnances &c. concernant le Canada. Vol.I.4°. Quebec. 1803
Edits, Ordonnances &c. concernant le Canada. Vol.II.4°. Quebec. 1806
Canada, Public Acts relative to. 4°. Quebec, 1824
Canada, Upper, Statutes of, &c. 4°. Kingston. U.C. 1831
Beaubien (H. des R.) Traité sur lois civiles du Bas-Canada. Tom.I.12°. Montreal. 1832
Beaubien (H. des R.) Traité sur lois civiles du Bas-Canada. Tom.II.12°. Montreal. 1832
Beaubien (H. des R.) Traité sur lois civiles du Bas-Canada. Tom.III.12°. Montreal. 1833
Smith (Wm) History of Canada. Vol.I.8°. Quebec. 1815
Smith (Wm) History of Canada. Vol.II.8°. Quebec. 1815
Smith (Wm) History of Province of New York. Vol.I 8°. New York. 1829
Smith (Wm) History of Province of New York. Vol.II 8°. New York. 1829
Upper Canada, Seventh Rept. Committee of U.C. on grievances. 12°. Toronto. 1835
Sketch of Condition of U.S. of America. 8°. Baltimore. 1826
[Marriott] Plan of Code of Laws for Quebec. 8°. London. 1774
Thompson (Z) Gazetteer of State of Vermont. 12°. Montp. 1824
Lower Canada Watchman. 12°. Kingston. U.C. 1824
Laws of Vermont passed Oct. 1835. Montp. 1835
Laws of Vermont coming down to & including 1834. 8°. Montp. 1835
Vermont State Papers. 8°. Middleburg. 1823
Trial of David McLane for High Treason. 8°. Quebec. 1797
Quebec & its Environs. 8°. n.p. 1831
Upper Canada, Statistical Sketches of. 12°. Lond. 1832
Fairplay (Francis) Map of the Canadas. A Pamphlet. Lond. 1834
Statement relative to the Works of Chambly Canal. 8°. Montreal. 1836
First Report of Coburg Rail Road Co. Oct. 1835. 12°, Coburg. U.C
Doyle (Martin) Hints on Emigration to Upper Canada. 12°. n.p. 1831
Society, Third Annual Rept. for Converting &c. the Indians in U.Canada. 1833
Society, Fourth Annual Rept. for Converting &c. the Indians in U.Canada. 1834
Society, Fifth Annual Rept. for Converting &c. the Indians in U.Canada. 1835

Buchanan (James) Reasons for allowing Transmit of Merchandize to Mich. Toronto. 1836
Lower Canada. Proclamation to perform Quarantine. 8° n.p. ord
Anti-Gallic Letters to Earl of Gosford. 12°. Montreal. 1836
Petite Clique Dévoilée. 8°. Etats-Unis. Rome. N.Y. 1836
Lower Canada, Documents relating to Ld. Aylmer's Administration
Canada, Few Words on the subject of. 8°. Lond. 1837
Affairs of the Canadas. 8°. Lond. 1837
Canadian Portfolio. No. V. 8°. Lond.
Horton (Robt. W) Exposition &c. of Earl Bathurst's Administration. Lond. 1838
Canada, The Abstract. Jan. 1838. 8°. Lond.
Canada, Plain Statement of Quarrel with Canada. 8°. Lond. 1838
Canada, U. Messuages &c. to Sir H B Head on his Resign. 8°. Toronto. 1838
Head (H B) Address to H. of Lords against Union of Canada. 8°. Lond. 1840
Girod (A) Notes Diverses sur le Bas-Canada. Liv.1.8°. 1835
Observations de l'Hon. D B Viger contre la nomination d'un agent. Montreal. 1835
Quebec Auxiliary Bible Society. 11th Rept. of. 8°. Quebec. 1836
Society for Promoting Christian Knowledge, 17th Annual Rept. of Quebec Committee
Society for Promoting Christian Knowledge, 10th Annual Rept. of Quebec Committee
Stewart (C J) Charge to Clergy of Quebec. 8°. Montr. 1840
Esson (H) Sermon preached at Montreal. 30 Nov. 1835. 8°. Montreal. 1836
Observations on Proceedings of H. of Assembly. 8°. Montr. 1836
Society, Prospectus of in Montreal. 8°. Montr. 1836
Rept. of Comm. of U. Canada upon Address to King. 8°. Toronto. 1836
Address presented to Sir J Colborne. 8°. Toronto. 1836
Review of Rept. in 1828 by Canada Comm. 12°. Montr. 1835
Remarks on the Petition of the Convent. 12°. Montr. 1836
Entretien sur les Etablissemens du Bas-Canada. 8°. Montr. 1826
Dalhousie (Earl) Memoirs of Government of L. Canada. 8°. Queb. 1829
Perrault (J Fr) Le rédacteur de Gazette de Québ. 12°. [Queb. 1835]
Messuage du Gouverneur en Chef. 8°. n.p. or d
Aubin (M N) Chant patriot. du Canada. *On a Sheet*
Catalogue sur l'Hist. de l'Amerique. 8°. Queb. 1837
Society, Literary & Hist. Transact. of. Vol.III.Pt.IV. 8°. Queb. 1837
Soc. of Quebec. Lit. & Hist. By-Laws of the. 8°. Queb. 1832
Soc. of Quebec. Lit. & Hist. By-Laws Report &c.[Queb. 1836]
Soc. of Quebec. Lit. & Hist. By-Laws Meeting 11 Jan. 1837. 8°.n.p. or d.
Catalogue of Montreal Lib. 8°. Montr. 1833
Catalogue of Quebec Lib. 8°. Queb.n.d.
Regulations and Cat. of Queb. Garrison Lib. 8°. Queb. 1837
Catal. of Garrison Lib. of Queb. 12°.n.p. 1833
Lib. of Legislative Council. 12°.n.p. or d.
Lib. of Legislative Council. 1834
Armour & Ramsay. Catal. of Books 8°. Montr. 1837
Catal. of Books in House of Assembly. 8° Queb. 1831
Catal. of Books in House of Assembly. added to Lib. 1831. 12°.n.p. or d.
Catal. of Books in House of Assembly. 8°. Queb. 1835

Appendix II
Author coverage in the British Library

The figures given indicate the BL holding out of a possible total, *eg* AQUIN (Hubert) 5 books out of a possible 5 is given as 5/5.

ACHARD (Eugène) 7/63
AQUIN (Hubert) 5/5
AUCLAIR (Joseph Arthur Elie) 2/23
BEAULIEU (Michel) 14/14
BIBAUD (Maximilien) 8/25
BLAIS (Marie-Claire) 17/17
BOURASSA (Henri) 22/51
CARRIER (Roch) 12/13
CASGRAIN (Henri Raymond) 18/50
CHAMBERLAND (Paul) 8/8
CHARBONNEAU (Jean) 8/9
CHOQUETTE (Guy Robert) 11/15
CONAN (Laure) 11/17
DAVID (Laurent Olivier) 34/43
DESROSIERS (Léo-Paul) 15/15
DUBE (Marcel) 21/21
FERRON (Jacques) 24/26
GARNEAU (François Xavier) 6/9
GODBOUT (Jacques) 10/15
GROULX (Lionel) 29/37
HEBERT (Anne) 11/11
HERTEL (François) 20/32
LABERGE (Albert) 3/15
LAMONTAGNE (Blanche) 10/11
LANCTOT (Gustave) 16/19
LASNIER (Rina) 20/23
LEMELIN (Roger) 7/7
MAILLET (Andrée) 12/16
MAILLET (Antonine) 16/18
MALOUIN (Reine) 9/22
MARCOTTE (Gilles) 8/10
MORISSET (Gérard) 13/13
POTVIN (Damase) 23/32
ROY (Camille) 21/27
ROY (Gabrielle) 11/11
ROY (Pierre Georges) 46/113
RUMILLY (Robert) 28/35
THERIAULT (Yves) 43/67
TREMBLAY (Michel) 13/13
VIGNEAULT (Gilles) 13/14

Stephen P Green

Resources for advanced research in Canadian Studies in the British Library Reference Division: newspapers (A summary)

For many years, newspapers have been undervalued as library materials in research libraries, although the last decade has seen a considerable change in attitude to newspapers by both librarians and users. The pressure on the 80-seat reading rooms at the Newspaper Library at Colindale is a manifestation of this, and on frequent occasions the reading rooms are full with people waiting for seats to become free. The strength of the British Library's newspaper collections rests in:

1. Comprehensive coverage of United Kingdom newspapers from the 1830s onwards.

2. An exceedingly fine collection of newspapers from countries previously part of the British Empire.

3. A representative range of newspapers from other countries throughout the world.

The collections now stand at over 500,000 volumes and parcels and 150,000 reels of archival microfilm.

The retrospective holdings of the Newspaper Library in the field of Canadian Studies consist of about 350 titles, with a particular strength in the late nineteenth century. Many of these titles have been microfilmed at Colindale to the highest archival quality standards, and positive copies are available for sale.

On a current basis, twenty-two Canadian titles are taken. Of these, three are French language titles and nine are English language, the remaining ones being ethnic titles. Ottawa, Toronto, Vancouver, Winnipeg, and Montreal are represented. However, it is recognised that there is a need for a deeper examination of the value of the titles taken and a consideration of what further titles, if any, ought to be acquired. This will take place during 1984, as part of a world-wide review of the Newspaper Library's current subscriptions to newspapers, which started in late 1982.

Suggestions from users and other interested parties about those titles which should be subscribed, either current titles or past runs of Canadian newspapers, would be very much welcomed. The Newspaper Library has been immensely helped by advice it has received consequent upon the earlier colloquium on American Studies, and it is hoped a similar pattern will emerge from this colloquium.

The Newspaper Library is also keen to play its full part in improving the exchange of information between libraries of all types about significant newspaper collections. We read with great interest the results of the questionnaire recently circulated by the National Library of Canada on newspapers, and its paper giving an overview of the collection and preservation of newspapers in Canada. The questionnaire will act as a good model to the British Library when the time comes for it to undertake its own national survey.

The *Newsletter* of the Newspaper Library is designed to be a vehicle for communication between all those interested in newspapers, and any contributions from both librarians and users on Canadian newspapers would be very welcome. The *Newsletter* appears twice a year and is distributed free of charge to 3,000 institutions and people all over the world.

'Chief Duckhunter.'
Photographer A W Gelston. 1913

TOP '"Porcupine's Lady Prospector".' Photographer Henry Peters. 1911

BOTTOM 'Hauling spud weighing twenty-seven tons to Bear Creek for the Canadian Klondike Mining Company's dredge, the largest in the world.' Photographer Erling Olav Ellingsen. 1910

TOP 'Lieutenant Sousa (the composer) and Indians.' Photographer Howard Henry Allen. 1919

BOTTOM 'The beach Kelowna looking towards the grandstand and aquatic building.' Photographer G H E Hudson. 1910

TOP 'Dawson by the light of the Aurora Borealis.' Photographers Jerry Doody and M H Craig. 1908

BOTTOM 'Monsters of the deep, River John.' Photographer Edwin Clay Blair. 1918

TOP 'Group of Eskimo women and children.' Photographer Geraldine Moodie. 1906
BOTTOM 'John Baran's house.' Photographer Howard Henry Allen. 1913

British Library Add. MS 21880, ff. 197–8
A translation of His Excellency General Haldimand's speech to the Oneida Indians in the rebel interest, as delivered to them in the Iroquois language/Goragh Asharegowa tekawenadennion Tyoghtyaky nonwe yeghsagodadigh Oneayotronon.

A Translation *of His Excellency* General HALDIMAND's *Speech to the* ONEIDA *Indians in the Rebel Interest, as delivered to them in the* Iroquois *Language.*

BROTHERS,

BE very attentive, to what I Asharegowa the Great King of England's Representative in Canada am going to say.

By this String of Wampum I shake you by the head to rouse you, that you may seriously reflect upon my Words.

A String of Wampum.

BROTHERS,

It is now about four Years ago, since the Bostonians began to rise and rebel against their Father the King of England, since which Time you have taken a different part from the rest of the five Nations your confederates, and have likewise deserted the King's Cause, thro' the deceitful Machinations and Snares of the rebels, who intimidated you with their numerous Armies, by which Means you became bewildered, and forgot all your Engagements with, and former care and favors from the Great King of England your Father.

You also soon forgot, the frequent bad usage and continual Encroachments of the Americans upon the Indians Lands throughout the Continent. I say therefore that at the breaking out of these Troubles, you firmly declared to observe a strict Neutrality in the Dispute, and made your Declaration known to Sir GUY CARLETON my Predecessor, who much approved of it provided you were in Earnest.

I have hitherto strictly observed and examined your Conduct, and find that you did not adhere to your Assertion, altho' I could trace no Reason on the side of Government as well as the Indians why you should act so treacherous and double a part, by which Means we not mistrusting your Fidelity, have had many Losses among the King's Subjects and the five Nations your Friends and Connections; and finding you besides proud and haughty on the Occasion, as if you gloried in your perfidy, doubtless in sure confidence as if your Friends the Rebels were getting the better at last, and captivated with that pleasing Opinion of yours, you have presumed twice during the course of last Winter, to send impertinent and daring Messages to the five Nations, as if you meant to pick a quarrel with them.

In consequence of this your daring and insolent Behaviour, I must insist upon, by this Belt of Wampum, that you declare yourselves immediately upon the Receipt of this my Speech and Message, whether you mean to persist in this your daring and insulting course, and still intend to act as you have hitherto done treacherously under the Cloak of Neutrality, or whether you will accept of this my last Offer of reuniting and reconciling yourselves with your own Tribes the five Nations. Do not imagine, that the King has hitherto treated the Rebels and their Adherents with so much Mildness and Indulgence, out of any Apprehensions of their Strength or getting the better! No, by no Means! For you will find, that in

GORAGH ASHAREGOWA *Raoweana tekawenadennion Tyoghtyaky nonwe yeghsagodadigh* ONEAYOTRONON.

TYATADEKEA,

Atahoghtsíyoghts satahoghsatad tsiniyoriwa n'tgewenninegeane, Asharegówa yongyats keantho non we ni kideron r'iyatyadontaghkon ne Goraghwowa wagonoghrondawete wagonnoghketsko N'ighsarondagowa, Yensanigonghrayendane kadi tsiniyoriwa eaghskewennáronge.

Orongwaghsa.

TYATADEKEA,

Onea kayery Niyoghserágegh tsinahae tethoditackseaonk ne Goraghgówa ok Wastonghronon, ethone kady nadeyodeckhaghsyongh Sewanigónra ne Rodinoughsiyonni, Saghsyarongwea n'ise ne Nighserondagowa ne Goraghgowa Raoriwa, Yanikoghrodakweah ne Wastonhoronon, ne ne tsiniharighwaweyehhon, wakarihhóni ok ne ne tsinilhot'yoghkoweána;

Onea akwégon sesanikorhea, tsinihanoronghgwa tsinahhe n'Ongwehonwe ne Goraghgowa. Ok oni ne Wastonghrónon tsinihayadótea tsinahhe, onea ki oni wesanikorhea tsiniyawedaa, tsinightsisewayérea j'Ongwehonwe Oghwenja Aoriwa.

Ethone tsisadaghsawe ne sádonghs Kayannereghsera ok n'ii n'katsteriste, etho oni T'hodádygh Anigonghríyoh ne ne rawea tokeske etho na esewáyere ne neok kea thaesewayérea, Tekonkaghneraghtsihhon, tyotkon yaghetho tesayérea; ne kea ne saadonghs? Kayanneraghsera wakyenawágon waker'ighwayéwagh ne ne ii Ongawaríwa akeahagge tsi..tea aniyog': t'kakonde yaghtea Satadeweanayerídong:, sadonghs Kayannereghsera? Onea eso waghsk'yeaghte, eso oni ise Sariwa wahontkarooni Ongwadatekea-a Rodinoghsiyonni, yaghse onea kaneka nonwe n'ayesakarewaghton, ikeghre kady agwagh ki aniyogh kanáye Sanikónra otogeaonh serighwanonwax, Iseghre onea waghadeashani ne T'syatatekeá-a Wastonghronon? Onea teckeni yadeghsadádi ne Kanoghsiyoníge, agwagh yotsanigh tsnisaweanodeah, ne kadi wahhoni waghhi Shiweáneran onea n'onkyadadekea, ok oni onea yadekeweánakonde. Giron yaghnadeghyatshanighse ne Goraghgowa n'ighserondagowagh, netsi ne ok ne Karighwiyoh roghthare tsitsideron, ikeghre ranoronghwa teaghnoon tsioni nihayerha ne Wastonghronónke ne ne seko ok eskarighwíyo t'endakadadi ne tehonnoghyanicks. Agwagh kadi kerighwanhadeaghs, agwagh yaghongwadonghniokthaghse, ne ne tsi onea wakonyénhaghle, Takenigonghradógeaghst onea, kea kaye tsiron t'kakonde wetyaderíyol etho kadi Onea neayáweane, tokeske nikarighwesha kadi onea ok easatkaghton tsiniyeyadódean ne Kheyéongonwa ne ne tyotkon k'heghtoghraragon; ok oni karighwiyo segon ne togat eaghsiron onea ki Kanoghsiyoníge sakyéndaghgwe Akenigonra. Kadon onea yadekeweánakonde, ne kadi wakaderíendare ne togat tokeske enteghserighwakóndea ne aetyaderíyo yotkáde ne t'kakonde segon Kanoghsiyoníge kayendaghkon n'akonigónra, yoyannere kadi ne ne éne ayondadóoni, n'keyadeweyendon segea neanee; Segon Tondakatnanetta, ne kaadon onea Tagenigoghradogeagst, toghsa isi nonwe yaseríwayen.

Gonrighwanondonghs

Printed at Quebec by William Brown, 1779. The Oneidas, alone of the six Iroquois nations, 'deserted the King's cause' and supported the rebel American colonists in the American Revolution. Sir Frederick Haldimand (1718–1791), Governor of Quebec 1778–1786, reiterates the advantages of the King's Bounty and urges the Oneidas to repent for their past 'vile actions'. Tremaine 325.

in case you slight or disregard this my last Offer of peace; I shall soon convince you that I have such a Number of Indian Allies to let loose upon you, as will instantly convince you of your Folly when too late, as I have hardly been able to restrain them from falling upon you for some time past.

I must therefore once more repeat to you that this is my last and final Message to you, and that you do not hesitate or put off giving me your direct and decisive Declaration of Peace or War, that in case of the latter (knowing there are still some of your Nation who are Friends to the King and the five Nations) I may give them timely Warning to separate themselves from you.

BROTHERS,

Let me lastly convince you of the Deceit and Dissimulation of your rebel Brethren General Schuyler, Parson Kirtland, and others; have they not told you in the Beginning of the Rebellion, that they wanted not your Assistance and have your Blood Spilt, and you likewise declared that you would not join them, but remain Neuter. Have either of you stuck to your Words? No! you basely broke it and seemed from the beginning to be of mutual hostile Sentiments against the King and his Allies, and soon after manifested it by your Actions.—What confirms me in this Opinion, and proves your deceitful and treacherous Disposition, is your behaviour during the course of last War, when you likewise acted a double part, in clandestinely joining and carrying Intelligence to the French in this Country; which I myself am a Witness to, and also was told of it by your Friend the late Sir *William Johnson*, who notwithstanding your base Behaviour, upon promising that you would be true and faithful for the future, forgave you, and received you into favor again, advising you to be more prudent and honest in time to come, and frequently after that loaded you with the King's Bounty and Favors.

But he was no sooner dead, than you ungratefully forgot his good Advice and Benefactions, and in Opposition to his Family and Indian Friends, and every thing that is sacred, adopted the Cause of Rebels and Enemies to your King, your late Patron Sir *William Johnson* and your own Confederacy and Connections.

These are Facts, Brothers, that unless you are lost to every Sense of Feeling cannot but create in you a most hearty Repentance, and deep Remorse, for your past vile Actions.

The Belt.

Gonrighwanondonghs Tyatadegea? ne tyotkori saadonghs shagonoronghkwa ne Wastonghronon ne Ongwehonwe, yaghteghanówefe ne ayeneckwa Skaghstarat, yaghteghanonwefe ne ahonwayenawafe tsiroderigo Thaniendagáyen ok Onaghgwifakhon ne rodighthare, ok oniie sadonghs yaghnoweandon thiyahiyenawafe? Onghka onghtegh onnóweaghte? Tsyattadegea-a Wastonghronon Yaghristha kea tsinonwa nighsatyerha? Ok oni n'ise sadonghs kea? Yaghwahhi teghsenonwefe n'ayesayénawafe tsisateriyo? Ok Shiwakaderiendare Onówea tsinihoyerannyon ne Wastonghronon; raweron toghnóh oktheayondyérea onea eayeyádarane tsiroderíyo, Yakwerhaghgwe kadi ethone onghte tantsisewayadoreghte ne onea ensewadogeaghse, oriwakon ne raadon yaghtekenonwefe Ongwehonwe ayonkyenawafe; Agwagh kadi aniyogh tsideckhkanere tejaron seninonwele ne waenikorhátea. Ne wahoni kadon Takenigoghradogeaghst, aniyogh t'kakonde thayorighwaghnirhaghfere tsiteckhkanere tsinighsenikorhátha ne N'ighferondagowagh ne ne tsiyongwaderíyoh n'Onondíyo, etho are nen'ne nisatiyérea tsi are nonwanighsatyerha Teghsaderighwayendonghkwa kanikorhádon sayodeserighweahawefe efo eghtsiyenawafe n'Onondiyo; ne kadi ne onea skeanon safondon ok onea tsiniwadearonseródea ne Goraghne, ok on'ife tsifewaweanandáon tsireandero ne Goraghkeaha etho tsifewáyen Sewanigonra, efo tsinightsifewatfenoniyadeani Goraghgowa Raoweak. Agwagh kawonio sahadonhókte ne Goraghkeaha, oksaok agwékon fefewanikorhea ne tsinightsifewayeraseghhaghkwe tsinahotea Sewayannereghfera; Tokatonsefewatateghyaghraghkwa n'oghnáge nonkadi tsiniyaweáon, nonwa oni tsinontakadadi aefewarighwakaeayon: Yaghtea yawigh ne yagh thiyaont-tokáne ne Seweriáne.

Kayooni.

'T Longboat, the Canadian runner.' Photographer Charles A Aylett. 1907

Patrick B O'Neill

Canadiana deposited in the British Museum Library between 1895 and 1924

The history of copyright legislation in Canada is considerably documented but little attention has been accorded to the implication of Canada's copyright laws for sources of Canadiana. This paper will attempt to rectify that situation by focusing first on the history of the various copyright deposits created by the federal government, and secondly, on the copyright collection sent to the British Museum Library (now the British Library) between 1895 and 1924, which is the particular concern of our research project.

Copyright legislation in Canada

The first piece of federal copyright legislation was passed in 1868 when Parliament re-enacted the Copyright Act of the Province of Canada as stopgap legislation to apply in the new Dominion; publishers were required to deposit two free copies with the Minister of Agriculture who kept one in the Copyright Office and deposited the other in the Library of Parliament, established by the purchase of the Legislative Library of the Province of Canada for $200,000 in 1867. The first complete and original copyright legislation in Canada was the Canadian Copyright Act of 1875. This act, which was substantially re-enacted with some alterations first in the *Revised Statutes of 1886* and later in the *Revised Statutes of 1906*, supplied the basis of copyright in Canada between the years 1875 and 1924. It granted copyright for twenty-eight years from the time of registration to any person living in Canada or any other part of the British dominions; and recognised the copyright for a similar period of a citizen of any country having an international copyright treaty with the United Kingdom. The impetus for the legislation came from business interests and thus concerns itself primarily with the commercial aspects of printed and published works rather than the right by authorship to a written work.[1] To register a work and thus obtain copyright under the Canadian law, the person, often the publisher and not the author, must have complied with the following conditions: first, such literary, scientific or artistic works must have been printed and published, or reprinted and republished, in Canada; or, in the case of works of art, must have been produced or reproduced in Canada; and secondly, two copies of the book, map, chart, musical composition, photograph, print, cut, or engraving must have been deposited at the Office of the Minister of Agriculture: for paintings, drawings, statuary and sculpture, a written description of such work could have been substituted and sent to the Minister. The Act of 1875, as had the 1868 Act, instructed the Minister of Agriculture to deposit one copy of the work in the Library of Parliament and to retain the other copy in the Copyright Office. In 1895, section 10 of the Act was amended to require that three copies be sent to the Minister: the third copy was to be forwarded to the British Museum Library.

The deposit requirement under the 1875 Act and its Amendment of 1895 remained unaltered until the passing of the Act of 1921. The 1921 Act repealed and superceded all prior copyright legislation in Canada and, with its various amendments, is the basis of Canadian copyright law today. Sadly, the 1921 Act (which was not proclaimed until 1 January 1924) contained no provision requiring deposit copies of books, in Canada or elsewhere. The Library of Parliament, the Copyright Office, and the British Museum Library all lost their free copies of Canadiana on 31 December 1923. This situation obtained until 1931 when a bill was passed, 'not intended to revise generally the Copyright Act, but to amend that Act only in so far as is necessary to bring Canadian copyright legislation into conformity with the provisions of the Rome Convention' of 1928. In addition to its above stated purpose, the amendment included a provision to restore deposits to the Library of Parliament:

The publisher of every book published in Canada, within three months of the publication thereof, shall deliver or cause to be delivered, at his own expense to the Librarian of Parliament, who shall give a written receipt therefor, two copies of the first edition and two copies of each subsequent edition if such subsequent edition contains additions or alterations either in the letter press or in the maps, prints, or other engravings thereto belonging.

The rationale for this action was explained in a subsidiary note in the amendment: that such copies, when deposited, would form the nucleus of a National Library for Canada.

The dream of a National Library, shattered by the Depression and World War II, did not become a reality quickly. Not until 1952 did the National Library Act pass through Parliament. Section II of that Act gave the new library the responsibility of collecting and systematically preserving Canadiana by requiring Canadian publishers to deposit two copies of each publication in the National Library within one week of its release for public distribution or sale.

Copyright deposit collections in Canada

Everything copyrighted in Canada prior to 1924 or published in Canada after 1931 found its way as deposit material into official libraries. This system would seem to have guaranteed ready access today to all published Canadian material: time and circumstances, however, have served to offset the intent of the various Copyright Acts. The Acts produced three sets of collections: the Library of Parliament/National Library Collection; the Copyright Office Collection; and, finally, the British Museum Collection.

The Library of Parliament Collection

Unfortunately, the Library of Parliament has been diminished by two fires. The first fire in 1916 began in the Library and would eventually destroy the rest of the Parliament Buildings. The Report of the Joint Librarians indicates the extent of the damage:

The disastrous fire which destroyed the Parliament Buildings, in February, did not leave the Library unscathed.

The fire originated in the reading room, which contained a large and valuable collection of books, as well as the current newspapers.

When these took fire, the whole collection of books was hopelessly doomed to destruction.

During the night, the water thrown upon the burning buildings found its way ultimately to the Library, and the floor was flooded to the depth of many inches, during the two days which followed.

Much damage was done by this flood of water; but owing to the exertions of some members of the Library staff, who were on duty, the books on the lower shelves were, as far as time allowed, removed and placed in higher shelves.

A second fire began in the dome of the Library of Parliament in 1953 and water damage again caused most of the destruction as it cascaded down upon the collection.[2]

The collection was not totally destroyed by these two fires: the Report of the National Librarian in 1957 observes that several 'large transfers have been made by the Library of Parliament, and about 100,000 of these volumes have been unpacked and placed on shelves.'[3] By 1967, this transferred material had been catalogued simply in a composite file, known in the National Library as the 'In Process Catalogue', and included 86,223 items; the In Process Catalogue, however, was not integrated into the National Library Catalogue.[4] Michel Thériault of the National Library, in charge of the Canadiana 1867–1900 Project, stated during the Learned Societies' Meetings in Halifax in June 1981 that the transferal from the Library of Parliament does not contain a full set of deposit materials. Similarly, Maria Calderisi Bryce, Music Division, National Library, noted in correspondence in the summer of 1983 that 'a great number of legal deposit copies . . . have not been located in our own collection,'[5] and the National Library should contain the first deposit copy of every book published in Canada between 1868 and 1923 but, in fact, can not claim to house this full collection. Destroyed in the Parliamentary fires of 1916 and 1953, lost in transit to the National Library in the 1950s, or simply stored and forgotten in a warehouse at some intervening date, a complete set of the first deposit copies of Canadian material published prior to 1952 is not accessible in the Library of Parliament nor the National Library of Canada.

Copyright Office Collection

The history of the Copyright Office Collection, consisting of the second deposit copies received after 1868, is more tightly documented. With the assistance of the Hon Robert Stanfield, then member of Parliament for Halifax, a memorandum dating from 1937 was traced: because of its impending removal to new premises the Copyright Office requested direction on the disposition of its collection of deposit material, since the new offices lacked the necessary storage space. Forces of Continentalism outweighing Nationalism in 1938, the Committee of the Privy Council determined that few of the 'several thousands of volumes of books, catalogues, periodicals, pamphlets, sheet music, maps' etc. had any value. An Order-in-Council, signed by Lord Tweedsmuir and Prime Minister MacKenzie-King, ordered that the material be offered for selection to the Secretary of State Library and that the Copyright Office dispose of what remained. The Secretary of State Library observed shortly thereafter that: 'One hundred and fifty-five books of prominent Canadian statesmen and the history of Canada were obtained from the Copyright Office, together with some sixty volumes of Canadian fiction.' A search of the Public Records Office did not reveal further correspondence on this subject; the remaining 40,000-odd pieces were, we must presume, destroyed.[6]

Perhaps confusing Canadian with American and English copyright law requirements, some applicants continued to submit deposit copies after the legal obligation to do so ceased in 1924. Items that continued to accumulate in the Copyright Office after 1938 were collected by the Department of Indian Affairs in the mid-1960s and distributed to schools and libraries, particularly in the North West Territories.[7]

The formation of the British Museum Library Collection

Now let us consider the third deposit copy received by the Copyright Office. The disposition of these items provides the second focus for this paper, the British Museum Library Collection. The deposit copies for the British Museum Library began arriving in London in 1895: 'The works transmitted to the British Museum commence with those registered on July 23, 1895, viz. nos. 8035–8040 or the latter nos. of the list in the Patent Office Record vol. 23, no. 7, July 31, 1895. (Signed) F.B.C.'[8] In Valerie Bloomfield's valuable *Guide to Resources For Canadian Studies in Britain*, she reported that 'coverage of Canadian publication is virtually complete for the years 1842–1886,' in the British Library collection. The information supporting this assertion had been supplied to her by a staff member of the British Library, but the deposit of these Canadian materials to which the Library was entitled by the Imperial Copyright Act of 1842, and which was actively desired by Library staff at the time, had not, in fact, ever arrived.

In 1886, an Imperial Act removed the requirement of copyright deposit copies from all Colonial publishers including the self-governing Dominions. Since Imperial legislation could not guarantee colonial deposits the British Museum Library now looked to diplomatic channels in the various dominions as a means of assuring transmission of such materials. In 1889 an amended Canadian Copyright Act had passed through Parliament, but failed to receive Royal Assent. During the considerable discussion in England and Canada that followed, the proposed bill came to the attention of the Trustees of the British Museum. On their behalf, E Maunde Thompson, then Director of the British Museum, wrote to the Marquess of Ripon at the Colonial Office requesting that he 'keep the interests of the British Museum in view in the course of the negotiations with the Canadian Government' and 'that, if the Canadian Government obtain any realisation of copyright regulations in their favour, they should undertake on their part to comply with the law as regards the deposit of books in the British Museum.'[9] The Marquess of Ripon forwarded the request to the Earl of Aberdeen:

I have the honour to transmit to you, to be laid before your Minister, a copy of a letter from the British Museum, respecting the supply to it of copies of books first published in Canada. . . . The collection in the British Museum is, as you are aware, the only national collection, and I am sure your Ministers will agree with me that it is important that it should be complete, and especially in respect of works issued in the most important of Her Majesty's Possessions.[10]

Although the 1889 Act failed to receive Royal Assent, Canada's Parliament did agree that works published in Canada should be part of the British Museum Library's collection. An 1895 amendment to the 1875 Canadian Copyright Act directed that three copies of each work be deposited with the Minister of Agriculture – the third copy to be deposited in the British Museum Library. The rationale motivating the Canadian legislators to require a third copyright deposit copy for the British Museum Library was, according to the Report of the Privy Council, that it 'would be the means of introducing the works of Canadian authors to the large and influential class of readers who frequent the library.' In actuality it was probably a political move to gain concessions from the Canadian authors and the British government who had both opposed the proposed 1889 Canadian copyright legislation.

The unpublished 'Canadian Copyright Lists' of the British Museum Library indicate nearly 100% receipt of the deposits there between 1895 and 1924. A memorandum of 27 March 1899 stated that 'It is not proposed to ask for "Insurance Plans" (Canadian), in as much as their value is purely local – nor for English Novels published in England, which are reprinted in Canada.' Despite this disclaimer, these materials continued to be sent by the Canadian Copyright Office, and, for the most part, to be received by the British Museum. The 'Lists' for 1914 reveal that 'Copyright exhibit Nos. 28790–28806 registered between May 14 and 19 have not been received – they were presumably lost in the wreck of the *Empress of Ireland* on May 30.' In addition, dozens of incendiary bombs fell on the British Museum on 10 May 1941 and the resulting fires in the south-west quadrant caused the loss of some 200,000 volumes. The principal destruction among Canadian copyright deposit books was in the shelves containing law, stenography and cookery. Despite its losses, the British Library collection of Canadian copyright deposit material remains, we believe, the most complete, of both English and French published materials, for the period between 1895 and 1924.

The British Library Collection today

THE DEPARTMENT OF PRINTED BOOKS

Our project has completed the check of cards compiled from the 'Canadian Copyright Lists' against the British Library catalogue, and the cross-check against the list of materials destroyed during the blitz. We are now searching for the materials not located in the British Library catalogue. The reasons for a non-appearance in the catalogue are threefold: first, errors or omissions on our cards; second, British Library practices at the time; and third, uncatalogued material. Regarding the first, errors made by the clerks in the Copyright Office at the time of registration are the most annoying since an incorrect entry of the author's name means checking other possible spellings – time-consuming but not impossible. In addition, the author's name is occasionally omitted and replaced by the name of the person or persons holding the copyright: the British Library catalogue places the work under the author's name, but we do not know that name. Regarding the second, many shortcuts for cataloguing have been developed by the British Library over the years: all Directories, for example, were catalogued under one heading and, at one time, many appeared without individual pressmarks. We have located a number of these 'group deposits' but have not completed an inventory of the items. Finally, regarding the third, because of the enormity of its accessions, the British Library does not catalogue all the material it receives, and uncatalogued material is placed in subject area 'dumps'. One of these 'dumps' measuring some three hundred linear feet at Woolwich produced over four thousand pieces of Canadiana – primarily photographs and trade material – but including a fiction work by Gilbert Parker. The major detriment to the completion of the project is the possibility that such uncatalogued 'dumps' were destroyed in the blitz – with no catalogue records, there would likewise be no records of their destruction and loss.

Although its various staff librarians insist that the British Library does not collect photographs, we have located about 3,500 of the 5,000 received under copyright deposit. The collection was primarily uncatalogued and loose on shelves and many of the remaining photographs are undoubtedly lost forever. We have gathered together all these uncatalogued photographs, dusted them and placed them in acid-free envelopes. Although individually uncatalogued, some photographs are mounted in guardbooks which necessitates checking each one for the Canadian copyright number, another time-consuming operation. We located twelve Canadian photographs in a thirty-five volume set of British photographic material. The largest collection of catalogued photographs is held in the Map Room which houses approximately one thousand Canadian photographs. The Canadian copyright number has been removed from many of these photographs making identification difficult. The major problem with the photographs will be determining what has been lost, as opposed to what has been removed. The Museum of Mankind (formerly the Department of Ethnography of the British Museum) now has over one hundred of the photographs of Canadian native peoples received by the British Museum Library, but we need to check other possible recipients of Canadiana.

THE MAP LIBRARY

To inventory the map collection, I had to read the entire map library catalogue, but this led to the simultaneous location of books, photographs and maps. The most important discovery in the map collection is the Goad Insurance Plans. In 1977 Robert J Hayward published his study *Fire Insurance Plans in the National Map Collection* which details the holdings of the Public Archives of Canada with regard to the Charles E Goad Ltd Insurance plans. In his introduction to the work Hayward explains why these large-scale urban maps are now the most sought-after documents in the National Map Collection and how they had been systematically destroyed when returned by the subscribers to the Goad company. Fire insurance plans are maps or a set of maps of a community showing in detail, by means of colour and symbol, the character of the outside and inside construction of buildings, passages, fire walls, openings in walls, height and occupancy or use of the building or groups of buildings. They are invaluable to historians interested in morphologic changes, urban land use, architecture and urban demography. The collection at the British Library numbers over fourteen hundred plans of which, Louis Cardinal and Robert J Hayward of the Public Archives estimate, only 30% exist in Canada.

THE MUSIC LIBRARY

This year, we have attempted only to trace the location of Canadian music throughout the history of the music collection in the British Library and we hope to inventory the collection during the winter of 1984. Beginning in 1885, staff shortages forced the British Museum Library to begin selective cataloguing of copyright instrumental music (be it British, foreign, Canadian, etc.). The music collection continued to catalogue all copyright vocal music until the end of 1889, but thereafter introduced selection in this area also. In the 1920s when the Music Library moved into its present quarters, the uncatalogued music was organized to form two series of ten-year parcels (1890–1899, 1900–1909, etc.) arranged according to date of copyright receipt. Within each decade the pieces were filed alphabetically by composer's name. The instrumental music series is not indexed; the vocal music series is indexed, by title or first word followed by the name of the composer and the date of copyright receipt. The process of locating Canadian pieces will be dust-producing, and as always time-consuming, but otherwise straightforward.

None of the copyright deposit material thus collected was catalogued until Edward Sington, a retired civil servant, joined the Music Library staff in 1957 as a volunteer part-time worker. Over eighteen years he catalogued all the deposit material published before 1909, and vocal music by composers A to D in the decade 1910–1919. He read the proofs, did most of the press-marking himself, and made up the sheet music into binding size batches, which produced a total of 490 folio volumes besides a long series of boxes for unbindable band parts. A collection of some 62,254 pieces of music. The task of locating Canadian music to 1909 has been greatly assisted by Sington's preliminary work, but remains formidable.

Conclusion

The significance of the collection in the British Library is not that individual items are unique, but that the whole collection, for the most part, is housed complete in one library. Our current plan is to publish a series of checklists of the materials in the British Library: printed books, maps, sheet music, photographs, etc. The National Librarian of Canada observed in his annual report for 1960:

One of the chief purposes and responsibilities of a national library is to collect systematically and preserve the total output of the nation's publishers.

The British Museum Library systematically collected the published output of Canadian publishers for the period between 1895 and 1924. Undoubtedly the collection should prove beneficial to scholars in all areas of Canadian Studies in the future, and all Canadians should be thankful that the British Library has preserved our heritage.

References

1. See 'Canadian Copyright' in Proceedings and Transactions of the *Royal Society of Canada for the Year 1892*, Section 11 (Ottawa, 1893), 3–18. In it Sir Daniel Wilson, President of the University of Toronto wrote: 'It is treated as a mere question between English and Canadian printers and publishers as though the "Idylls of the King" . . . were the mere work of the type-setters.'
2. For a short history of the Library of Parliament, see the *Encyclopedia Canadiana*, vi (Toronto, 1966, 132–138
3. *Report of the National Librarian*, 1957 (Ottawa, 1958)
4. Dorothy Benson, 'Instant Cataloguing,' *Canadian Library*, 22:6 (May 1966), 419–421
5. Information supplied by M Theriot and M C Bryce of the National Library in correspondence
6. Information supplied by B McDowell, Administrative Assistant to the Hon Robert Stanfield
7. Information supplied by C White, Consumer and Corporate Affairs, Ottawa
8. Memorandum in the Canadian Copyright Deposit Lists held by the British Library
9. *Parliamentary Papers*, 1895, 1xx,90
10. *Parliamentary Papers*, 1895, 1xx, 90–91

John R T Ettlinger

Checklist of Canadian copyright deposits 1895 to 1924 in the British Museum Library: a note on format

The principal list will include books, pamphlets and single sheets, with the exception of the following types of material, which will be listed in separate groups: maps; insurance plans; sheet music; serials; photographs; directories; catalogues; prints, art work and other pictorial matter. Each of these groups will require a distinctive format for the assistance of users which is not described here.

The model for entry will be the information provided in the British Library Catalogue, but this will be expanded by incorporating information derived from the Copyright Register. Where physical examination of the actual items or information derived from standard bibliographical sources, such as the National Union Catalog or Tod and Cordingley, supplements or corrects this substantially, appropriate changes will be made. This has been done to assist future bibliographical work, such as the compilation of RETRO, and also researchers in Canadian research libraries, until the checklist has been superseded by complete bibliographical investigation for the period. This accounts for a measure of eclecticism and inconsistency in the format.

Personal forms of main entry have been preferred, and in many cases authorship has been assigned on the basis of the Copyright Register. Where this differs from the British Library entry, it is distinguished by the symbol [cop.]. Doubtful cases have been entered in a note, and not used as the entry. No record has been made of copyrighters who are publishers, printers or their agents.

The first index will record added entries, including subject entries, as follows: added entries are made for co-authors; contributors noted; editors; illustrators; pseudonyms and copyrighters where these are not adopted as the main entry; and other persons or institutions having a connection with the work. Subject entries are made only when specific for persons, institutions, and Canadian places. A second index will include titles and series. A third index for publishers and printers is not yet planned, but this information will be available from the entries when required.

Other titles which are in the British Library by the authors listed have not been noted. Other editions of the titles listed have not been noted except editions of the same year or of the preceding or following year. This is to assist investigators into 'simultaneous' publication of books in Canada, Great Britain and the United States; the phrase 'another edition' must be construed as including states, impressions, variant title-pages or other differentiations. The identification shows the British Library shelf location, and also the Copyright Register number. 'D' [destroyed] or 'Missing' indicates that the BL catalogue so states; 'Not Located' means that the compilers have not found the copyright item in the British Library. Some items were recorded by the British Library as 'Not Received' and they have been indicated as such.

Keith Barr

The British Library Lending Division and Canadian Studies

Introduction

The British Library Lending Division (BLLD) was formed in 1973 from two existing libraries, the National Central Library (NCL) and the National Lending Library for Science and Technology (NLL). The NCL dealt mainly with monographs, with public and academic libraries and with the humanities and social sciences. It used a union catalogue approach to pass on requests to holding libraries. The NLL dealt with science and technology, though it had covered social science serial literature since 1967, with serials and report literature more than monographs, and with special, industrial and academic libraries. It worked on the principle of having in its own stock everything for which a significant demand existed. The two libraries thus complemented each other.

On the amalgamation of these two libraries to form the British Library Lending Division, one organization came into existence which dealt with all aspects of interlending and document supply for all types of literature in all subject fields.

Since the Lending Division concentrates on satisfying the demand on it without being particularly concerned with the type of material requested, it does not have a great deal of subject- or area-based information on its collections or on the use of those collections. These collections are however very rich and very extensively used; its users rather than the Library itself probably best appreciate the strengths of the Lending Division.

Serials

The Lending Division's general policy is to collect research level serials in all languages wherever published. At present over 54,000 current serial titles are received, of which around 1,600 are published in Canada. Unfortunately there is no breakdown of Canadian titles by subject, nor is it known how many of the 110,000 dead serial titles held by the Library are Canadian. Full listings of current serials can be found in the annual publication *Current Serials Received*, and full listings of all the Library's serial titles both dead and live can be found on KIST (Keyword Index to Serial Titles), through which keyword access is available to any serial title held. Many journals from countries other than

Canada will of course be of great importance to students and scholars of Canadian Studies, and the Library's collections are very often used by those searching for peripheral material which is not contained in their own more specialised local library research collections.

Books

The general policy for the purchase of books is the same as that for serials with the major exception that foreign language titles are not bought except on demand, and only then when there are no locations in the UK listed in the Union Catalogue of Books. The NLL had been buying English language books at research level in the fields of science and technology from Canada since 1960, and since 1972 the Lending Division has been acquiring research level English language monographs from Canada in all subject fields through a blanket order with a Canadian supplier who is able to provide a particularly good service for Canadian books. It is believed that the coverage of Canadian research level monographs since 1975 has been very wide indeed.

The Lending Division's Union Catalogue of Books contains some 3.5 million entries, and includes not only the stock of the Division but also location information built up by the National Central Library from 1920 through to 1973. Since 1973 locations have continued to be added for new accessions by the majority of British university libraries of pre-1972 English language monographs and of all foreign language monographs. The Union Catalogue is therefore the main tool for the discovery of locations in Britain of Canadian books in English published before 1972 and of Canadian books in French published at any time. Unfortunately no figures are available for the Lending Division's holdings of Canadian books or of books published in other countries which relate to Canadian Studies. It is thought, however, that the Division has one of the best collections of research-level monographs published in English since 1972 anywhere in the world.

Although the comprehensive collecting policy for the Division has only been in existence since 1972, very large amounts of material published before that date have been obtained by the Lending Division and its predecessors by purchase and donation. Although the Division does not currently buy antiquarian books, or books on the secondhand market, the NCL did buy extensively books from North American university presses published from the mid-1960s through to the early-1970s. In addition the Lending Division (and before it the NCL) is at the centre of the British national gift and exchange scheme, and continues to act as a redistribution centre for books being discarded by libraries in Britain.

Through this redistribution service the Division is adding to its stock some 40,000 books per annum, although once again it is not known what proportion of these relate to Canadian Studies. One particular category of Canadian books which the Division hopes to be able to provide more readily in the future is pre-1900 material. This will be available through the cooperative purchase by the British Library Reference and Lending Divisions of the CIHM Pre-1900 Canadiana microform collection, distributed in the UK by University Microfilms International. Arrangements are being made for any item in this collection to be made available by the Reference Division to the Lending Division for loan purposes.

At present there is no access for outside users to details of the Lending Division's holdings of books. However, the Division is planning the implementation of an automated monograph acquisition and record system from the beginning of 1984. A GEAC system has been purchased and in due course the Lending Division will provide microfiche and possibly on-line access to its holdings of post-1979 books and also to its Union Catalogue of foreign language books published after the same date. This will allow research libraries in Britain immediate access to locations for French Canadian books in Britain (if held in the main university library collections) and will also allow libraries to know whether or not the Division holds recent English language Canadian books.

Conference proceedings

The Lending Division has always made special efforts to obtain as many as possible of the world's published conference proceedings in all languages, and has a very comprehensive collection. The published *Index to Conference Proceedings Received* lists all these proceedings. The number of items in this Index relating to Canadian Studies is again not known.

Reports and translations

The Lending Division has always been concerned with obtaining report literature as widely as possible. From Canada the Division receives the unlimited reports of the various establishments of Atomic Energy of Canada Limited (AECL); the unrestricted reports of the Defence Research Board; many of the series produced by the National Research Council of Canada; reports from Canadian universities (with the University of Toronto Institute of Aerospace Sciences (UTIAS) probably the largest single series); reports and translations from the Fisheries Research Board, Environment Canada, and many other organizations. There is an exchange of translations and information on translations between the Lending Division and CISTI. Since May 1983 the Division has subscribed to the Federal Canadian section of the *Microlog* microfiche document supply service. This includes all federal reports, both from government and from government research institutions, which are likely to be of reference interest. The documents in this series are well indexed in the *Microlog Index*.

Theses

The Lending Division is one of the main repositories of theses in the UK, and includes large collections of both British and US doctoral theses and smaller collections of theses from Canada and other countries. For many years the Division has been receiving copies of all doctoral theses from the majority of British universities which it has itself filmed and subsequently made available on loan or sale to its customers. This will include a number of theses of interest to students of Canadian Studies. For non-British theses the policy has been to acquire only those theses which have been requested by users and over the last three years the Division has purchased approximately 200 Canadian doctoral theses each year through the National Library of Canada.

Music

The Lending Division acquires music scores extensively, with particular reference to current publications. Although British publications are acquired more comprehensively, a large amount of foreign material is also added to stock. Canadian music is treated in the same way as any country's output; the holdings will depend on the availability of the material.

Valerie Bloomfield

A Guide to Resources for Canadian Studies in Britain

GUIDE TO RESOURCES FOR CANADIAN STUDIES IN BRITAIN (with some reference to relevant collections in Europe), by Valerie Bloomfield. Second edition. British Association for Canadian Studies, 1983. xxi, 252 pp. maps. bibl. ISBN 0-9509063-0-1. £5. Orders handled by the Library and Resources Group of the British Association for Canadian Studies, c/o Royal Commonwealth Society Library, Northumberland Avenue, London WC2N 5BJ.

The first edition of this *Guide* published by the Canadian Department of External Affairs in Ottawa in 1979 contained 137 entries. In the second edition due to appear later in 1983 under the auspices of the British Association for Canadian Studies the number of entries in the British section has increased to 182, with a further 82 entries in a new section on European holdings. Existing entries have been expanded and up-dated wherever possible, and a special effort has been made to improve the coverage of scientific and audio-visual materials. There are 100 collections in London and 82 in other parts of the country. As the project was based in London there is a natural bias towards the capital, but it is evident that London has by far the greatest concentration of resources. Other main centres are Edinburgh (16 collections), Oxford (10), Cambridge (7) and Glasgow (4).

These institutions which contribute to the national coverage of Canadiana are of many kinds: national, university, government, special and public libraries, diplomatic offices, learned societies, religious organizations, museums and archives. They are funded in various ways, by central government, local authorities, individual subscriptions and in some cases by, or with the support of, the Canadian Federal and Provincial governments. Among them they cover all subjects and a wide range of materials and services: books and pamphlets, periodicals, newspapers, government publications, manuscripts, theses, maps, audio-visual materials (films, filmstrips and slides, pictorial sources, sound recordings), microforms, machine-readable data banks and online bibliographical services. Many of these libraries themselves undertake bibliographical activities which are noted where relevant, and the entries also include published references used in the preparation of the *Guide*.

The collections vary greatly in size, scope and level of interest, from the comprehensive coverage of the British Library to the Fawcett Library's specialized holdings on the subject of women. The following examples illustrate the range:

The National Library of Scotland concentrates on all aspects of the Scottish-Canadian connection and has a particular interest in Gaelic language material published in Canada; the National Library of Wales, because of the linguistic situation in its own country, makes a special effort to collect material on bilingualism and minority languages; the National Film Archive preserves a selection of feature films, documentaries and newsfilms relating to Canada; The Social Science Research Council Data Archive at the University of Essex has a growing collection of machine-readable data files with a Canadian content; the Foreign and Commonwealth Office and the Public Record Office between them hold the most complete runs of Canadian and Provincial official series such as Acts, Sessional Papers, Debates, Government Gazettes, Legislation and Statistical blue books, and the PRO's map collection contains some 1,850 printed and manuscript maps of Canada; Canada House Reference Library provides a focus for the study of Canadian life and culture and the High Commission offers an extensive range of information and other services; the Offices of the Provincial Agents General in London (Alberta, British Columbia, Nova Scotia, Ontario, Québec and Saskatchewan) act as sources of current information on their respective Provinces; Edinburgh University Library's long-standing interest in Canada has received added stimulus from the establishment of the Centre of Canadian Studies; the University of Birmingham, a Regional Centre for Canadian Studies, has developed a particular interest in French Canada, and in addition material on Canadian sport will be found in the library's Sports Documentation Centre; the University of Leeds, another Regional Centre, specializes in Canadian literature and history; the Royal Commonwealth Society Library receives an annual grant from the Canadian Government for the purchase of current Canadiana to complement its strong historical holdings, while its published catalogue makes a significant contribution to the bibliography of the area; the Scott Polar Research Institute at the University of Cambridge collects extensively on the Canadian Arctic; the Imperial War Museum's research collections (printed books, documents, photographs, film, art, sound records) cover Canada's participation in the two World Wars and other twentieth-century conflicts; the Commonwealth Institute's multi-media Library and Resource Centre contains material particularly suitable for use in schools as well as for more advanced study; the House of Lords Record Office holds on deposit the Beaverbrook Papers which are of exceptional interest for Canadian affairs; the Press Library of the Royal Institute of International Affairs adds some 1,000 cuttings annually on Canada. Some 'unexpected' collections include the School of Oriental and African Studies' holdings on Inuit and Canadian Indian languages and the Polish Library's printed and manuscript resources on Poles in Canada.

In addition to describing holdings the *Guide* also attempts to establish links between related collections. For example, the National Film Archive holds a selection of documentary films associated with John Grierson who later went on to become the first Commissioner of the National Film Board of Canada. Grierson's personal papers are deposited several hundred miles away in the John Grierson Archive at the University of Stirling. The Archive in Stirling works in close cooperation with the John Grierson Project at McGill University in Montreal, which adds an international dimension to the location of material.

Another function of the *Guide* is to identify sources of information. The entries on the National Register of Archives, the Business Archives Council, the Public Archives of Canada (London Office) and the Slade Film History Register at the British Universities Film Council fall into this category.

The survey on which the *Guide* was based was concerned to discover gaps in holdings as well as to record existing strengths. This was to enable librarians and others with an interest in Canada to improve coverage, possibly on a cooperative basis. Provincial publications and newspapers both appeared to be under-represented. The Library and Resources Group of the British Association for Canadian Studies is currently developing plans to place the acquisition of Provincial publications on a more systematic basis, in some cases with the support of the Provincial governments themselves. The newspaper problem has not yet been tackled, principally because of the lack of demand. Recommendations for future bibliographical projects include the preparation of a guide to manuscripts relating to Canada (this was before the Public Archives of Canada announced its own initiative), a listing of British academic theses on Canadian topics, and a union list of periodicals and major government serials. The listing of theses is under active consideration but the union list of periodicals is seen as part of a wider problem and awaits further developments at the national level.

In the new European section entries are based largely on replies to a questionnaire sent to the national and specialist institutions, and in certain instances the amount of material on a country reflects the nature of the response rather than the extent of the resources. Germany, for example, returned a high proportion of questionnaires whereas Italy is barely represented.

Sufficient replies have been received to reveal the complementary nature of British and European resources. In France the range of material parallels that in Britain, comprising as it does records of government and administration as well as works of scholarship. There are rich holdings of printed books, official reports, manuscripts and archives, maps and plans, with the emphasis on French Canada, more specifically Québec and Acadia. Many of these documents have been listed in a recent guide: *Guide des sources de l'histoire du Canada conservées en France* (Ottawa, Public Archives of Canada, 1982. xix, 157 pp).

The holdings of other countries are more specialized but they illuminate many aspects of Canadian history. Spain and Portugal preserve in their archives some of the earliest records on the discovery and exploration of Newfoundland and Labrador and the development of the whaling and cod-fishing industries, while Italy has early material on missionary activity in Canada. Collections in the USSR relate in the main to political and economic matters; from the 1780s when Russia founded permanent settlements on the North West coast of America, until 1867 when she sold Alaska to the United States, Russia was actively concerned with North American affairs as well as an interested observer of their repercussions in Europe. Records of the period contain reports on political and military events in Canada, on the progress of the Russian-American Company and on the expansion of the fur trade. German holdings cover a range of topics and periods: there are eighteenth-century records on Hessian, Brunswick and other auxiliary troops recruited to fight in North America; nineteenth-century commercial documents on transatlantic trade; diplomatic correspondence on German relations with Canada; and military archives on World Wars I and II. Under the subject specialization scheme organized by the Deutsche Forschungsgemeinschaft, the University of Göttingen has been assigned English-language Canadiana. Göttingen also has significant holdings of eighteenth-century Americana including many items of Canadian interest and is cooperating with the British Library in the preparation of the Eighteenth-Century Short-Title Catalogue (ESTC). Other German libraries with specialist responsibilities include the University of Bonn (French Canadiana) and the Prussian Cultural Foundation (law, foreign newspapers, official publications and topographic maps).

A major theme which helped in the identification of Canadian sources is European migration to Canada. Printed, manuscript and audio-visual materials have been collected by institutions in the countries of origin, particularly on cultural matters. The National Library of Iceland, for example, has a special collection on the Icelandic communities in Canada; the University of Helsinki collects printed works on Finns in North America while the University of Turku acquires related manuscript material; the Federal Archives in Bern hold documents on Swiss settlements in Canada; and the Polish State Archives preserve records on Polish organizations in Canada. Again there is a parallel with collections in Britain; the Polish Library in London, as noted above, has printed and manuscript material on Poles in Canada, and in Scotland collections of national or local interest frequently contain material on the activities of Scots in Canada from the seventeenth century to the present day.

The arrangement of the British section of the *Guide* is first by place and then by name of institution. An exception to this is the British Association for Canadian Studies which precedes the general sequence as its location changes with its office holders.

In the European section the arrangement is alphabetically by country, then by town and finally by name of institution. Exceptions are the Canadian Studies Associations of France, Germany, Ireland and Italy which head their country sequences. There are separate indexes for the British and European sections.

Martin Callow

Material on Canada in the Foreign and Commonwealth Office Library

Introduction

The Foreign and Commonwealth Office Library came into existence as a result of the merger of the Foreign Office and the Commonwealth Office in 1968. The Commonwealth Office had itself only recently been formed as a result of the fusion of the Colonial Office and the Commonwealth Relations Office, formerly the Dominions Office, in 1966. The FCO Library thus inherited the libraries of three government departments, two of which, the Foreign Office and the Colonial Office, dated back to the late eighteenth century.

The FCO Library is jointly administered with the Overseas Development Administration Library and forms part of the FCO Library and Records Department which is also responsible for departmental records and their transfer to the Public Record Office after the statutory period of thirty years. The FCO Library is spread over several buildings: the Main Library in Sanctuary Buildings, Great Smith Street, which houses the majority of the bookstock; the Legal Library in Downing Street, with its comprehensive collection of the legislation of Commonwealth countries; the Overseas Development Administration Library in Eland House, concentrating on aid matters; and a Cartographic and Map Section in Matthew Parker Street.

Holdings of Canadian material in the FCO Library fall into the following categories:

- Books and periodicals
- Official publications
- Legislation, official gazettes and law reports
- Photographs and drawings
- Petitions and loyal addresses
- Maps and atlases

'Manuscripts' have not been listed although the petitions and loyal addresses may be considered to fall under this heading. Apart from these there is little manuscript material in the FCO Library. Departmental records are normally made available to the public at the Public Record Office after a period of thirty years, and the records of the FCO's predecessor departments up to and including the year 1952 at present, are, with few exceptions, to be found there. Records within the thirty-year period are not open to the public.

The Collections

BOOKS AND PERIODICALS

The Library has a remarkable collection of books and pamphlets published in and about Canada and its provinces, including many early and rare works dealing especially with travel and exploration but also with many other aspects of the early development of Canada. It is possible to note here only a few examples to give a flavour of the collection:

Several editions in French and English of the works of Father de *Charlevoix* (1682–1761) the French Jesuit traveller who twice visited Canada

Ellis, Henry: 'A voyage to Hudson's-Bay . . . for discovering a North West passage . . . ' (London, 1748)

'The Canadian freeholder: in three dialogues, showing, the sentiments of the bulk of the freeholders of Canada concerning the late Quebeck-Act . . . ' (London, 1776–79)

'Motives for a subscription towards the relief of the sufferers at Montreal in Canada, by a dreadful fire on the eighteenth of May 1765 . . . '(Montreal, 1765)

Lafitau, Joseph François: 'Mémoire concernant la precieuse plante du ginseng de tartarie decouverte en Canada . . . ' (Paris, 1718). [Including a sketch of the plant.]

Vancouver, George: 'A voyage of discovery to the North Pacific Ocean and round the world . . . 1790, 1791, 1792, 1793, 1794 and 1795.' (London, 1798. 3vols.)

Howard, James S: 'A statement of facts relative to the dismissal of James S Howard . . . late postmaster of the City of Toronto.' (Toronto, 1839)

The library has complete sets of the publications of the Champlain Society (Toronto) and the Hudson's Bay Record Society.

Current acquisition policy regarding Canada, is, as with other countries, to concentrate on history, politics, economics, and foreign relations. The library takes about 60 current periodicals relating to Canada, including statistical serials.

OFFICIAL PUBLICATIONS

Apart from legislation and gazettes which are discussed below, the main categories of Canadian official publications currently received in the FCO Library are parliamentary and legislative assembly debates, and departmental and administrative reports. Holdings of Canadian Federal parliamentary debates commence in 1870 and are virtually complete from that date. There are also collections of provincial assembly debates and journals but these are not so comprehensive.

Departmental and administrative reports are received from Canada and the provinces but are very incomplete for several provinces. These are transferred to the Public Record Office after approximately 20 years.

There are many official publications of a monograph nature, *eg* reports of committees and commissions of enquiry and these are in the catalogued stock, including early material of the Colonial Office Library.

The Canada treaty series (1928–   ) is held, as are all the censuses of Canada dating back to 1851/52.

British official publications relating to Canada are to be found in the sets of parliamentary papers of interest to the Colonial Office which were bound in annual volumes by the Colonial Official Library. The Foreign Office Library had a similar practice which is still continued by the FCO Library today.

The series known as British and Foreign State Papers (1821–1968) compiled by the Foreign Office Library and amounting to 170 volumes, latterly published by HMSO, contains Canadian material.

LEGISLATION, OFFICIAL GAZETTES AND LAW REPORTS

The legal library holds a complete collection of both Federal and provincial main legislation including the two Territories. The collection extends to approximately 300 linear feet and contains laws dating from 1777. It includes the laws of the defunct political units of Vancouver Island (1853–1865)m Cape Breton (1793–1809) and the Isle of St John (1773–1797).

Canadian Federal sub-legislation is collected from 1947 onwards.

Federal and provincial official gazettes (including all supplements) are received and kept on file for approximately twenty years after which time they are transferred to the Public Record Office. The sub-legislation included in the provincial gazettes is not extracted in any way. Gazettes are not received at present from the two Territories.

The Library has sets of the Canadian Supreme Court reports (1878–1979), the Exchequer Court reports (1923–70), the Federal Court reports (1971–79) and certain miscellaneous law reports of the first half of the nineteenth century, *eg* Lower Canada 'Court of King's Bench and Courts of Appeal reports' (1810–1835).

Of particular interest is a framed illuminated copy of the Canadian Bill of Rights (1960) signed by John Diefenbaker. A recent acquisition is the 'Proclamation on the Constitution Act, 1982', signed by Pierre Trudeau and André Ouellet, Registrar General of Canada.

PHOTOGRAPHS AND DRAWINGS

In its collection of photographs and drawings the FCO Library has 30 volumes concerned with Canada. There are two especially interesting and valuable items. One is an album of 16 views of Toronto in 1856 by the firm of Armstrong, Beere and Hime. This album was lent to the Public Archives of Canada in 1980 for an exhibition in Ottawa entitled 'City Blocks, City Spaces'. Their research was unable to locate any other such early photographs of Canada. The other noteworthy album of photographs contains views of

British Columbia taken by Frederick Dally, a Victoria photographer, in 1867–8.

The collection also includes a volume of 12 sketches of New Brunswick published in 1836.

PETITIONS AND LOYAL ADDRESSES

Of historic and antiquarian interest is the collection of petitions to the monarch or the Secretary of State for the Colonies and loyal addresses to the monarch on accession or coronation and other special occasions. These petitions and addresses from the colonies or dominions dating back to 1891 were often beautifully illustrated and presented. Canadian material includes such items as a resolution of the City Common Council of St John, New Brunswick on the death of Queen Victoria, 1901 and an address of the Royal Ancient Order of Buffaloes of Winnipeg to George v on his coronation.

MAPS AND ATLASES

The Library has a working collection of current maps, charts, atlases, gazetteers and pilot's guides.

The Colonial Office Library possessed a remarkable collection of early maps and charts, many in manuscript, of the former colonies and dominions, but all the items dated earlier than 1910 have been transferred to the Public Record Office (Class CO 700).

Services

The FCO Main Library, Legal Library and the Library of the Overseas Development Administration (ODA) are open to the public from Monday to Friday, 9.30 am to 5.30 pm (ODA: 5 pm), for reference purposes only. Photocopying facilities are available.

The Main Library houses the major part of the bookstock, including all books and periodicals acquired prior to 1950. It houses official publications (apart from legislation, gazettes and law reports), photographs, petitions and loyal addresses. The Legal Library in Downing Street has the comprehensive collection of the legislation of Commonwealth countries and dependent territories as well as certain law reports. The Library of the Overseas Development Administration (ODA) consists largely of material on aid and technical matters.

The Main Library holds a series of catalogues to the collections. The union catalogue to post-1980 material is held on microfiche. Certain earlier catalogues which contain details of Canadian material have been published by G K Hall of Boston, Massachusetts, as follows:

Catalogue of the Colonial Office Library (1964) 15 vols.
—*First Supplement, 1963–1967* (1967)
—*Second Supplement, 1967–1971* (1972) 2 vols.
(Including accessions to the FCO Library from 1969)

Catalogue of the Foreign Office Library, 1926–1968. (1972) 8 vols.

Foreign and Commonwealth Office: accessions to the library, 1971–1977. (1979) 4 vols.

The other published catalogues are:

Catalogue of printed books in the Library of the Foreign Office. (London: HMSO, 1926).

Robertson, Colin L: *A short title catalogue of books printed before 1701 in the Foreign Office Library* (London: HMSO, 1966)

The Overseas Development Administration Library produces a list of Commonwealth official publications (including legislation and gazettes) received in the FCO Library system as a whole. This is published monthly by the ODA and entitled 'Technical Cooperation: a monthly bibliography of Commonwealth official publications'. It includes details of all the Canadian Federal and Provincial official publications received in the Library.

Note on the National Sound Archive

Mr Jonathan Vickers of the National Sound Archive also spoke in this session. He gave an outline of the Archive and emphasised its function as a resource and information centre, pointing out that it is open to everyone and that no charge is made. A wide variety of Canadian recordings is held, ranging from political speeches to music to sounds of wild life and the elements. Selected BBC broadcasts are taken, including those of the World Service, and also CBC transcriptions. Lectures and poetry readings with Canadian speakers are recorded live in this country; he cited as an example the recordings made of Margaret Atwood at the Cambridge Poetry Festival. He referred also to the importance of sound recordings in providing source material for the study of oral history and said that this was especially true of Canada.

Discussion

In the subsequent discussion, a number of points were raised: there was a problem of access to official publications (particularly federal ones) and this had been exacerbated by the withdrawal of selective depository status from the British Library of Political and Economic Science, but it was then confirmed that this status would be restored; a review had been made of the use which libraries in Canada and in the UK made of their selective depository status and some libraries would be re-instated although others would not; there are only two libraries outside Canada with full depository status, the BL and the Staatsbibliothek Preussischer Kulturbesitz in West Berlin; demand for material is also a matter of access and of information about it; the consignment of official publications in BLRD to Woolwich may be one reason for the lack of demand for them; there was a strong case for improving coverage of provincial publications and also for providing better guides to, for example, official publications; the question of demand arose also in connection with the availability of newspapers; Cambridge University Library is used as the first 'back-up' of BLLD; the National Library of Scotland is open to all; Mrs Bloomfield's *Guide* would be useful in aiding knowledge of access to material; the BACS Library and Resources Group welcomed colleagues from other libraries to its meetings to make known their problems.

The following people took part in this discussion: Mrs Bloomfield; Mr Clarke (London School of Political and Economic Science); Mr Cox (Leeds University Library); Mr Hamilton (BLRD); Mr Hellyer (Canada House); Mrs Howe (National Library of Scotland); Dr Lyon (Institute of Commonwealth Studies); Mr Noblett (Cambridge University Library); Professor Quinn (Liverpool); Mr D Simpson (Royal Commonwealth Society); Dr Sylvestre (National Library of Canada); Mr Wilson (BLRD).

Anne B Piternick

Bibliographic access for Canadian Studies: overview of current developments in Canada

Introduction

The emphasis in this part of the Colloquium programme is on bibliographic access to resource materials for Canadian Studies. My task in this session is to present an overview of current developments in this field in Canada. According to my old Concise OED, a development is a 'gradual unfolding', and some of the developments I shall describe seem to be unfolding very gradually indeed. However, I shall try to present a summary of major recent events and ongoing projects in the field which I hope will indicate the directions of current efforts in Canada.

I propose to summarize first of all the major developments in retrospective and then in current bibliography in a comprehensive sense. (I include in the term 'bibliography' indexing projects and related projects to bring materials under control.) Some problems relating to the bibliographic control of special types of materials will be covered next. I shall briefly mention analytic projects such as indexes which are concerned primarily with subject access. After this, developments in area and thematic bibliography for Canadian Studies will be examined. I shall describe here the objectives and operation of a special program introduced by the Social Sciences and Humanities Research Council of Canada (SSHRCC) to support the preparation of bibliographies and other tools to aid the researcher in Canadian Studies. Finally, I shall make an attempt to identify the requirements of researchers in developing areas of Canadian Studies as I see them.

We have available to us two documents which attempted to assess the state of Canadian bibliography at different points in time. The first of these is the proceedings of the National Conference on the State of Canadian Bibliography which was held at my home university in Vancouver in 1974.[1] The second is the proceedings of the Conference on Bibliography for Canadian Studies held at Dalhousie University in Halifax in 1981.[2] For convenience, these conferences will be referred to as the 1974 and 1981 Bibliography Conferences, respectively, throughout.

In this paper I shall make reference to several Canadian online systems; these are CAN/OLE, QL/SEARCH, Informatech and UTLAS, which is a bibliographic utility. Not all of these are currently accessible in the United Kingdom or Europe. The Quebec databases mounted by Informatech are not accessible outside Canada, and there are no plans so far to make them available in the UK or Europe. Technically, CAN/OLE can be accessed by any international network supporting X.25 protocol, but legal restrictions make this impossible without significant modifications in software to prevent users accessing databases for which they have no access authorization. QL/SEARCH is accessible throughout Europe, and has some subscribers in the United Kingdom. UTLAS, to my knowledge, has no subscribers anywhere in Europe at the present time.

Retrospective Bibliography – General

One of the major concerns of the 1974 Bibliography Conference was the lack of a comprehensive retrospective bibliography of Canadiana. Now, nine years later, we hve a great deal to be proud of. Other speakers at this session will give details of 'RETRO' – the National Library's retrospective bibliography of Canadiana covering so far monographs published from 1867 to 1900 – and of the retrospective *Bibliographie du Québec* which will complete the publishing record for that Province to 1967, to link up with the current series of that name which started in 1968. A description will also be given of the Canadian Institute for Historical Microreproductions (CIHM) and its project to produce microfiche copies of items of Canadiana wherever they may be held, and to provide a catalogue to accompany the fiches.

There is obviously no problem for the user of the CIHM file in obtaining a copy of the material listed in the CIHM catalogue. RETRO assists the user by indicating locations for items it lists. No locations are given in the *Bibliographie du Québec*, but two related projects aid in locating copies of items published to 1820. The Bibliothèque nationale du Québec has prepared a catalogue of its own holdings of Laurentian imprints to 1821 – *Laurentiana parus avant 1821*[3] and is also participating in a joint project with CREPUQ (Conférence des Recteurs et Principaux des Universités du Québec) to prepare a union catalogue of Quebec imprints published from 1764 to 1820.[4]

The fact that all these bibliographies are being compiled in machine-readable form means that a multiplicity of indexes are available in print form and that eventually online searching will be possible. As online searching of ESTC has demonstrated, machine manipulation can greatly enhance subject access. Both RETRO and the *Bibliographie du Québec* provide indexes to proper names as subjects, and the latter uses a classified arrangement by the Library of Congress Classification with modifications for Canadian History and Literature. The CIHM Catalogue provides Dewey class numbers and subject headings in French and English to Canadian standards for each item. Standard subject headings in French are also being provided for the entries in the *Catalogue collectif des Imprimés québécois 1764–1820*.

Two other projects are of interest here. We have already heard from Dr O'Neill and Dr Ettlinger of their work in identifying in the British Library Canadian items received by legal deposit between 1895 and 1924. Their work will help to supplement Tod and Cordingley's *Checklist of Canadian Imprints, 1900–1925*, and provide a basis for a future extension of RETRO. Yet to come is a description by Dr Fleming of her project to continue the work begun by Marie Tremaine in her *Bibliography of Canadian Imprints* by extending the record for Upper Canada imprints from 1801 to 1840.

Current Bibliography – General

Central to current bibliography is, of course, *Canadiana*. This is now available in print and microfiche versions issued eleven times a year and in a weekly tape version which is limited to monographs. All versions include Cataloguing-in-Publication (CIP) data where available for forthcoming books and these records are revised once an item has been published.

The print and fiche versions are divided into two parts for Canadian and foreign imprints. Access is by author, title, series title, Dewey class, English and French subject headings, ISBN and ISSN. The print version cumulates annually; the fiche version is based on a register arrangement, the indexes for which are issued monthly and cumulate entries for all previous months. Each year, a cumulation of fiche entries from 1981 on will be issued; a ten-year cumulation unit is eventually foreseen.

The tape version, besides being available for purchase, is also searchable online through the CAN/OLE searching system back to January 1973.

A microfiche cumulation of *Canadiana* for 1973–1980 is available in the same format as the current fiche version. This covers all records for the period which were compiled in machine-readable form.

Canadiana now presents some enhancements over previous years. For example, all items are listed in classified order; for many years government publications were listed alphabetically by jurisdiction and had no controlled subject access. And almost all materials except pamphlets are now catalogued at the second level of description. Libraries and bibliographers handling Canadian materials will already be familiar with *Canadiana Authorities* for names, which has been issued separately on microfiche from 1979, and is accessible online through UTLAS.

Aids to acquisition

The unrevised CIP entries which appear in *Canadiana* are also published as a 'Forthcoming Books' insert in *Quill & Quire*, the monthly magazine of the

Canadian book trade. They also appear in *Canadian Books in Print*, which is now issued as an annual printed catalogue with quarterly updates on microfiche. The latest service of value for ordering material is a microfiche listing service offered by the Canadian Telebook Agency. This lists English-language trade books available in Canada, including Canadian imprints, gives the names of Canadian distributors from whom a particular item is available, and also indicates whether items are in stock, out of stock, out of print, or not yet published. The CTA database can now be searched online through UTLAS.

One interesting feature about the CTA service: I understand it tags items which publishers consider to have Canadian authors. Although *Canadiana* includes foreign imprints which the National Library considers to have Canadian authors, it does not in any way indicate Canadian authorship in any of its records. Canadian authorship is indicated in some of the RETRO entries, which is important because RETRO has a rather broad definition of what constitutes a Canadian author.[5] As far as current listings are concerned, however, the issue of indicating the nationality of a living author is a far more complex problem than one might imagine. This issue has recently been explored by a Committee of the National Library Advisory Board on behalf of scholars of Canadian Studies who would find a printout of books by Canadian authors to be very useful; I have to report that no action on this seems possible at the present time.

The National Library has prepared and mounted a file of CIP data on the TELIDON videotex system. This has been done as part of the iNet experimental networking project, which is now in the process of evaluation.

Special materials

NON-PRINT MATERIALS

Details of the current scope and coverage of *Canadiana* are provided in the front of the January 1983 printed issue. This will reveal that certain types of material are not covered by *Canadiana*. Films have not been included since 1976, but have been listed in *Film Canadiana*, compiled to 1979/80 by the Canadian Film Institute. The Institute has now discontinued this service and a recent agreement has been signed between the National Library, the Public Archives and the National Film Board whereby all three organisations will compile data for *Film Canadiana*. The Board will enter the data into its FORMAT system and will provide a printed service as well as disseminating records online through UTLAS. Details of the new agreement and the FORMAT database are given in the March 1983 issued of *National Library News*.[6] The FORMAT database, incidentally, includes bibliographic data on filmstrips, Canadian and otherwise, available on loan from the NFB.

Media kits which include visual materials have been listed in *Canadiana* since 1978, but filmstrips, videotapes, slide sets, transparencies and prints are not at present subject to legal deposit and are not listed unless they form part of a kit. Visual materials are important for teaching at all levels as well as research; the lack of a truly comprehensive system for collecting such materials and providing bibliographic access to them is a concern to teachers in particular.[7] At the 1981 Bibliography Conference, several speakers stressed the importance of bibliographies of non-print sources for Canadian Studies. This topic will be addressed again later.

MICROFORMS

The National Library has plans to extend legal deposit to microforms produced in Canada. The creation of a union list of microforms is also proposed. The implementation of this program will depend on the availability of resources.

SERIALS

Entries are made in *Canadiana* for new serial titles received on legal deposit, but we have no recent listing of Canadian serials as such. The second edition of the *Canadian Serials Directory* for the year 1976 will be the last, unless a new compiler and publisher are willing to undertake a new edition. The National Library now verifies and enters records for Canadian serials into the CONSER database and distributes CONSER tapes and fiche products, but produces no separate Canadian list. On the plus side a *Union List of Serials in the Social Sciences and Humanities held by Canadian Libraries* was published on microfiche by the National Library in 1980; a second edition appeared in December 1982. Both this file and the companion *Union List of Scientific Serials in Canadian Libraries* (ninth edition, 1981, in a printed version) are available online through CAN/OLE. This means that Canadian serials, once identified, can be rapidly located. UNION also includes information on the interlending/copying policies of individual libraries.

NEWSPAPERS

Newspapers are a special category of serial with special problems. The Resources Network Committee of the National Library Advisory Board has been working on a policy for decentralized control and preservation of local and regional newspapers. Legal deposit at the national level is considered impractical as a means of accomplishing these objectives in a country with Canada's size and pattern of jurisdiction. The policy is intended to be as flexible as possible so that it can be adapted to special circumstances in each province or region.

In a letter dated 20 May 1983 sent to provincial and regional libraries and other agencies, the National Librarian outlined the main features of the plan as follows:

At the National level, the National Library would be responsible for coordinating and publicizing the program; providing contract funds to develop provincial plans or pilot projects; developing standards and guidelines for microfilming, storage and handling, and bibliographic control of newspapers; delineating collecting guidelines at the national, provincial, and local levels; purchasing one copy of each Canadian newspaper microfilmed; lending microfilmed newspapers interprovincially and internationally; and creating and updating a union list of Canadian newspapers and register of microform masters (with contributions from provincial/regional participants).

At the provincial or local level, appropriate library agencies within a region would be responsible for initiating a specific program, possibly with the assistance of National Library contract funds; coordinating and implementing the program; collecting all current newspapers and preserving all newspapers published in the province; microfilming the newspapers (by any means and with any funds available); promoting indexing projects for individual newspapers; creating a checklist of provincial newspapers; and making newspapers available for on-site consultation and lending within the province.

It is hoped that this pragmatic approach to a very difficult problem will eventually have good results. Meanwhile, it may be noted that the National Library did produce a *Union List of Canadian Newspapers held by Canadian Libraries* in 1977. Rider notes three retrospective bibliographies for newspapers published in Nova Scotia and Québec which have been compiled in recent years.[8]

MAPS

The National Map Collection in Canada is under the jurisdiction of the Public Archives, not the National Library, and maps do not come under legal deposit, although published atlases do so. Thus atlases are listed in *Canadiana* but not maps. The NMC used to compile an annual bibliography of Canadian maps which was included in the *Bibliographie Internationale Cartographique*, but the *Bibliographie* ceased publication with the 1975 issue and the last Canadian listing was issued as a separate for the year 1976.

The Catalogue of the National Map Collection was published in sixteen volumes in 1976. This covers largely sheet maps and maps in atlases and books, classified by area with author and subject indexes. Series maps and government maps are not included. The collection also issues specialized catalogues from time to time – to its holdings of township plans, maps of Indian reserves, and so on. At the present time, plans are being made to enter cataloguing records for items added to the Collection into the UTLAS database, starting at the end of August 1983. Eventually it is intended to spin off an annual bibliography of Canadian maps from the UTLAS records, but this is a long-term project and will show no immediate results.

GOVERNMENT PUBLICATIONS

Canadiana includes federal and provincial government publications. Municipal publications are not systematically included, and inclusion of provincial publications depends a great deal on the cooperation of provincial government publishers, or provincial libraries. For this reason, checklists or catalogues of provincial publications are extremely important. These are now issued by the government printers or provincial/legislative libraries in most provinces – exceptions are Newfoundland, and the Yukon and Northwest Territories. However, not all lists are issued monthly, and some are only annual.

MICROLOG, a commercial service, offers microfiche copies of federal, provincial and municipal publications and reports from other bodies, and provides a monthly *Index* to them. The *Index* is accessible online through CAN/OLE. Both the *Index* and *Canadiana* are widely used for identifying federal government publications since the official *Government of Canada Publications Catalogue* changed from a monthly to a quarterly in 1979.

Rider notes retrospective bibliographies of Ontario government publications, and of Royal Commissions in Ontario and Alberta, in her 1981 survey of Canadian bibliography.[9]

The National Library is concerned particularly about access to municipal documents which are generally not subject to any kind of systematic control. A decentralized approach to collection, preservation, and control has been suggested, on the lines of the decentralized system being tried for newpapers. We await further developments in this area.

THESES

Researchers and librarians alike no doubt welcomed the recent appearance of *Canadian Theses* for the academic years 1976/1977 up to and including 1979/1980. Theses are now catalogued by the National Library using the DOBIS database management system, and future bibliographies will be prepared in fiche form, starting with the one for the year 1980/81 which is expected to appear early in 1984. *Canadian Theses* lists all masters and doctoral theses accepted in Canadian universities and, from 1981 on, will include foreign theses of Canadian authorship or Canadian association. Foreign theses so listed will be available on interlibrary loan from the National Library. The bibliography also covers theses which are part of the Canadian Theses on Microfiche service; copies of such theses may be ordered from the National Library.

The arrangement of *Canadian Theses* is by subject groupings which correspond generally to classes in the nineteenth edition of Dewey. Canadian theses on microfiche are also listed in *Canadiana* as they are processed by the National Library; the arrangement here is by Dewey class number. A separate listing of theses on microfiche is available to former subscribers to the *Canadian Theses on Microfiche Catalogue*, which is no longer produced.

We should soon see publication by the National Library of a compilation by Jesse J Dossick of 10,000 doctoral dissertations on Canada and Canadians accepted by British, Canadian and American universities. Publication of this bibliography, together with the new arrangements for listing Canadian theses, should greatly assist researchers on Canadian Studies. However, identification and location of foreign theses is an expensive and time consuming task and will no doubt require a good deal of international cooperation to be completely successful.[10]

GREY LITERATURE AND RESEARCH IN PROGRESS

Theses constitute a special category of material which is 'unpublished' in a traditional sense. It is inevitable that this should bring to mind other unpublished materials, especially so-called 'grey literature' which often also originates in universities. No comprehensive system – comparable, say, to SIGLE (System for Information on Grey Literature in Europe) – exists in Canada. This situation is receiving the attention of the National Library Advisory Board's Committee on Bibliography and Information Services for the Social Sciences and Humanities (CBISSSH). A check through both *Canadiana* and the *Microlog Index* will reveal some report series from some universities and research institutes, but neither service collects such material in a systematic or comprehensive way. Scholars who wish to obtain reports of current research in their fields must generally rely on personal knowledge of who is doing what research, or else turn to directories of research to identify projects of interest, and then write to the project directors. A *Directory of Federally Supported Research in Canadian Universities* is published annually by the National Research Council of Canada, and this provides a subject index based on keywords in the project titles and lists the name of the project director, affiliation, supporting agency, and amount of grant for each entry. The file can also be searched online (as IEC) through CAN/OLE. A *Canadian Register of Research and Researchers in the Social Sciences* will shortly be available for searching through CAN/OLE. This database is not available in printed form. It includes up to six reports or publications for every researcher listed, and subject searching can be carried out using codes representing academic disciplines as well as by keywords in project titles and descriptions.[11]

A database of current and recently completed research relating to the Prairies is maintained by the Canadian Plains Research Centre in Regina. This database is searchable on QL; searches will also be performed by the Centre on request. The Centre maintains a manual file of completed research once records for such research have been removed from the database.

The Association for Canadian and Quebec Literatures is currently compiling an Inventory of Research on Canadian/Quebec Literatures. Previous inventories carried out by ACQL have focused on research carried out by anglophone and francophone members of the Association respectively. Compilers of the current Inventory are working with Canadian Studies associations outside Canada in an attempt to make contact with all scholars working in the field, whether or not they are members of ACQL. The result should provide a truly comprehensive picture of the state of research in the field.[12]

MACHINE-READABLE DATA FILES

It might be appropriate here to note the growing concern among researchers for the preservation of and access to machine readable data files (MRDFS). These are files of quantitative data which result from surveys of all kinds. As far back as 1976 the Canada Council issued a report by its Consultative Group on Survey Research which made recommendations on deposit of data files resulting from surveys, provision of questionnaires, documentation and code books to permit access to the data in the files, release and re-use of data, and so on.[13] There is no one centre where files can be deposited; the Public Archives of Canada has a Machine Readable Archives Division, but other institutions across the country have also set up data archives or libraries. At my own institution, for example, the Data Library is part of the university library system; at Carleton the Social Science Data Archive is part of an academic faculty.

The Department of Communications recently funded a 'consultation' in Vancouver to discuss questions relating to survey data, at which the need for a union file of holdings of MRDFS was stressed as well as ancillary matters such as agreement on standards for description of files. During the late 1970s the Data Clearinghouse for the Social Sciences was compiling such a union file, and published the first of a proposed annual series of Social Science Data Inventories in 1977. Unfortunately the Clearinghouse was compelled for financial reasons to close its doors in 1978. Over the past year the Social Science Data Archive at Carleton University has been preparing inventories of MRDFS in three areas: Mental Illness, Canadian Native Peoples, and Federal Election Outcomes and Electoral Districts, These compilations were funded by the Social Sciences and Humanities Research Council; at the time of writing they have not yet been published.

Abstracting and indexing services

Comprehensive indexing of Canadian periodicals did not begin, except for sporadic attempts, until 1938; this is the starting date of what is now the *Canadian Periodical Index*. Retrospective indexing has been done before this date chiefly for individual titles or in special subject areas. Now the Canadian Library Association is sponsoring the compilation of the *Index* back to 1928, and will publish a 20-year cumulation for 1928–48 (superseding the 1938–47 cumulation). Also under way is a project to index Canadian art and architecture periodicals, funded last year by the Social Sciences and Humanities Research Council. The Council has also from time to time awarded grants to aid Canadian research journals in the preparation of retrospective indexes to their contents.

Some help for retrospective searching may come eventually from a project being undertaken by the Association of Research Libraries with funding from US foundations. This will add to records in the CONSER serials file a note to indicate which abstracting and indexing services currently index an individual periodical. Several Canadian indexes are included in the sources to be covered and the National Library will be responsible for these. The Committee on Bibliography and Information Services for the Social Sciences and Humanities has welcomed this development and has asked that this information be compiled by the National Library on a retrospective as well as a current basis, as an aid to searching older material.

As far as current indexing goes, the most comprehensive coverage of Canadian periodicals would be provided by a combination of the *Canadian Periodical Index, Canadian Business Index, Canadian Education Index* and RADAR – *Repértoire d'Analyses de Revues du Québec*.[14] Recent years have seen the demise of the *Canadian Essay and Literature Index*, of which only three volumes were published, and of the index to federal government periodicals which appeared in the *Monthly Catalogue* from 1963 to 1978. Canadian music literature is indexed in RILM – *Répertoire Internationale de la Littérature de la Musique* – by volunteer Canadian music librarians under the sponsorship of the Canadian Association of Music Libraries. Fine arts literature was indexed in RILA – *Répertoire Internationale de la Littérature de L'Art* by the curatorial staff of the National Gallery, but the Gallery ceased contributing to this service after the 1981 issue.

By no means all articles on Canadian Studies are published in Canadian periodicals, and the major Canadian research journals at any rate are covered by disciplinary abstracting and indexing services of international scope. But a study of Canadian indexes can provide an interesting insight into topics and concerns which inspired publication in Canadian sources at a given time. This is particularly true for newspaper indexes. The *Canadian News Index* selectively indexes 7 major newspapers across Canada. The French-language service *Index de l'Actualité* indexes 3 major Quebec newspapers, and also provides summaries of articles.[15] Since the end of 1977 we have been able to search and print out items from the full text of each day's Toronto *Globe & Mail* online through the INFO GLOBE service, and QL/SEARCH offers NEWSTEX – the full-text database of the Canadian Press News Agency's news stories (including stories from CP's broadcast news service). This database includes stories from January 1981 to date; work is in progress to extend the file back to 1974. The INFO GLOBE database, in particular, provides a rapid way to locate the dates of specific events, and such dates can be used to locate news stories and editorials in other newspapers.[16] Incidentally, I understand that the NEWSTEX database (which includes news stories whether or not they were actually published in a newspaper) uses a label for one category of stories which is the equivalent of the television warning: 'parental guidance advised'. An analysis of such stories could perhaps provide an interesting research project for Canadian Studies.

None of these services is much use for local news. In September 1981 the

Newspaper Division of the National Library conducted a survey of Access to Newspaper Collections across Canada. A report prepared in February 1982 includes a list of newspapers indexed selectively by libraries, with information on the subject and geographic characteristics of items indexed, and also a list of newspapers regularly clipped for vertical files with topics covered.[17] The Newspaper Division is now preparing to distribute questionnaires for a survey of newspaper indexes held by libraries, archives, newspaper offices, genealogical societies and other institutions.

As well as the NEWSTEX database, QL/SEARCH also mounts several other databases of special interest to students of Canadian law and public affairs. These are full-text files of federal and some provincial statutes and law reports, as well as the English and French versions of *Hansard Oral* and *Written Questions* and *Standing Orders of the House of Commons*.

Thematic bibliography

The 1974 Bibliography Conference provided an assessment of the state of thematic bibliography in the subject disciplines and in regional and provincial bibliography. For the 1981 Bibliography Conference, Lillian Rider produced an update: a 'Summary of developments in Canadian subject and area bibliography since 1974'.[18] This Conference also included papers on the state of bibliography for some areas not considered at the 1974 Conference. These are the developing, interdisciplinary areas of Native Studies, Ethnic Studies and Women's Studies, for which papers were prepared by Harvey McCue[19], Judy Young[20] and Veronica Strong-Boag[21], respectively.

Altogether Rider's review listed (according to my count) some 95 subject bibliographies and a further 136 area bibliographies. These range in size from the 780-page second edition of Bruce Peel's *Bibliography of the Prairie Provinces to 1953* to the 18-leaf catalogue of an exhibit of Canadian children's picture books, prepared by Irene Aubrey at the National Library. Size is, of course, no measure of importance to, or usefulness for, Canadian Studies. It is also no indication of bibliographic quality, as Rider is at pains to point out.

Rider's review includes some items like union lists (*eg* of atlases) and surveys of collections in special subject areas. The subject categories used (which follow those for the 1974 Conference) are somewhat artificial: for example, some items under 'area bibliography' could well fit under 'history'; Olga Bishop's *Bibliography of Ontario History, 1867-1976* is a case in point. Nevertheless, some general observations on developments to 1981 may be drawn from the evidence presented here.

Many of the area bibliographies emphasize local imprints, as well as items about the region. They include checklists and bibliographies of government publications, of Royal Commissions, and of newspapers. Some major accomplishments are noted; publication of the new edition of Peel; Strathern's bibliography of Alberta, 1954-1979, starting where Peel left off (now published);

the Bishop bibliography for Ontario mentioned above. There is much current activity on materials relating to the North, although still no one source which could replace the *Arctic Bibliography*.

The Western Canadiana Publications Project at the University of Alberta, as a preliminary to seeking funding, recently canvassed scholars and librarians on the idea of an annual Prairie bibliography. I am also aware that a group of historians, bibliographers and others have begun to discuss the possibility of a bibliography of Manitoba starting from the termination date of Peel. Perhaps these projects might be actually under way by the time the next report on bibliography for Canadian Studies is prepared.

As far as subject bibliography is concerned, Rider notes some 'gap-filling' in areas such as Children's Literature, Fine Arts/Architecture, Linguistics and Canadian Drama and Theatre History. She lists few personal or author bibliographies, although she includes compendia such as the *Dictionary of Canadian Biography* (of which Dr Halpenny will have more to say in her paper) and *The Annotated Bibliography of Canada's Major Authors*. However, it can be said that the kinds of scholarly, definitive, author bibliographies which were called for by Landon at the 1974 Conference have, with very few exceptions, not materialized. Rider also notes a dearth of bibliographies in the broad fields of Sociology and Anthropology except for Folklore, and in Geography, except for some bibliographic sources for maps and atlases.

It has been noted elsewhere that Canadian bibliographies and indexes are generally not commercially attractive.[22] This is borne out by an examination of Rider's list. A number of the book-length bibliographies are published by university presses rather than true commercial publishers, and a fair proportion of other items are published by federal and provincial government libraries, departments or agencies. Libraries and other institutions such as art galleries and archives appear as publishers as well as library associations and other societies – especially historical societies. A high proportion are compiled and published by university departments and research institutes.[23]

The National Library has announced its intention in the future to take a more active role in promoting Canadian bibliography, in part by undertaking and issuing more compilations, and in part by publishing or assisting the publication of bibliographies compiled by others. The importance of this policy can be seen from the foregoing. We should, incidentally, be grateful that the National Library published the Proceedings of the 1974 Conference and provided funds for the publication of the 1981 Proceedings.

Also worth noting from the data on publication is the increasing involvement of university research institutes in compiling and issuing bibliographies. There is no doubt that some of these are excellent, and the subject expertise necessary for selecting items is undoubtedly available in such departments and research institutes. However, the quality of the bibliographic records and observance of bibliographic standards in some bibliographies from these sources is not always up to the quality of coverage. The National Library

Advisory Board's Committee on Bibliography and Information Services in the Social Sciences and Humanities is concerned that instruction in bibliographic compilation, as well as in the use of bibliographies, should be provided to university students. A survey of university departments was recently carried out to assess the current level of instruction, and the results of the survey should be available shortly.

One or two of the items listed by Rider were published in scholarly journals. In developing areas of Canadian Studies, in particular, the journals serve a very important function not only by publishing bibliographies and reviews of the literature on an annual or irregular basis, but also by commissioning compilations and taking on the responsibility for their continuity. Librarians and scholars alike have been grateful over the years for the 'Recent Publications Relating to Canada' section in the *Canadian Historical Review* and the 'Letters in Canada' review section of the *University of Toronto Quarterly*. We have also watched in dismay the efforts of the annual bibliography of Canadian Literature to find a permanent home after it lost its haven in the journal *Canadian Literature*.[24] Judy Young, in her paper on Ethnic Studies at the 1981 Conference noted that 'many ethnic group bibliographies have been published in periodicals'; she also appends 'A Selected List of Associations and Periodicals which Publish Bibliographical Information in the Area of Ethnic Studies'.[25] Veronica Strong-Boag notes the publication of two bibliographies in *Resources for Feminist Research* which listed special issues of periodicals devoted to women, and points to the usefulness of *Resources* itself for identifying 'critical reading' in a number of issues devoted to topics focusing on women.[26]

The value of a conference such as that held in 1981 is that it makes possible a broad overview of developments – a sort of bibliographic stock-taking, one might say. It is not easy to summarize more recent developments since then as there is no one place to check what is going on. And here I should mention that the National Library has before it a proposal from the Committee on Bibliography and Information Services for the Social Sciences and Humanities setting forth specifications for a Clearinghouse on Canadian Bibliographic Projects in Progress. The Clearinghouse would be a machine-readable database which could provide details of such projects and which would be searchable by a number of access points, especially by subject. Projects once completed would be transferred to *Canadiana* if published, or to a directory of databases or other appropriate source. It is unfortunate that, in a time of restraint such as the present, a project of this kind cannot receive a high priority.

One development which has had a marked effect on bibliography for Canadian Studies is the introduction in the Fall of 1981 by the Social Sciences and Humanities Research Council of Canada (SSHRCC) of a program to support the compilation of research tools for Canadian Studies. 'Research tools' are defined as bibliographies, retrospective indexes, catalogues of collections, guides to the literature, and guides to or inventories of archives. This program is a new departure for the Council, which previously only supported bibliographic projects which were preliminary parts of research projects or which could be considered research projects in their own right. So far, three competitions have been held under the program; the results of the third have not been announced at the time of writing and will not therefore be commented on here except in general terms.

Awards made in the three competitions total approximately $3.8 million. More than 80 projects have received or will receive support. These range in amount from a few thousand dollars to the maximum of $75,000 per year for three years. In the first two competitions, library projects accounted for two-thirds of the funds awarded and archival projects for one-third. Perhaps I should mention here that the Council made a policy decision to exclude provincial and territorial archives and libraries from support through this program, and this policy undoubtedly affected these results.

Because the Social Sciences and Humanities Research Council is known to scholars for its support of research and for its fellowship programs, it is not surprising to find a fair proportion of projects being undertaken by university-based teams which may or may not include librarians. In some cases, in fact, the Council last year required consultation with professional librarians or archivists, or inclusion of professionals in research teams, as a condition of grants to such groups to ensure that bibliographic/archival standards and methods were properly employed.

Projects supported to date may be categorized as follows:

- those which fill gaps in the national bibliography (such as the Fleming and O'Neill/Ettlinger projects);

- those which provide the basis for definitive studies of Canadian writers and public figures; these include projects to prepare guides to collections of literary manuscripts and personal papers;

- those which provide the foundations for new and developing areas of research in Canadian studies; these include projects in:
– Native Studies (including two bibliographies of imprints in native Indian scripts);
– History of Science and Technology;
– Theatre History;
– Art and architecture (both bibliographic and archival projects);
– Film, TV and radio;
– Ethnic Studies;
– regional projects, both bibliographic and archival.

Materials covered by the projects include all kinds of printed documents, manuscripts, audiovisual materials of various kinds and machine-readable data files which contain survey data which may be used for secondary analysis. The actual research tools developed from these projects are beginning to appear now; they should be listed as they are published in the Council's Annual Report – and, of course, in *Canadiana*.

The Council also funds a program to support purchase of research collections by Canadian academic libraries, to the limit of $75,000 per library per year. The program is not restricted to collections of Canadiana, and comparatively few such collections have been purchased in this way.

Requirements for research in Canadian Studies

At this point I am changing gear, so to speak, to turn from what has been achieved to some assessment of requirements for research in Canadian Studies. I have chosen to examine requirements from the point of view of scholars working in established fields such as Canadian History and Literature, and of scholars working in developing areas of Canadian Studies. In doing so I shall draw on my own experience in working with academic colleagues and on the evidence presented by researchers who introduced us to the needs of developing fields at the 1981 Bibliography Conference.

REQUIREMENTS FOR ESTABLISHED FIELDS

The division of researchers into those working in 'established fields' and those working in 'developing fields' is admittedly a very arbitrary one. It is not intended to imply that someone in an established field does not seek to develop new perspectives on or new approaches to his field; the development of subdisciplines such as Urban History, Business History, Labour History and the like clearly show this. In fact, the kinds of bibliographic and other sources needed are precisely those which should provide the means of access to collections which will open up new areas for research within the discipline.

Such sources include, for example, guides to collections of the kind compiled by Valerie Bloomfield for the United Kingdom[27] and Lillian Rider for McGill University.[28] (It is a pity that more Canadian libraries have not followed the example of McGill.) The Resources Surveys carried out by the National Library of Canada[29] have not been directed specifically to Canadian Studies, although Canadian collections of importance in areas such as Law have been identified in this way. (The exception is the Native Studies Resources Survey, which will be described below.)

Very important for this group are catalogues of important library or archival collections. In progress at the moment, for example, are projects funded by the Canadian Studies Research Tools Program to produce catalogues of the Canadian Labour Union Collection at the University of Toronto Centre for Industrial Relations and the collection of Acadiana at l'Université Moncton. The Research Tools Committee recognizes that network access to collections such as these could certainly be enhanced if systems such as UTLAS were used to create catalogues and to add records to the database at the same time. The costs of doing this are, however, high, and the Committee has had to refuse requests to use UTLAS in this way when it has judged that using, say, a word-processor to create a published catalogue in hard copy or fiche form would provide adequate access, taking into account the significance of the collection involved and the total demands for funding.

Researchers in various fields of Canadian Studies will welcome the funding of projects to produce catalogues or guides to the National Archives of the Canadian Jewish Congress, the folklore archives at Laval, and a collection of business archives at Dalhousie, not to mention an inventory of the papers of former Premier 'Joey' Smallwood of Newfoundland at Memorial, and a detailed index to the scientific correspondence of geologist Sir John William Dawson.

The Program has also awarded grants to Queen's and Calgary to produce catalogues of collections of literary manuscripts held in their University Libraries. These awards are interesting because they require both insitutions to collaborate in developing compatible machine-readable formats for their records. I may say here that the problem of the lack of universally-recognized standards of archival description is one which is causing much concern to the archival community at present. This concern is shared by the Canadian Studies Research Tools Committee and its parent Council, all of whom would like to see the development of archival standards which would permit networking among archives in parallel and in conjunction with library networks.[30] Projects funded by the Council are required to report to the Union List of Manuscripts where appropriate, but network access to machine-readable records would increase the value of dollars spent on such projects.

Workers in established fields also welcome the appearance of retrospective indexes or bibliographies in broad fields of research: comprehensive in the sense of covering a broad theme rather than blanket coverage of Canadian periodicals. I have mentioned a Council-funded indexing project for Canadian art and architecture periodicals; another example would be a cumulated bibliography of literary criticism of Quebecois and French-Canadian literature. A further indexing project of interest is one which will concentrate on Ontario rural society from 1867 to 1930 as seen through non-technical articles published in agricultural and farm magazines published in that province.

Where appropriate, the Canadian Studies Research Tools Committee requests that project directors use computers or word processors for indexing to allow as far as possible for extended subject access to, and bibliometric uses of, the records they are creating. The compilers of a bibliography of Canadian Science and Technology, for example, have been asked to bear in mind such questions as the extent to which documents in this field were published in Canada. A project to produce a *Bibliography of Ontario Research Scientists, 1914–1939*, indexes not only the research topics on which the scientists worked, but also personal data such as place of birth, membership in various societies, and so on.

REQUIREMENTS FOR DEVELOPING AREAS

Developing areas of Canadian Studies are typified by fields such as Women's Studies and Native and Ethnic Studies which are characterized by their multidisciplinary approach and their new perspectives on established fields. They need research tools which are highly selective but which draw from a broad range of disciplines and which reflect the special viewpoint of their users in some cases by the use of specialized indexing vocabularies and innovative arrangements.[31]

The multidisciplinary approach of Canadian Studies in general is well illustrated by an examination of publications of the Association for Canadian Studies. For example, *Canadian Issues* No 3, published in the Spring of 1980, focussed on 'Canada and the Sea' and included papers on marine resources, fisheries policy, marine culture (in the anthropological sense) and marine law. Young stresses the multidisciplinary approach to Ethnic Studies, suggesting that researchers in this area need to be familiar with disciplines such as 'history, political science, sociology, economics, psychology, linguistics, the fine arts and anthropology – to name the major ones.'[32] McCue, in speaking of Native Studies, makes the point that, whereas traditional studies of native peoples developed out of anthropology and focused on ethnographic research on different tribes and cultures, the contemporary approach represents an attempt 'to provide an Indian/Metis/Inuit perspective to historical and contemporary analysis of native issues.' He points to the need for 'Canadian bibliographies on specific topics such as Urbanization Studies, Health, Reserve and Community Studies, and Native Politics, to name only a few.'[33]

Strong-Boag draws attention to the fact that existing classification schemes are of little or no help for the identification and classification of materials in Women's Studies and points to the need for a special perspective. An additional problem is the difficulty of identifying in most available bibliographies which materials are Canadian in scope or content.[34] She notes with regret the failure of the *Canadian Periodical Index* to cover sources which reflect the current interests of Women's Studies exponents. At the same time, she comments that inclusion in that *Index* of sources such as ' . . . *Chatelaine, Canadian Home Economics Journal, Homemakers' Magazine* and *Canadian Nurse* as the only journals focussing explicitly on women means inevitable disappointment for those seeking information on the state of Women's Studies in this country.'[35]

Drawing from a broad field implies covering a wide range of materials as well as subject areas. McCue and Strong-Boag in particular note the importance of oral and audio-visual materials in their respective fields of study. They also stress the importance of archival materials.[36] McCue calls further for bibliographies of government and native organizations' published and unpublished reports on native issues as well as those of special and public interest groups.

Two initiatives should greatly improve access to research resources in Native Studies. The National Library's Resources Survey Division recently undertook a survey of Native Studies resource collections in Canadian libraries. Questionnaires were sent to more than 400 Canadian libraries and a high rate of response was achieved. The survey report is scheduled for publication in January or February 1984. It will include a directory of collections in libraries and other institutions and a list of native periodicals with locations across the country. The National Library has also taken over the collection assembled by the Indian Claims Commission and has hired an expert who is a native Indian to organize and service it.

Young spells out the problems involved in compiling bibliographies in Ethnic Studies: 'the variety of languages in which many of the published (and unpublished) materials are written; out of the way, inaccessible publications; lack of written records; secretiveness of individuals or groups; intra-group conflict; group dispersal (or its opposite, ethnogenesis); difficulty of defining group identity or affiliation; incomplete or inaccurate listings in already existing bibliographies.'[37] Some of these problems would be pertinent to other areas of Canadian Studies.

The necessity for coverage of materials in languages other than French and English seems essential for Ethnic Studies bibliographies. Strong-Boag notes also the importance of adequate coverage of French-language material to present a balanced view of developments in Women's Studies right across Canada.

One of the difficulties of coverage of developing fields is that of establishing standards of quality for material to be included. Whiteside accused librarians of paying more attention to form than to content by generally ignoring publications of native organizations because of their fugitive nature, and relying on materials from major publishing houses for their collections on native affairs.[38] Strong-Boag faces squarely the dilemma of selection in the absence of established standards. She writes that 'The innovative character of Women's Studies also means that it is still in the process of formulating appropriate standards of judgement. Not only the choice of women as a legitimate area of interest but the accompanying need for new methodologies and interpretations challenge many of the accepted standards by which new entries are to be judged. The result can be both the potential omission of valuable but unorthodox studies from consideration and equally unwarranted attention to other works whose real merit is their topicality.'[39]

The problem of standards goes beyond what to include and what to ignore in compiling a bibliography. In the Canadian Studies Research Tools Committee we have had a number of discussions about whether or not we serve the field better by supporting what one member has called 'working bibliographies' rather than 'fine bibliographies'. (Presumably the latter serve only bibliographers.) The 'working bibliographies' are assembled as the field begins to develop and take on an identity; Strong-Boag, for example, mentions the usefulness of something as simple as inventories of articles on women published in nineteenth-century Canadian periodicals. Exchange of reading lists is another mechanism, encouraged by meetings of the learned societies. The Canadian Research Institute for the Advancement of Women (CRIAW) is sponsoring an electronic bulletin board project to facilitate information exchange, and has also decided to undertake a 'current contents' service with KWIC index for Canadian feminist periodicals.[40]

Bibliographic activity at the 'working' level is almost always voluntary, although publication of bibliographies may be made possible because of support given to publication of journals and newsletters as a method of communication incidental to developing teaching programs or promoting research.[41] As the volume of material published in the field begins to grow, the task of bibliographic control becomes too great for voluntary, informal and sporadic efforts, and there is usually an attempt to find support for some formal mechanism. For Women's Studies, the 1981 Bibliography Conference called on the National Library Advisory Board's Committee on Bibliography and Information Services for the Social Sciences and Humanities to 'pay special attention to the possibility of creating a National Women's Bibliographic Resource Project in order to identify and eliminate gaps in bibliographic coverage'.[42] No action has been taken on this recommendation to date. CRIAW recently sponsored a study to examine the feasibility of setting up a national database on women. Although the concept has been accepted in principle, the CRIAW Board is further examining the study report in the light of the information needs of the field, and hopes eventually to find funding to develop such a system.[43] Because of its highly specialized coverage there is really no hope that a database of this kind could ever be self-supporting.

There is much that librarians and bibliographers can do to assist researchers in developing fields. Basic to this assistance is an appreciation of the special needs of the field at each stage of development. Above all, assistance in compiling bibliographies to the most appropriate standard for each stage is an important contribution.

Conclusion

In a previous report on developments in this area I stressed two major problems: that of ensuring the continuity of current Canadian bibliographies, and that of bibliographic standards.[44] Before an audience such as this I need not dwell on the problem of standards, which has become especially acute in the age of machine-readable records. I would like to comment, however, that we are facing a problem of considerable dimensions in ensuring not just the continuity of current bibliographies but the continuity of support for Canadian bibliographic efforts in general. The CIHM needs assurance of new grants to develop its coverage from its present base. The National Library has delineated a number of areas of support for Canadian Studies for which funds have been requested from the Federal Government over a five-year period, including acquisition of materials not at present in the collection, enhanced bibliographic records for materials which are presently brieflisted, acquisition and control of microforms, appointment of additional subject experts, and other projects, some of which have already been remarked upon. The priority afforded some of these projects will obviously depend on the resources made available to the National Library for Canadian Studies. The Social Sciences and Humanities Research Council received special funding for Canadian Studies which permitted establishment of its Research Tools Program among others, but the funds available to this Program will be halved next year in comparison with this year, and could conceivably disappear altogether unless government funding is maintained. The Secretary of State in 1981 allocated special funding for a National Program of Support for Canadian Studies over a three-year period which will soon expire. Although this last program has had no direct impact to date on research tools in the area, it is nevertheless indicative of government priorities for Canadian Studies.

It is important that all who are interested in the development of research in Canadian Studies make sure that we do not lose ground after the many steps forward that have been taken over the past few years. We in Canada look to our overseas colleagues to assist in identifying collections and compiling research tools which will facilitate research in Canadian Studies. We also look to you for support in demonstrating to our government the value of the programs described here and in encouraging the Minister of Communications (responsible for the National Library and SSHRCC) and the Secretary of State to maintain and increase funding for such projects.

References

1 National Conference on the State of Canadian Bibliography, Vancouver, Canada, 1974. *Proceedings*. Ottawa: National Library of Canada, 1977. (Available in English- and French-language versions.)
2 *Bibliography for Canadian Studies: Present Trends and Future Needs/Bibliographie pour les Etudes canadiennes: situation actuelle et besoins futurs; proceedings of a Conference held at Dalhousie University, Halifax, N.S., 1981*. Willowdale, Ont.: Association for Canadian Studies, 1982. (*Canadian Issues* Volume IV)
3 Bibliothèque nationale du Québec. *Laurentiana parus avant 1821*. Par Milada Vlach avec la collaboration de Yolande Buono. Montreal: Bibliothèque nationale du Québec, 1976
4 Lavigne, Lise. 'Bibliographie retrospective pour les études canadiennes: la contribution de la Bibliothèque nationale du Québec.' In *Bibliography for Canadian Studies* . . . ; 124–136
5 Thériault, Michel. 'Canadiana 1867–1900: Monographies. In *Bibliography for Canadian Studies* . . . ; 124–136
6 'Film Canadiana.' *National Library News 15*(3): 10–11 (March 1983)
7 Rogers, Lorelei M. 'Bibliographic services and Canadian audiovisual materials.' In *Bibliography for Canadian Studies* . . . ; 124–136
8 Rider, Lillian M. 'Summary of developments in Canadian subject and area bibliography since 1974.' In *Bibliography for Canadian Studies* . . . ; 2–27
9 Rider, Lilliam M. *Op. cit.*
10 Rider also lists two bibliographies of theses in Canadian Literature – by Gnarowski (English Canadian Literature) and Naaman – in her 'Summary . . . '
11 Mitchell, Paula S. 'A Note on the development of the Canadian Register of [Research and] Researchers in the Social Sciences: purpose, general dimensions, and applications.' In *Bibliography for Canadian Studies* . . . ; 108–111
12 Those interested in the inventory should contact Barbara Godard, ACQL Research Committee, English Department, York University, Downsview, Ontario, M3J 1P3

13 Canada Council. Consultative Group on Survey Research. *Survey Research; Report* . . . Ottawa: The Council; 1976
14 At present, only RADAR of these indexes is searchable online; it can be accessed in Canada through Informatech
15 Full title is *Index de l'Actualité vue à travers la Presse écrite*. This database is searchable online through QL
16 INFO GLOBE is being accessed by some European customers; at the time of this writing it is not being accessed by any source in the UK
17 *Access to Newspaper Collections: Results of a Survey by the Newspaper Division, National Library of Canada, Ottawa, February 1982*; Annexes 9, 10 and 11. [mimeo.] For a note on the forthcoming survey of newspaper indexes see: *National Library News 15* (9):7 (September 1983)
18 Rider, Lillian M. *Op.cit.*
19 McCue, Harvey A. 'Native Studies.' In *Bibliography for Canadian Studies* . . . ; 30–37
20 Young, Judy. 'Some thoughts about the present state of bibliography in the area of Canadian Ethnic Studies.' In *Bibliography for Canadian Studies* . . . ; 38–47
21 Strong-Boag, Veronica. 'The fugitive female: an introduction to the bibliography of Canadian Women's Studies.' In *Bibliography for Canadian Studies* . . . ; 48–57
22 Piternick, Anne B. 'Spreading the word: some problems of bibliographic control of Canadian publications.' In *The Written Word; Proceedings of 22nd Symposium, 1980*. Ottawa: Royal Society of Canada, 1981; 104–114
23 This analysis also holds true for the bibliographies on Native Studies, Ethnic Studies and Women's Studies provided by McCue, Young and Strong-Boag in the same source
24 See the entries for this publication in the section on Canadian Literature in Rider, p.23
25 Young, Judy. *Op.cit.*
26 Strong-Boag, Veronica. *Op.cit.*
27 Bloomfield, Valerie. *Guide to Resources for Canadian Studies in Britain*. Ottawa: Department of External Affairs, 1979. [Second edition now available]
28 Rider, Lillian M. *Canadian Resources at McGill*. Montreal: McGill University Libraries, 1980
29 National Library of Canada. Resources Survey Division. *National Library News 15* (5–6): 4 (May/June 1983)
30 See, for example:
Social Sciences and Humanities Research Council. Consultative Group on Canadian Archives. *Canadian Archives: Report* . . . Ottawa: Supply and Services Canada, 1980. See especially p.98: 'The need for research in the development of standard forms of description, indexing and arrangement for archival materials is urgent. . . . The lack of uniformity of descriptive and cataloguing methods seriously hinders the creation of an information system at the national level.'
Caya, Marcel. 'La diffusion par la publication des instruments de recherche en archivistique.' In *Bibliography for Canadian Studies* . . . ; 58–74
31 An earlier, excellent study of the problems of researchers in the developing areas of Anthropology and Sociology was presented by Marchak at the 1974 Bibliography Conference: Marchak, Patricia. 'Subject bibliography – Anthropology and Sociology. In *National Conference on the State of Canadian Bibliography* . . . ; 232–258
32 Young, Judy. *Op.cit.*
33 McCue, Harvey A *Op.cit.*
34 This brings to mind problems encountered with the Library of Congress Subject Headings (LCSH) before the National Library Published *Canadian Subject Headings* (CSH) in 1978. Gerda Ferrington, editor of CSH, notes that according to LCSH, Canda had nothing to do with the War of 1812! for a discussion of the compilation of CSH see:
Ferrington, Gerda. 'A list of Canadian subject headings.'
Libraries with Canadian collections will also be glad to know of the recent publication of:
Haycock, Ken and Lighthall, Lynne Isberg. *Sears List of Subject Headings: Canadian Companion*, second edition N.Y.: Wilson, 1983
35 Strong-Boag, Veronica. *Op.cit.*
36 In this connection, the catalogue of a recent exhibition mounted by the Public Archives of Canada with support from the National Library should be noted:
l'Espérance, Jeanne. *The Widening Sphere: Women in Canada, 1870–1940*. Ottawa: Supply and Services, 1982
37 Young, Judy. *Op.cit.*
38 Whitside, Don. [sin a paw] 'A case for the collection of fugitive material about and by Indians.'

In *The Bibliographical Society of Canada. Colloquium III/IIIe Colloque*. Toronto: Bibliographical Society of Canada, 1979; 71-75
39 Strong-Boag, Veronica. *Op.cit.*
40 Hall, M Ann. Personal communication, 13 July 1983
41 For example, the Association of Canadian Community Colleges received support from the W K Kellog Foundation, the Canadian Studies Foundation and the Secretary of State (through the Canadian Studies Project at the Ontario Institute for Studies in Education) to publish several issues of *Comuniqué: Canadian Studies* which contain a series of bibliographies and lists of resource centres (including archives and museums) for topics ranging from Folk Culture to Military History. (This publication is no longer issued.) *Resources for Feminist Research* receives assistance from the Women's Programmes of the Department of the Secretary of State, which also gives support to CRIAW
42 *Bibliography for Canadian Studies . . .* ; 193
43 Hall, M Ann. Personal communication, 13 July 1983
44 Piternick, Anne B 'Social science information services: an overview of new developments in Canada.' Paper presented to the Social Science Libraries Section, International Federation of Library Associations, Annual Meeting, Montreal, August 1982. [IFLA 128/SOC/4-E/96]

Francess G Halpenny

The Dictionary of Canadian Biography/ Dictionnaire biographique du Canada

The very title *Dictionary of Canadian Biography/Dictionnaire biographique du Canada*, reflecting as it does the honourable tradition of the *Dictionary of National Biography* (DNB), would seem to provide in itself a definition of the project and indicate its method of procedure. Even its particular use for students and scholars as a reference work would seem to be apparent. There are, however, departures from the tradition in the creation of the DCB/DBC which have had profound effects for users of the volumes and therefore for scholarship. It is important to understand these differences in order to see what place the project takes in Canadian studies, and its relation to further research in that field in Canada and abroad.

The DCB/DBC is an historical survey of the Canadian people through biography, its form being a many-volumed work with entries on individuals. It is a national project, covering all parts of the country, and it deals with all kinds of people, including the known and the almost forgotten. Its particular originality (followed, though with a difference, by the Australian national dictionary) is the chronological arrangement of volumes, with death dates determining the siting of biographies within them. This decision, taken in the 1960s, was in large part a practical one, the concentration on a period being seen as making publication of individual volumes faster, sales of particular volumes as soon as they were published more attractive, and eventual revision easier. In the event those advantages have been realized, but the editorial consequences of the decision were more profound. Each volume of the DCB/DBC becomes a great cross-section of society, a complex web of people whose lives are connected by virtue of their personal interactions or the simple fact of their living through the same events and responding to similar pressures. When the biographies for a volume are selected their role in providing a cross-section is an influential factor.

The lists of candidates for a volume are prepared on the basis of the types of people that should be represented in it in order to reflect the society of the period – fur traders, early colonizers, merchants, military, clergy, officials, artisans and artists, lawyers and doctors, Arctic explorers, surveyors and geologists, agriculturists, industrialists, or educators. The lists also take into account a need to reflect the areas of Canada and the particular stage of their history (the Maritimes, for instance, are seeing the end of the golden age of trade by sailing vessel when the west is only beginning to feel the pressures of European settlement). Within the areas of the country we try to represent the growth of communities at critical stages – in volume v, for instance (dates 1801–1820), a number of its biographies show the importance of Kingston and the Niagara peninsula and the Windsor area in the first years of Upper Canada. Our planning lists reflect too the issues and events that bulk large in the years being covered (volume v is thus much preoccupied with the development of a new economy after 1763 and with the coming of the Loyalists after 1783), and often the institutions that are developing (in the nineteenth century the founding of universities or the creation of railways are examples).

When the biographies for a volume are submitted and are being edited, the structure of that volume as a whole, and the relation of the structure to the cross-sections of society provided in other volumes, become clearer and the editors now give much attention to the provision of the cross-references which weave biographies together within a volume and link them to neighbouring volumes. One way to read the DCB/DBC volumes, indeed, is to take up a biography and trace all the leads that cross-references can provide to make a fuller story.

For students the advantages of access to societies of different periods through the DCB/DBC are very real. Access comes by way of stories of individuals who built those societies and the narrative aspect eases the approach. The biographies are relatively short so that students can approach a group of people and then a topic speedily. The special indexes now accompanying volumes, though they may seem to some arbitrary in construction, are also recognized as helpful finding aids. The volumes of the DCB/DBC up to 1900, as a group, can be seen now to form a pattern which students can usefully study (I am confining my attention in this paper to volumes I-XII, the scope of our past and present research and the funding we have received). Volumes I to IV take readers through early exploration and the rise of colonies in Newfoundland, the Maritimes, and New France, and they record the final years of the French régime. Volumes v to VIII are the years of the establishment of British North America, of its survival from the shock of invasions, of the influx of settlers to the eastern and central colonies, and of the expansion of the fur trade west and north. Volumes IX to XII are the years of consolidation in territory and settlement and society, and yet also of growth and changes that were often rapid: in numbers of people, in towns and cities, in industry, in transportation (especially with the railways), in social institutions of all kinds, in forms of government. Canada from sea to sea is now a reality.

There are other aspects of coverage in the DCB/DBC which its chronological arrangement makes evident, and which are important in relation to the concerns of a colloquium such as this. Its volumes are full of persons who may be called 'newcomers'. They contain biographies of native peoples, of Indians and Inuit, of course, to the extent that documentation is available, and some of those biographies are major contributions. Moreover, there are the many descendants of original families in Acadia and New France who perpetuate the farms and towns, institutions and crafts of l'Acadie and Québec. Two of the fathers of Confederation, Tilley and Tupper, like many persons of their region, were born in the old provinces of New Brunswick and Nova Scotia. Sir John A Macdonald's life, however, represents a pattern very familiar in the opening paragraphs of DCB/DBC biographies for the seventeenth, eighteenth and nineteenth centuries: he was born in Glasgow and came to Canada with his parents in 1820. Indeed for volumes I-XII the largest number of persons receiving biographies have come from elsewhere: from France and Great Britain especially and from the United States and Europe, some as children, some as mature persons with families intent upon obtaining land and a secure abode, some as fur traders and entrepreneurs ready to explore and exploit the resources of large and promising colonies, some as professional people pursuing their careers in a new setting. Many newcomers stay in what will be Canada and their story becomes its story. Their antecedents are often important factors, however, determining the education and attitudes they bring with them and continuing to affect their reactions to the society they join. In some instances connections between the New World and the Old may be maintained more closely. To take one example, Canada at all periods has been an exporter – of furs, of fish, of timber, of wheat – and an importer of goods. This trade has depended on overseas connections: with ports in France, with the merchants of the West Country ports, with Glasgow and the Clyde shipbuilders, with Liverpool, with the Caribbean. In religious matters, to take another example, the overseas as well as United States connections and relationships of Anglicans, Presbyterians, Methodists, and Catholics are constantly evident, from the French and British support of missionaries and parishes in the New World to questions of the applicability of doctrine and legal status in the colonies. Similarly, the achievements of many writers and artists who came to Canada can only be understood and properly evaluated if their continuing interest in the subject-matter and standards of writers and painters in Great Britain and Europe is remembered and studied.

There are, however, also in volumes I-XII many persons whose coming to what is now Canada is an incident, short or long, in careers centred elsewhere. The prevalence of such figures would be expected in the histories of colonies. Prominent among them for the DCB/DBC is a procession of governors with varying mandates, most of whom have already seen service in outposts of France or Great Britain or Spain and who move from Canada to other territories. Amherst, Durham, and Elgin would be familiar examples. And then there are the military who have fought the wars of the home country in the Caribbean, the Netherlands, India, the Crimea, the Iberian peninsula, and the field of Waterloo and who come to Canada to defend frontiers or assault them or to develop systems of defence. Montcalm, Bougainville, and Wolfe, Carleton and Haldimand, Isaac Brock and Colborne, even Edward Augustus, Duke of Kent, are among their number. Merchants and entrepreneurs who move easily between colony and *métropole* with the latter as their base are often met – Joshua Mauger and Brook Watson, Edward Ellice, and Sir John Rose; Lord Selkirk too could be included. Canada over these centuries received a disparate host of other visitors: explorers such as Cook, Vancouver, and Franklin; travellers such as Lafitau and Palliser who wrote often celebrated accounts of what they had seen; minor officials; scientists such as Sir Joseph Banks and Sir John Henry Lefroy.

The DCB/DBC volumes do not have unlimited space of course, and so for our purposes the accounts of the careers of persons who came to Canada and stayed or who came temporarily and yet affected its development have to focus on the years in Canada. The events and the importance of time spent elsewhere have to be given briefly. Moreover, the position from which most of our authors start in viewing these careers is Canada – their point of view, and their general understanding of place and theme, are those of Canadians. Thus when the DCB/DBC takes up subjects that appear in the DNB the scope of the coverage and also the treatment will likely differ. The DCB/DBC volumes have a special contribution to make in offering to students at all levels an opportunity to view the panorama of historical events as they affect Canada and are experienced by Canadians. But yet there must be a sense of balance. For we must not lose sight of the significance of all the connections of Canada with the world beyond its borders past and present, connections which often fundamentally determine the course of its history. The consequences for Canada of conflict in the eighteenth century and early years of the nineteenth century between England and France and between Great Britain and the Thirteen Colonies or the United States are, for instance, what give volumes V and VI many of their themes. For those concerned with Canadian studies, in Great Britain or in Canada, it is important to look in two directions: out to Canada from Europe and back to Europe from Canada.

I think it can fairly be said that contributors to the DCB/DBC, in tackling these thousands of individuals who lived in Canada (3,883 of them now in published volumes), have made significant advances in the understanding of the history and culture of this country. It should be stressed that a great deal of new research for all areas and periods has been incorporated into the biographies – they are not by and large simply an arrangement of previous work. Some of this research has been necessary because the careers of persons to be included, often in shorter biographies, have not been studied previously in any detail and such people have been known largely by allusions in general works or biographies of major figures or by references in the compendia biographical volumes that flourished in the late nineteenth and early twentieth centuries in Canada. Moreover, the record of Canada's past is still lacking full-length modern biographies of even major figures let alone those in the second and third ranks, and there are many issues and events in political, social, cultural, and intellectual history that still await authoritative contemporary discussion. In this aspect of scholarly contribution the volumes of the DCB/DBC differ from the original volumes of the DNB at the time they were published in the nineteenth century and certainly as those volumes exist today. Our contributors have had to work in most cases with original documents, to pry out the complexity of incidents, to test and sometimes correct the assertions of local historians, to develop a firmer understanding of issues in certain periods in order to place their subjects more truly. To obtain the benefit of current research into Canada's past a reading of the DCB/DBC volumes is essential. It is in those volumes that the fullest and most up-to-date record of Newfoundland is appearing; it is there that such themes as the land question in Prince Edward Island or the constitutional dilemmas in central Canada after 1763 or the patterns of overseas trade are being addressed by contemporary scholarship.

As users of DCB/DBC volumes will know, we lay stress on the bibliographical record of sources used – more stress perhaps than other biographical projects of similar type. Such amplification was the wish of the first benefactor of the project, the man whose bequest initiated our work. But it also reflects the conviction in 1959 when the project began that bibliography in Canada was not sufficiently developed for us to shirk a responsibility to contribute to it in ways that would help readers. That situation has changed greatly in recent years – as projects such as those represented at this colloquium demonstrate – but we believe our bibliographical work to be essential still. The individual bibliographies list the most important sources used by the authors of the entries as the back-up for their texts as a service to our readers, with students especially in mind; the general bibliography in each volume picks up items that appear more frequently in the individual bibliographies and provides the full citations for them in one place. It also presents more general information about the archival collections, the reference works, and the newspapers and serials which our contributors consult. We issue a caveat that our general bibliographies should not be taken as bibliographies for the period covered in each volume; they are guides to the sources used by contributors and editors. Nevertheless the scope of the research represented in each volume and the effort made to provide full and accurate bibliographic citations do bestow an independent value upon the general bibliographies considered as a whole.

The necessity for accuracy, it should be stressed, means that all the listings are fully checked by our staff, who maintain a file record of verified citations and an archive of title-pages in photocopy. In the course of this work of verification they carry on a considerable correspondence with archives and libraries in Canada and abroad. The British Library is one of our correspondents (at this stage in the life of the BL printed catalogue we often find direct inquiry about bibliographical problems more useful in ensuring accuracy), as is the Public Record Office and the Scottish Record Office, and we also deal with many other collections at the county or municipal level.

A similar effort in accuracy is made with all proper names – of persons, institutions, and places – that appear in the biographies, and the DCB/DBC volumes are now being recognized as a kind of special 'authority file'. For this purpose we have thousands upon thousands of slips or fiches to guide us from volume to volume. The *Historical Atlas of Canada* project, with which we maintain an association, will, when complete, constitute a mammoth published authority file in another style.

Canadian history has a special challenge in the area of reference because of the two official languages. Institutions, for instance, from 1841 onwards may have an official name in both languages; if only in one, we use what is the formal name in both English and French editions of a volume. It should also be noted that publishing two editions of each volume requires an immense work of translation (with each volume, the equivalent of a year to do the translating and to check it for absolute fidelity to meaning and nuance). The translation process involves a constant run of decisions about how to render terms: the terms to be used in presenting in English the government, army, and parish system, and the social institutions of New France and later Lower Canada and Québec, and the terms to be used in French for the fishery and the fur trade, the church organization, the judicial systems, and the business operations of the maritime colonies, Upper Canada, and the west. What do you do in the French edition with the term 'Pedlars' used by Hudson's Bay Company men for the Nor'Westers or in either edition with the terms 'Canadiens' and 'Canadians', familiar designations for some years after 1763 for the French-speaking inhabitants of Lower Canada? How do you present in English the overtones of the word 'pays' for our French authors? The DCB/DBC volumes are thus a source book for Canadian studies of yet another kind that does not have a parallel in Canada or elsewhere.

There is a further aspect related to translation. Contributors make use of quotations in their texts to confirm information or to give a reflection of contemporary opinion and means of expression. Thus the seventeenth or eighteenth or nineteenth centuries can speak in their own voices. We check as many of the quotations as we can. They will ultimately be translated from English to French or French to English to serve the needs of both editions. It is true, of course, that some documents, official publications, or books already exist in English and in French and we try to use accepted translations for quotations from such sources. We do discover, however, that sometimes these accepted translations are not faithful renderings of the original and the discrepancies have to be dealt with, especially if factual information in the original has been distorted in the move to the other language.

The implications of the DCB/DBC as a national biographical project, as a set of chronologically organized volumes, as a bicultural/bilingual enterprise, and as a reference work of scope and reliability were certainly not all anticipated before its official founding in 1959 and 1961 – the year in which Université Laval and its press entered into association with the University of Toronto and its press and in which the editorial office in Québec joined the office in Toronto. The project's life since those two key years (and since 1973 when the grants of the Canada Council, then of the Social Sciences and Humanities Research Council of Canada enabled expansion of its work) has been one of challenges, curiosities, adventures, and discoveries. The requirements of each new volume as we proceed to put it together add to the complexity of the overall undertaking.

One important factor needs always to be taken into account in looking back to study what the project has been and what it yet may do: that is the scholarly context of the 24 years of its life to date. When the project began Canadian history as a scholarly discipline was well established even if its effective life was brief by comparison with the discipline in other countries. The Canadian segment of the department of history at the University of Toronto, a leader for many years in the field of Canadian history, had been given initial impetus with the appointment of Professor George Wrong in 1894 and with his establishment in 1897 of the *Review of Historical Publications relating to Canada*, which was succeeded by the *Canadian Historical Review* in 1920. The Canadian Historical Association was founded in 1922. In Québec, the *Bulletin des recherches historiques* had begun in 1895, the *Cahiers des Dix* in 1936, and the *Revue d'histoire de l'Amérique française* appeared in 1947. Moreover, over these years archival collections had been built up and the reports of the Public Archives of Canada and the Archives nationales du Québec had recorded much valuable material. By the Second World War important document series existed such as the *Jesuit Relations*, published 1896–1901, Shortt and Doughty's volumes relating to constitutional history, issued in two languages 1907–35, the series of the Champlain Society, founded in 1905, and the collections of the Hudson's Bay Record Society inaugurated in 1938. Scholars of the calibre of Burt, Brebner, Stacey, Creighton, Neatby, Lower, Trudel, Frégault, Martin had set standards. Yet it was true that historians of my generation at the University of Toronto, who graduated into the Second World War, by and large obtained their doctorates outside Canada. With their eventual addition to the staffs at the older Canadian universities, with the expansion and creation in the late 1950s and 1960s of universities across the country which incorporated sizeable history departments, with the introduction of more doctoral programmes and the arrival of graduate students in quantity to plunge into research, and with the major expansion of a Canadian university press which was building a strong history list, the setting in relation to Canadian historical studies for the creation of the DCB/DBC seemed favourable indeed. At the same time other related disciplines in the social sciences were undergoing development in Canadian universities which were to have similar scholarly consequences for the work of the DCB/DBC: historical geography, anthropology, the history of science and technology, and to some extent sociology are examples in point.

It was not so for Canadian literary studies unfortunately. Canadian literature, even for some years after the Second World War, was given short shrift in time and respect as far as curriculum and recognition of academic value were concerned. The first important journal for the field sponsored in

English Canada, *Canadian Literature*, was not founded until 1959 and it was very much the personal enterprise of a literary critic, George Woodcock. When the field of Canadian literature, present and past, did begin to receive something of its rightful place in literary studies at the universities, those who dealt with work written in English were at first preoccupied with their needs as teachers and felt a responsibility to assist in creating the necessary paperback texts such as the New Canadian Library. For Canadian literature in English the groundwork survey represented by Watters' *Check List of Canadian Literature* came in 1959, and it provided the impetus for research as well as teaching. So too did the *Literary History of Canada*, the successor to the surveys of Baker, MacMechan, and Stevenson; it was first published in 1965, with Northrop Frye's seminal concluding chapter. One of the first full-length major critical works in contemporary modes on Canadian literature in English was D G Jones's *Butterfly on Rock* and that was in 1970. The preoccupation with twentieth-century literature among students especially was for some years a real concern – however, recently more concerted attention to the earlier centuries is being given. Only in the last decade or so are editions of letters of Canadian authors in English and literary biographies at last being achieved. Descriptive bibliography is still lacking. Critical editions have finally begun with the impetus of the work of the Centre for Editing Early Canadian Texts at Carleton University, the results of which are not yet available in publication. The record in studies of Canadian literature in French shows a similar pattern of scattered initial efforts giving way to studies which would encourage more concentrated research. To take two significant events: the first edition of Gérard Tougas's *Histoire de la littérature canadienne-française* appeared in 1960 and the *Dictionnaire des œuvres littéraires du Québec* put out its first volume in 1978. It was fortuitous that the early volumes of the DCB/DBC had few Canadian authors to review, although we had Aubert de Gaspé and Octave Crémazie in volume x, the third volume to be published (1972); volume IX, published in 1976, brought Haliburton and Garneau. Later volumes have now been able to take advantage of the development of Canadian literary studies and contributors from this field will become increasingly important. It might be noted here that a similar late start has to be recorded for Canadian art history of scholarly significance, with Harper's important survey *Painting in Canada/La Peinture au Canada* appearing in 1966, called forth by Canada's centennial. We would have welcomed an earlier beginning. Fortunately, when volume X was in the making, Harper had just completed his major study of Paul Kane.

Our contributors, tackling the earlier history of Canada and facing up to its overseas connections, have had the benefit of a number of essential services undertaken in earlier years. Given the significance of Canada's ties with Europe it was invaluable that they could find in the Public Archives of Canada the transcripts of important series of documents in the British Library, the Public Record Office, and the Archives nationales in Paris, and finding aids for them. But the decision to have our volumes 'begin at the beginning', as Professor G W Brown, the first general editor, used to say, soon revealed that consultation overseas on a large scale was still going to be essential. Much of the source material for the early history of Newfoundland was not available in Canada – we had to depend on the resources being studied in, for example, Liverpool by David Quinn and his students such as Gillian Cell. The Hudson's Bay Company Archives were then in London, and we came to rely on Alice Johnson and Glyndwr Williams. The DCB/DBC was founded just when historical investigation of Louisbourg was being given significant priority at that site and a major effort at identifying the location of source material in Europe and copying it was not yet ended. Much information about New France was still only available in archives and libraries in France and help had to be sought through the good offices of Étienne Taillemite and others. The Archives of the United Society for the Propagation of the Gospel in Westminster had essential manuscript material. So too did the Scott Polar Research Institute where Alan Cooke and Clive Holland proved good friends.

The development in Canada of interest in and study of all the many areas in which our history interconnects with Europe has, however, been made increasingly possible and speeded up by the use of microfilm and photocopy, neither of them available until after the war. Without these two aids the DCB/DBC as we have tried to create it would really have been impossible. The necessary access to documents and printed materials abroad would have been beyond the physical and financial reach of all but a few contributors, and our own staff would have been severely crippled in their efforts to obtain and check information from Toronto and Québec. Our readers are the beneficiaries of the persistent efforts over the years of persons in our own archives, in Europe, and in Great Britain to identify and make available in copy the source materials needed for the study of our history. They are also the beneficiaries of the PAC's distribution of copies to archives across Canada. The availability of printed materials through interlibrary loan is another development in accessiblity which makes a project like the DCB/DBC possible. The National Library of Canada came into being in 1952, just seven years before the DCB/DBC, and the building up of its collections and its bibliographical services has been an essential aid to research. So too has been the formation of the Bibliothèque nationale du Québec, which occurred in 1967. It is the fervent hope of the DCB/DBC that the enormous work in preservation and cataloguing represented by the Canadian Institute for Historical Microreproductions will be maintained to add its contribution of knowledge.

And yet much historical research remains unaccomplished so that we are only too conscious of the vagaries of historical chance. We are sure that a great deal remains to be discovered in sources abroad. In recent years the DCB/DBC has had the benefit of the researches in France's port cities – La Rochelle, Bordeaux – of J F Bosher, Dale Miquelon, and Tim Le Goff who have been tracing the transoceanic trading patterns of France with her colonies. Investigation in many similar places would have informed our scholars and our volumes. The Maritime History Group at Memorial University of Newfoundland has added immensely to knowledge of the connections between the West Country and our early maritime colonies, so that Poole is almost as familiar a name to the DCB/DBC as Harbour Grace. Their work should be an example for other enterprises yet to be designed. When J M Bumsted was in Edinburgh at the Centre of Canadian Studies he found his way into sources, yet to be fully exploited, that would tell much about the motives and methods of emigration to Canada, and we were at a point where we could use what he had been able to turn up during his residence. One could go on with these tantalizing possibilities.

A continuing source of frustration for us is the lack of adequate published guides and finding aids to collections in Europe. For Great Britain users have had the benefit of such publications as the *Guide to Manuscripts relating to America in Great Britain and Ireland* (1961, 1979), the *Guide to the Contents of the Public Record Office* (1963–68), and the volume *Britain and the Dominions: A Guide to Business and Related Records in the United Kingdom* (1978). We are grateful for such aids as Valerie Bloomfield's *Guide to Resources for Canadian Studies in Britain*. But as the number of useful sources grows by discovery, and the curiosities of scholars change, the need for detailed guidance about the contents of sources old and new increases. Thus if we and our contributors are to be able to make inquiries that are capable of answer by the staffs of depositories abroad there must be more, and more detailed, guides to content. Such a plea is a familiar one wherever archives and special library collections exist and try to serve scholars. We make it with special urgency because we and our contributors have to work at long range, but within confined time schedules, and we are not able to afford special research efforts on the spot.

A constant concern on our part is to try to validate dates and places of birth, marriage, and death. Given the characteristics of Canadian history I have already described, our lot is to write hundreds of letters to Great Britain and France seeking and verifying information. Our files have an imposing array of copies of certificates of birth and marriage or of wills. The letterheads of correspondence reaching our office identify French departmental offices, British parishes and county registries. The staffs of these registries have always tried to be helpful, and often, when our request is reasonably detailed, they have sent answers that add precision to the opening paragraphs of our biographies. But just as often we are told that they cannot undertake to do what our inquiries would need for reasons of lack of staff or because they are not the right registry, and 'please note the enclosed list of qualified searchers who will act for a set fee'. The searchers, whom we would not be able to brief effectively at a distance, would in any case want fees that might exceed what most of our contributors receive as an honorarium. Luck, then, plays a greater part in the documentation we can provide than we would like, and we wonder if a colloquium such as this has any suggestions about how our national project could get some coordinated assistance in one of the countries which houses the vital statistics of so many of our subjects.

Filling out the early history of persons in the DCB/DBC who came to Canada with accounts that go well beyond vital statistics is, may I suggest, a promising line of activity for students in Great Britain near the documentary sources and interested in the development of this country. So much could be done in discovering the facts and exploring the significance of the early life before emigration and the attitudes to the homeland that persisted. But in addition to the interest of figures who happen to be in our volumes and could receive further investigation from other points of view are small and large themes of Canada's interconnections yet to be studied: themes for an essay, a thesis, or a monograph. Not enough is known yet of the components and experiences of many of the groups who came to Canada; not enough is known about the attitudes to and knowledge of Canada among the many persons in Great Britain who were responsible for her government and her defence through more than two centuries. Not enough is known about the characteristics and significance of the persons associated with the Privy Council who had an important role in making judgements on Canadian affairs. Too little is known of the publishing history of the many works related to Canada that were issued in Great Britain by authors living there or in Canada and of the effect of those works upon British and upon Canadian audiences. Not enough is known of the reality and significance of relations among families attempting to maintain communications across the ocean. And I myself, after years of immersion in DCB/DBC work, have become intrigued with the surprising absence of a proper maritime history of Canada – although this is a country whose development has been profoundly affected because it fronts on three oceans and has an impressive system of inland waterways.

The list of topics could be extended to great length, and the items on it would offer possibilities for original work in areas not crowded with other inquirers. The DCB/DBC would welcome discussion of such work where and when it might occur and put the resources of its files, as far as possible, at the disposal of researchers. An exchange of points of view could not fail to be stimulating and constructive for all concerned. We have always interpreted our role to include the encouragement of research though our priority and energy have to go to fulfilling our mandate to publish volumes on a schedule. We shall be offering volume V in the autumn of 1983 and volumes VI, VII, VIII, and XII, in preparation now, will, I hope, stimulate research of the kind suggested here.

Hope E A Clement

Canada's Retrospective National Bibliography

Canadiana, Current and Retrospective

Canadiana, Canada's national bibliography, first appeared in January 1951 published by the Canadian Bibliographic Centre, the forerunner of the National Library, and covered materials published in 1950. In 1953, the National Library of Canada was created by an Act of the Canadian Parliament. Section 7(1)(c) of the National Library Act, amended in 1969, authorizes the National Librarian, among other things, to 'compile and publish a national bibliography in which books produced in Canada, written or prepared by Canadians or of special interest or significance to Canada may be noted and described'.[1] In this context, 'book' refers to 'library matter of every kind, nature and description and includes document, paper, record, tape or other thing published by a publisher, on or in which information is written, recorded, stored or reproduced.'[2]

Section 11 of the Act also establishes a legal deposit requirement beginning in 1953, whereby Canadian publishers are required by law to send copies of their publications to the National Library within one week of their release for public distribution or sale. Only publications which have been at least partially manufactured in Canada or which have the imprint of a Canadian publisher on the title page are subject to deposit, normally in two copies. The National Library of Canada is the only legal depository for Canadian publications.

As a general rule, current Canadiana is considered (for bibliographical purposes) to include material published since the year in which it began to be listed in *Canadiana*, the current national bibliography. This date varies with the type of material, and is often (though not always) related to the year in which it became subject to enforcement of the legal deposit regulations. For monographs, serials and Canadian government publications, this date is 1950; for sound recordings, 1969; and for educational kits, 1978.

Works published before the year in which that type of material began to be listed in *Canadiana* are considered to be retrospective Canadiana. For works published in Canada, coverage of the retrospective national bibliography dates from 1751, the introduction of printing in Canada. For works of interest to Canada published in Europe, coverage dates from the sixteenth century.

Canadiana 1867–1900: Monographs

The first segment of the retrospective national bibliography to be actively researched and compiled is that of monographs published between 1867 and 1900. The choice of this segment was based partially on its sociopolitical interest, spanning as it does the period between the year of Canada's Confederation, considered its founding as a nation, and the turn of the century. The period was also chosen for early treatment because of its relative lack of bibliographic coverage. *A check list of Canadian imprints, 1900–1925* by Tod and Cordingley,[3] and the Toronto Public Library's *Canadian catalogue of books*,[4,5] covering the period 1921 to 1949, while by no means comprehensive, do provide a measure of bibliographic control of Canadian works published between 1900 and 1949. Marie Tremaine's *Bibliography of Canadian imprints, 1751–1800*[6] is a basic text providing coverage of the pre-1800 period, and the Toronto Public Library's *A bibliography of Canadiana, being items in the Public Library of Toronto, Canada, relating to the early history and development of Canada*[7] and its *First supplement*[8] cover the period from the discovery of Canada to confederation of the provinces in 1867.

HISTORY

The 1867–1900 monographs segment was first undertaken on a part-time basis in 1953 by Dr Raymond Tanghe, then Assistant National Librarian, with the help of his associate, Madeleine Pellerin. Dr Tanghe retired in 1964 and Mlle Pellerin died in 1971; during these years the project continued on a very limited basis due to lack of resources.

In 1974, the National Library established on a formal basis the Retrospective National Bibliography Division, and a decision was made to continue work on the 1867–1900 monographs segment until it was substantively complete. In the same year and reinforcing this decision, a National Conference on the State of Canadian Bibliography was held in Vancouver, which passed a recommendation 'that this Conference advise the National Library of Canada, through the Secretary of State, of the importance of completing *Canadiana 1867–1900*, and of the necessity of providing adequate funds to the National Retrospective Bibliographical Division of the National Library of Canada to enable it to finish this project and to undertake other similar projects, in order to complete Canada's retrospective national bibliography.'[9]

In 1975 the task began of converting a card file of some 20,000 entries to machine-readable form. Between 1975 and 1980 the number of records doubled to about 40,000. In 1980 publication of the bibliography began on Computer Output Microfiche (COM) and a total of nine supplements were published at quarterly intervals until December 1982. Further supplements will be published on an irregular basis while a final cumulation is in preparation, expected to be published late in 1983. The National Library is also considering the publication of a printed edition of the bibliography, a costly undertaking, provided that funds requested for 1986 are granted.

SCOPE

The criteria for inclusion of materials in this segment of the Retrospective National Bibliography (referred to as RETRO) have been broadly applied, using the maxim 'When in doubt, include', as it is felt to be much easier to delete inappropriate entries later than to search for missing items.

As its title implies, *Canadiana 1867–1900: Monographs* includes monographs published at least in part between the years 1867 and 1900 inclusive. A monograph is defined as a separately published work issued in what is now called the private sector. However, the definition encompasses not only commercially-published works and works published by non-profit groups and individuals but also pamphlets, leaflets, broadsides, works by government officials and parliamentarians if the author's name is identified on the item, atlases, printed music (including sheet music), reports of annual meetings, municipal and county government publications and non-Canadian government publications. Municipal and county publications, broadsides and translations of works by Canadian authors published outside Canada are included when encountered, but are not systematically sought.

Excluded from *Canadiana 1867–1900: Monographs* are most Canadian federal, provincial and territorial government publications (unless by personal authors identified on the publication), serials, newspapers, manuscripts and unpublished theses, maps, audio-visual materials and patents.

The definition of Canadiana is more complex in that it contains an element of subjectivity. In compiling the current national bibliography, a rule of thumb for selecting items for inclusion is that the content be at least one-third Canadian. For the retrospective bibliography this 'one-third rule' for Canadian content is discarded in favour of a more inclusive policy as it is important for historical research to identify all works relating to Canada. Because of the relatively small amount of Canadian publishing in the early years it may be that even a portion of a work constitutes the only information on a particular Canadian subject or area. All works published in Canada (as defined by its present-day boundaries) in all languages are included, even if the Canadian imprint is not the first or prominent one on the title page. Also included are works published outside Canada but written by Canadians, defined as persons born in Canada, or those who spent some time in Canada if their stay was not considered of a temporary nature. Works by persons staying temporarily in Canada, published either in Canada or abroad during the period of their Canadian sojourn, are also listed. Thus works by British military personnel, university and college professors and clergy during the period of their temporary assignment in Canada, are normally included. Non-Canadian publications of Canadian association are also included: a work is of Canadian association when its subject is Canada or a Canadian, and when references to Canada are more than passing. For example, works related to the period of French influence in the Mississippi Valley, to the French-Canadian settlements in Montana, Minnesota and Michigan, to French-Canadian Roman Catholic missionary work in Oregon, and to northern explorers who drifted into Canadian waters, to cite a few, would be considered of Canadian association.

METHODOLOGY

The project began with a page by page search by Madeleine Pellerin during the 1950s and 60s of the one hundred and sixty-seven volumes of the basic set of the Library of Congress Catalog, copying appropriate entries by hand onto index cards.

Many other subject and local bibliographies were searched over the years as they were published. In early 1983 about eighty bibliographies of varying lengths are yet to be searched. Of these remaining bibliographies, some are separately published and others are bibliographies within works; they cover specialized subject areas or local history, and none are considered major.

The Canadian Union Catalogue of Books, maintained by the National Library in card form, was consulted for locations for each entry identified, and this process yielded many new entries as other editions of a work, or other works by the same author, surfaced.

In 1976 the bibliographical files of the noted Montreal antiquarian bookseller Bernard Amtmann (1907–1979) were acquired, adding some 5,000 titles to the retrospective bibliography.

It should be stressed that compilation of the retrospective national bibliography began in the very early years of the National Library's existence, when its collections were far from extensive. The present policy is to attempt to obtain comprehensive coverage of retrospective Canadian materials as resources permit and as opportunities arise. National Library staff regularly attend book auctions and endeavour by other means to fill gaps in the retrospective collection. As well, the preservation microfilming activities of the Canadian Institute for Historical Microreproductions have afforded an opportunity to obtain in microfilm otherwise unavailable materials.

However, the first segment of RETRO was of necessity compiled from secondary sources, very often without the book in hand. For this reason the bibliographic data are not always complete and contain some inaccuracies. It is meant to stand as a checklist, subject always to revision and correction by its users, and is in fact continually upgraded to reflect new information supplied by researchers and librarians. Future segments of the Retrospective National Bibliography will be compiled in standard cataloguing fashion with the book in hand.

In general, because of the date of the commencement of the project, bibliographic descriptions are composed according to AACR1, the *Anglo-American Cataloguing Rules. North American Text*[10] with its revised Chapter 6, issued in 1974, providing for use of the *International Standard for Bibliographic Description for Monographic Publications* or ISBD(M). However, some exceptions have been made to accommodate the nature of the project: in most cases, full forms of forenames and surnames are used; the form of the author statement is subject to correction, having been transcribed without the book in hand, for this reason as well the distinction between publisher and printer is not made in the imprint; generous added entries are provided for charters, acts of incorporation and similar documents which create or legislate the behaviour of corporate bodies; the corporate body has been chosen as the main heading with an added entry for the legislative body.

THE PUBLICATION

Canadiana 1867–1900: Monographs/Canadiana 1867–1900: Monographies is published on COM with 42x reduction from a machine-readable database of records in modified Mini-MARC format (a scaled-down version of the Canadian MARC (Machine Readable Cataloguing) format for bibliographic records). The one-time price of $48.00 (Canadian) in Canada, $58.00 elsewhere, includes all quarterly updates issued since 1980 and the final cumulation in 1983; thereafter annual or biennial recumulations incorporating updates and corrections will be produced and sold separately.

Canadiana 1867–1900:Monographs is published as a register of complete entries in a computer-assigned numeric sequence, accompanied by five indexes.

Index A (Author/Title) provides access to entries by author and title. Index B (Chronological) lists each item by the year of its publication. Index C (Publisher/Printer) provides access by names of publishers and printers and in the final edition will gather together under one form of a publisher's or printer's name works published by that firm over the years covered. Index D (Place of Publication/Printing) lists items under the name of the locality in which they were published or printed using the location name as it appears in the imprint; *eg* both Quebec and its Latin form Quebeci, Montreal and its Latin form Marianopoli. Index E (Subject) provides access by names of persons and corporate bodies associated with the work as subjects. No other topical approach is provided.

Indexes B, C and D can be used for such historical studies as, for example, the printing history of a given city, region or publishing firm. It should be noted that certain filing anomalies are present in the indexes due to the filing programs used to sort the machine-readable records. The National Library expects to resolve these problems shortly.

To date, 236 copies of *Canadiana 1867–1900: Monographs* have been sold, of which 204 were sent to Canadian institutions; the remaining 32 outside Canada.

The future of Canada's Retrospective National Bibliography

1867–1900 MONOGRAPHS

As is mentioned earlier, the National Library is considering publication of the 1867–1900 monographs segment of RETRO in a printed edition at some future date. Apart from the perennial problem of cost this option would present other difficulties in that a printed document is less easily updated. Even if microfiche supplements were to be issued it is feared that such supplements would tend to be disregarded. For this reason a printed version would only be considered once the coverage of publications is nearly complete and the majority of bibliographic records have been updated and corrected.

PRE-1867 MONOGRAPHS

RETRO's next segment will cover monographs published before 1867. For Canadian monographs works will date from 1751, the introduction of printing in Canada, while for European documents works dating from the sixteenth century may be included if they are of significance to Canada. This segment of RETRO is to begin in 1984 or 1985 in cooperation with the Canadian Institute for Historical Microreproductions (CIHM). For this segment full AACR2 records will be created in CAN/MARC format from the book in hand.

OTHER SEGMENTS

The National Library is actively seeking the advice and views of scholars, researchers and librarians on the relative priority which should be accorded the remaining segments of RETRO, depending on the degree of historical and bibliographic interest they present. For example, focus on retrospective serials may engender renewed interest or increased activity in the preserving, microfilming and indexing of serials.

Materials which have not yet been covered by the retrospective national bibliography project include a substantial body of government publications, although the current segment (1867–1900 monographs) does include certain publications of that period by government officials and parliamentarians who are identified by name in the publication. Government publications have been divided tentatively by period into three segments: pre-1867, 1867 to 1900, and 1901 to 1949, with the latter group perhaps further subdivided by date.

Also to be tackled are monographs published between 1901 and 1949, and all serials published before 1950 when they were first included in *Canadiana*. Bibliographic control of serials may be undertaken in cooperation with the CONSER (CONversion of SERials) project by some twenty North American libraries to create and maintain a machine-readable database of North American serials. The National Library of Canada is the Canadian participant, contributing records for Canadian serial titles as well as authenticating records for Canadian items contributed by other libraries. About 36,000 records for Canadian serial titles reside in the database.

Listing of retrospective (pre-1950) newspaper titles will be coordinated with the preservation and bibliographic control activities sponsored this year by the National Library Advisory Board's Resource Network Committee. The Committee has launched a decentralized programme designed to encourage the coordinated collection and microfilming of Canadian newspapers and the compilation of checklists of newspapers published in each province or region of the country. An eventual aim of the plan is the production of an up-to-date union list of Canadian newspapers held by Canadian libraries, combined with a register of microform masters.

Other materials yet to be covered by the retrospective national bibliography include pre-1950 theses, phonorecords issued before 1969 (when they began to appear in *Canadiana*), pre-1950 audio-visual materials, retrospective microforms and pre-1978 educational kits. The listing of retrospective maps and plans would involve collaboration with the National Map Collection of the Public Archives of Canada.

The National Library welcomes suggestions from scholars and librarians on priorities for beginning work on these historical documents.

Cooperative arrangements

The magnitude of the task of compiling a nation's retrospective bibliography has led in recent years to greater reliance on cooperative arrangements with other agencies engaged in similar or associated ventures.

CANADIAN INSTITUTE FOR HISTORICAL MICROREPRODUCTIONS (CIHM)

The Canadian Institute for Historical Microreproductions (CIHM) was formed in 1978 by the Canada Council as an independent not-for-profit corporation to assist in the preservation of sixteenth-, seventeenth-, eighteenth- and nineteenth-century Canadiana. CIHM's mandate to microfilm and to provide bibliographic access to early Canadian materials converged with the National Library's aims in compiling the retrospective national bibliography, and in 1980 a two-year contractual working relationship between the two institutions was formed. CIHM makes use of National Library collections and automated systems, and its cataloguing group is housed in the National Library's Cataloguing Branch where it has received training by National Library staff in bibliographic standards. CIHM has created AACR2 machine-readable records for the pre-1900 Canadian monographs and pamphlets filmed as part of its preservation microfilming activities. Records in this database are used to upgrade the bibliographic data in *Canadiana 1867–1900: Monographs*.

The records are available in machine-readable form on magnetic tape to purchasers of the microform documents, and are generally available online through the bibliographic utility UTLAS and in the form of a microfiche catalogue titled *Canada: the printed record/Catalogue d'imprimés canadiens*. The National Library expects to mount the CIHM database on the bibliographic system DOBIS (Dortmunder Bibliotheks-Informations-System) in the near future.

Since June 1982 when a new five-year contract was signed, the working relationship between the National Library and CIHM has continued and expanded. Under the terms of this contract, CIHM has undertaken for the National Library the conduct of bibliographic research and creation of machine-readable catalogue records for monographs of Canadian origin or interest published before 1867 (the next RETRO segment). CIHM records refer to microreproductions of documents, so will require modification by the National Library to reflect the bibliographic details of the original documents, for use in the retrospective national bibliography.

EIGHTEENTH-CENTURY SHORT-TITLE CATALOGUE

The emergence of the Eighteenth-Century Short-Title Catalogue (ESTC) in recent years has indirectly influenced the course of Canadian retrospective bibliography by stimulating the interest of historians, researchers and librarians in that period. The increased level of bibliographic activity for this period may lead to greater opportunities for collaboration and pooling of resources.

OTHER COOPERATIVE OPPORTUNITIES

Embarkation of the Resource Network Committee of the National Library Advisory Board on a programme to encourage local initiatives in acquiring, microfilming and providing access (via checklists, etc.) to Canadian newspapers has been mentioned. This effort should pave the way for that segment of RETRO devoted to newspapers and may influence its timing as well. A future RETRO publication on newspapers could conceivably combine the cataloguing and union list functions.

Conclusion

The National Library recognizes the need for a comprehensive and authoritative retrospective bibliography of Canadian works and of publications of Canadian interest, as an essential aid to the historian and scholar in search of Canada's past. Progress in this direction has been slow because of the National Library's need to accord priority to the bibliographic control of current Canadiana when assigning scarce human and financial resources. However, the variety of cooperative arrangements into which the National Library has entered in recent years in the field of retrospective

Canadian bibliography attests not only to the Library's abiding interest in this endeavour but to its growing recognition of the need for the involvement of many players. For example, the National Library has sponsored publication of a number of subject bibliographies and related works, both by its own staff and by other researchers. National Library staff publications include Dorothy Ryder's *Checklist of Canadian directories 1790–1950*[11], Maria Calderisi's *Music publishing in the Canadas, 1800–1867*[12], Edward B Moogk's *Roll back the years: history of Canadian recorded sound and its legacy: genesis to 1930*[13] and Joyce Banks' *Books in native languages in the collection of the Rare Books and Manuscripts Division of the National Library of Canada.*[14]

The National Library also published the earlier-mentioned Tod and Cordingley work, as well as Cimon Morin's *Canadian philately: bibliography and index, 1864–1974*[15] and its *Supplement*[16] and Olga Bishop's *Publications of the governments of Nova Scotia, Prince Edward Island, New Brunswick, 1758–1952*[17] and her *Publications of the government of the province of Canada, 1841–1867.*[18] Current plans are to publish a bibliography of doctoral theses on Canada and Canadians, 1884–1982, compiled by Jesse Dossick.

The National Library, then, views its own general retrospective bibliographic project as part of a two-pronged effort in collaboration with the many individual scholars and librarians working in specialized fields of knowledge.

The relatively recent emergence in Canada of a national consciousness and an attendant interest in Canadian Studies both past and present have brought to the fore the National Library of Canada's long-standing commitment to collecting, preserving and making known the literary heritage and documentary evidence of a nation which has yet been little examined. The wealth of scholarly opportunity represented by the unexplored avenues of research into the Canadian condition is well worth seeking and exploiting, and RETRO will provide some of the very necessary tools along the way.

References

1 National Library Act, R.S.C. ch. N–11
2 *Ibid*
3 Tod, Dorothea D and Audrey Cordingley. *A check list of Canadian imprints, 1900–1925/Catalogue d'ouvrages imprimés au Canada*. Ottawa, King's Printer and Controller of Stationery, 1959
4 *The Canadian catalogue of books published in Canada, about Canada, as well as those written by Canadians, with imprint 1921–1949*. Consolidated English language reprint edition. Toronto, Toronto Public Libraries, 1967
5 *Notices en langue française du Canadian catalogue of books 1921–1949*. Montréal, Bibliothèque nationale du Québec, 1975
6 Tremaine, Marie. *Bibliography of Canadian imprints, 1751–1800*. Toronto, University of Toronto Press, 1952
7 Toronto Public Library. *A bibliography of Canadiana, being items in the Public Library of Toronto, Canada, relating to the early history and development of Canada*. Edited by Frances M Staton and Marie Tremaine, with an introduction by George H Locke. Toronto, The Public Library, 1934

8 – *First supplement.* Edited by Gertrude M Boyle, assisted by Marjorie Colbeck, with an introduction by Henry C Campbell. Toronto, The Public Library, 1959
9 National Conference on the State of Canadian Bibliography, Vancouver, Canada, 22–24 May 1974: *Proceedings.* Edited by Anne B Piternick et al. Ottawa, National Library of Canada, 1977. p.463
10 *Anglo-American Cataloguing Rules. North American Text.* Chicago, American Library Association [c1967].
11 Ryder, Dorothy E. *Checklist of Canadian directories 1790–1950.* Ottawa, Supply and Services Canada, 1979
12 Calderisi, Maria. *Music publishing in the Canadas, 1800–1867.* Ottawa, Supply and Services Canada, 1981.
13 Moogk, Edward B. *Roll back the years: history of Canadian recorded sound and its legacy: genesis to 1930.* Ottawa, Supply and Services Canada, 1975
14 Banks, Joyce M. *Books in native languages in the collection of the Rare Books and Manuscripts Division of the National Library of Canada.* Ottawa, National Library of Canada, 1980
15 Morin, Cimon. *Canadian philately: bibliography and index, 1864–1974.* Ottawa, Supply and Services Canada, 1979
16 – *Supplement.* Ottawa, Supply and Services Canada, 1983
17 Bishop, Olga Bernice. *Publications of the governments of Nova Scotia, Prince Edward Island, New Brunswick, 1758–1952.* Ottawa, National Library of Canada, 1957
18 – *Publications of the government of the province of Canada, 1841–1867.* Ottawa, National Library of Canada, available from the Queen's Printer, 1963

Acknowledgements and bibliography

The author acknowledges the substantial assistance of her special assistant Elizabeth McKeen in the preparation of this paper, as well as the assistance and publications of Dr Michel Thériault, Chief, Retrospective National Bibliography Division, Cataloguing Branch, National Library of Canada.

The reader is referred especially to the following articles.

Lochhead, Douglas G. 'National bibliography – retrospective' *in* National Conference on the State of Canadian Bibliography, Vancouver, Canada, 22–24 May 1974 *Proceedings.* Edited by Anne B Piternick et al. Ottawa, National Library of Canada, 1977. pp.1–16

National Library of Canada. *Canadiana 1867–1900: Monographs: Canada's national bibliography: microfiche edition (an introduction).* Ottawa, 1980

Thériault, Michel. 'Canadiana 1867–1900, Monographs.' *Canadian library journal*, vol.40, no.3, June 1983, p.126–131
– 'Canadiana 1867–1900: Monographs, or the past in modern dress.' Paper presented to the 48th General Conference of the International Federation of Library Associations and institutions, Montreal, 22–28 August 1982
– 'Canadiana 1867–1900, Monographies, ou tout ce qu'il faut connaître sur les voyages, aventures, tribulations et douleurs de croissance d'une bibliographie nationale rétrospective depuis 1953 jusqu'à aujourd'hui.' *Canadian issues*, IV (1982), p.124–136

Louise Filion

La Bibliographie du Québec, 1764–1967

In the context of this Colloquium on Canadian Studies, I would like to introduce briefly the project of retrospective bibliography at present in progress at the Bibliothèque nationale du Québec (BNQ). These notes will give you a general idea of our programme of bibliographic compilation and of its constituent parts. Its contents, scope, methodology and publication programme will illustrate the characteristics of this bibliography which blazes the trail for a true history of publishing in Québec.

By retrospective bibliography, we mean that part of the national bibliography prior to the current bibliography, that is, before 1968. The year 1968 marks the boundary between the two parts of the national bibliography: the current bibliography and the retrospective bibliography.

The retrospective bibliography aims at listing everything published, printed or produced in Québec before 1968. This bibliographic compilation goes back as far as 1764, the year of publication of the first printed document in Quebec City: an order published by the printers Brown & Gilmore. During the period when Canada was a French colony (New France), it was forbidden to import presses and therefore to print. It was only after the Treaty of Paris, which ceded New France to England, that the English authorized Canadians to buy presses and to publish.

This period, covering 204 years of retrospective publishing, is divided into two parts: the first part, from 1764 to 1820, covers 57 years of publishing; the second part, from 1821 to 1967, represents 167 years of publishing: treble the number of years and even more than treble the number of titles. The transition year – 1820 – may be considered arbitrary by some, but it is a stage in the social evolution of the country as well as in the sphere of typographical processes: it marks the passing from the hand-press to the machine-press age.

A former prime minister of Québec, Pierre-Joseph-Olivier Chauveau (1820–1890) along with some writers and bibliophiles is said to have taken the initiative in designating as Canadian incunabula everything published before 1820. In fact, in 1880, Dionne stated that 'it is now recognized that Canadian incunabula do not go beyond the year 1820'.[1]

A. Le Catalogue des impressions québécoises antérieures à 1821

The first part of the retrospective bibliography is known by the title *Catalogue collectif des impressions québécoises antérieures à 1821*. This cooperative project is under way and is coordinated by BNQ with Québec university libraries, the Library of the City of Montreal, and the Library of the Séminaire de Québec. In the first stage, the aim is to put together a collective catalogue of Québec printing prior to 1821, and in the second stage, to make an inventory of documents printed outside Québec but related to Québec by their subject. Started in 1981, the first stage should be complete by the end of 1983. As for the second stage, it will be undertaken eventually.

CONTENTS OF THE COLLECTIVE CATALOGUE

The aim of this catalogue is to list every printed document considered as a monograph, and published from the beginning of printing up to 1820. The collective catalogue will describe the following categories of documents: books, pamphlets, single sheet publications, official publications and annual serials (almanacs and calendars). The 29 magazines and newspapers that began publication before 1821 are excluded from this catalogue.

The number of titles to be contained in this catalogue is estimated at about one thousand two hundred (1,200), of which more than 650 are located at BNQ. The listing of ephemeral publications (prospectuses, administrative forms, calendars and notices of all kinds) constitutes a major contribution to the record of this period of printing. John Hare and Jean-Pierre Wallot have recorded 1,189 printed documents located or known of, between 1764 and 1820; of those, 932 were from Quebec City (78.4%), 255 from Montreal (21.4%) and 2 from Three-Rivers (.02%).[2]

BIBLIOGRAPHIC DESCRIPTION AND INDEXES

The bibliographic description is done according to ISBD(A), the international standard bibliographic description for antiquarian books and to the Library of Congress *Bibliographic Description of Rare Books* for specifications for broadsheets. The specific characteristics of a particular copy belonging to each library are added in the notes. All copies have been seen and located.

This collective catalogue, to be published in 1984, contains eight indexes. They provide access points to the full bibliographic descriptions which are in alphabetical order. All the access points, whose headings are established according to the French edition of AACR2, furnish data for the following indexes:

1 Title index
2 Name index (main & secondary entries)
3 Subject index
4 Categories of documents index

5 Place of publication index
6 Printer-bookseller index
7 Printing date index
8 Provenance index

STATE OF THE PROJECT AND PUBLICATION PROGRAMME

We are in the process of completing work on the comparison of copies and most probably it will be finished by the end of 1983. All the bibliographic descriptions are loaded in the BNQ database and are in a format compatible with the Canadian MARC Format. Together with the collective catalogue, which will be published in early 1984, every participant in the project will get a magnetic tape containing the bibliographic descriptions of titles of monographs in their collections. BNQ is planning to send the bibliographic descriptions of titles prior to 1801 to the NAIP (North American Imprints Program) and to ESTC/NA (Eighteenth-Century Short-Title Catalogue/North America). Once all the data is on magnetic tape or in printed form, this catalogue will ensure not only the UBC (Universal Bibliographical Control) of documents of the 1764–1820 period but also the enhanced utilization, control and location in Québec of old and rare books, namely Canadian incunabula. This catalogue will be a research tool as well as being very useful for purposes of interlibrary loan. It will constitute a new landmark in the history of publishing and of books of the hand-press period.[3]

Now I would like to talk about the second part of the programme of the retrospective bibliography initiated at BNQ at the beginning of the 1970s. The programme of this second part, called the retrospective bibliography, will continue for many years. Started in 1980, this publication is entitled *Bibliographie du Québec, 1821–1967*.

B. The Bibliographie du Québec, 1821–1967

The aim of this bibliography is to compile a complete inventory of material published or printed in Québec between 1821 and 1967. The main purpose of this huge biblipgrahic work is to provide Québec with a complete inventory of its literary heritage. Let us note here that, at the beginning of the work in 1970, this project could not model itself on any other Canadian publication. Bibliographers and collectors had already written and published catalogues of their own collections. One need only mention Gagnon, Dionne, Tremaine. But these catalogues and inventories, though very useful, are incomplete, and cannot replace a true and complete retrospective bibliography of Québec, done 'book in hand'. By publishing this bibliography, we thus take it upon ourselves to assume bibliographic control. This bibliography records everything published whereas a catalogue lists the items of a collection or of a library.

CONTENTS

The aim of this retrospective bibliography is to establish the description of all non-official publications produced in Québec between 1821 and 1967. However, we intend only to describe items published in Québec, which had been estimated at about 150,000 titles. After fourteen years we have re-evaluated the situation and feel that the number is nearer 100,000 titles, including all editions and impressions given separate entries. The bibliography covers only non-official monographs, including the following:

1 Books
2 Pamphlets
3 Schoolbooks
4 Published university theses
5 Offprints
6 Publications which are part of a series
7 Illustrated books
8 Illustrated albums, books and pamphlets
9 Albums and books for children
10 Publications published for advertising (mainly literary or scientific texts)
11 Programmes of shows, exhibitions, fairs, etc; societies' statutes and schedules, guidelines, memorials, etc)
12 Printed music, provided that the text is more important than the musical notation
13 Atlases

The documents in all the above categories are published not only in French, but also in English, various Amerindian languages and languages of other ethnic groups. Subjects covered are predominantly literature, religion and history.

I would like to draw your attention to two types of documents: pamphlets and schoolbooks, both for their contents and the role they have played. In Québec, pamphlets have exerted an influence that deserves full evaluation some day. Their number is due, in great part, to the disputes which occurred throughout the nineteenth century, either between individuals or groups or between the government and individuals, or often between the Church and individuals or groups.

As for schoolbooks, which are relatively numerous and published in large print runs, they have never been listed anywhere. Often originating in religious communities, they have exerted a considerable influence. According to historians and scholars, the publishing of schoolbooks is connected with the appearance of publishing houses at the end of the nineteenth century, such as Beauchemin and Granger.[4]

Finally, I should like to mention two features of our bibliography. The first one is the publishing in Québec, during World War II (1939–1945), of works by French authors. In fact, following an amendment to the Berne Convention on

Copyright, a special exemption allowed Canadian publishers to reproduce works published by French publishers, provided that they were published unabridged and in accordance with the arrangements of the French editions. Of course, Québec publishers took advantage of these provisions. Consequently, works of authors like Victor Hugo, Claudel, Duhamel and others, published in Québec between 1939 and 1947 appear in our retrospective bibliography.

I should also like to mention the phenomenon of para-literature, also called mass or popular literature. Since 1925, this type of literature has been published in regular series. It is now being studied by the Littérature québécoise en fascicules (LIQUEFASC) group of Laval University. We are just beginning to discover this sector of Québec publishing, which was not highly regarded in the past in literary circles. Published in large numbers, some copies have been preserved by avid collectors. The *Aventures étranges de l'agent IXE-13* and many more, delighted Quebecers before the arrival of television in 1953.

This bibliography excludes serials, officially published monographs, maps, musical scores, records and theses. These will eventually be inventorized by BNQ.

METHODOLOGY

Our search for monographs is a two-stage process. First, monographs are searched for in the collections of BNQ whether they are catalogued or not. The library now owns about 42,000 monographs of that period, of which 20,000 are catalogued. Due to the work methodology adopted, which consists in grouping works under author, we started in alphabetical order of author's name. Therefore, works by authors with names beginning with the letter A or B are listed in the first volumes of the retrospective bibliography. Due to a recent move to a more spacious building, we have easy access to the uncatalogued books and we are completing the description of works by authors whose names start with the letters A, B, C, etc. In addition to improving the bibliography, we are, at the same time, making these books accessible to readers of the BNQ.

The majority of the documents described so far are located at the BNQ. When the first phase is completed, we will have described about 50,000 to 55,000 documents owing to increasing acquisitions. We will then begin the second phase consisting in unearthing and describing other monographs published in Québec but located in other libraries, centres and important collections in Québec, Canada, the US and possibly in England, but this all depends on the extent of the holdings of Québec documents. The list being prepared by Dr O'Neill and Professor Ettlinger will permit an evaluation of the BL collection. There are many unknown factors in this collection: the number of documents originating from Québec, the number of non-official monographs, the number of documents already partly or fully listed in the BL catalogue; the partial or selective application of the Copyright Acts to Canada, 1895–1924. To summarize, statistics based on the answers to these questions would give an idea of the size of this collection. According to the statistics that we have compiled, there could have been 19,000 monographs published in Québec between 1901 and 1925. How does the number of items in this collection compare with these 19,000 monographs published between 1901 and 1925?

Retrieval is the preparatory step to a bibliographic description done 'book in hand'. This 'book in hand' description is an important feature of our retrospective bibliography. It causes problems to bibliographers anxious to write a completely definitive description. Books are not always kept as they were when originally printed (missing covers replaced by library bindings, incomplete books, books *sine loco*, *sine nomine*, etc). In short they have suffered the ravages of time!

The bibliographic description follows the rules of ISBD(M) and headings are established according to the French edition of AACR2.

THE PUBLISHING PROGRAMME

Several options are open for those who want to publish a retrospective bibliography. They can publish it periodically, in stages, or in its entirety at the end of compilation. The decision depends mainly on the number of titles, the length of the period, the computer possibilities, and the financial and staff resources the library can afford. We have chosen to publish the retrospective bibliography in stages or by volume, according to the progress of the bibliographic work within a precise publishing programme.

This programme will be spread out over several years. Each volume is in two parts: one of 1,000 entries and one with 6 indexes. The first volume was published in 1980, the sixth and seventh will be published in 1983.

- *Main Entry volume*

The bibliographic records listed in each volume are systematically arranged. An alphabetical or chronological arrangement, recommended by some people, would not have been possible until the completion of the inventory of all monographs published in Québec during this period. However, as we preferred to make the bibliographic data available while the work was still in progress, the computer system, used in the compilation of this bibliography, reduces greatly the disadvantages of this arrangement. The 1,000 entries of each volume are listed alphabetically by author's name following the subdivisions of the Library of Congress classification.

- *Indexes volume*

Each 1,000-entry volume has its twin volume with six indexes. These indexes are compiled to facilitate multi-disciplinary research:

- Author, added entry, title index

This index contains references to personal and corporate names, and to titles. It is an indispensable addition to any national bibliography, be it current or retrospective.

● Publisher index

This index lists together under each publisher's name all the publications he has produced. It is often consulted for works about publishing history in Québec. It plays in part the role of inadequate reference works, which lack publishers' directories or statistics by publishing houses.

We have already made three findings from the work done:
1. There are few publishers still in existence from the period 1821–1967. Numerous publishing houses disappeared after World War II due to all kinds of difficulties.
2. Religious communities, who owned many schools, have published a lot of schoolbooks.
3. Finally, newspapers have acted as publishers of a certain number of brochures and books.

● Printer index

The publications of each printer are grouped together in this index which is complementary to the publisher index. This index shows the confusion that exists between the terms: in the nineteenth century, the same person often played the role of publisher, bookseller, printer.

● Chronological index

All items are listed chronologically. This index will later give interesting statistical data for the history of publishing in Québec. Hypotheses might then be confirmed or invalidated.

We can already give partial answers to two questions:
1. How many titles were published each year, every 10, 20, 25 years, during the 147 year period?
2. Can we notice a constant increase in the number of titles published from 1821 to 1967?

It is clear that a definitive answer to these two questions will be available in a few years when the work is more advanced. But fragmentary answers given in

Evaluation of the number of titles by period

PERIODS	VOLUMES I TO V	%	NUMBER OF TITLES ON 100 000
1821–1850	157	3.14	3 140
1851–1875	487	9.74	9 740
1876–1900	800	16.00	16 000
1901–1925	950	19.00	19 000
1926–1950	1 456	29.12	29 120
1951–1967	1 150	23.00	23 000
Total	5 000	100.00	100 000

1983 give some indication and allow for some extrapolation. Thus, from the first 5,000 entries (volumes 1 to 5) we have made cross-checks by periods of 25 years. From this compilation and with all due reservation, there seems to be a constant progression in the number of titles published. If we accept the fact that 100,000 monographs were published, about 19,000 monographs would have been published between 1901 and 1925. According to partial statistics, there would have been a constant increase of publications each year; around one hundred per annum between 1821 and 1850 and more than 1,353 between 1951 and 1967.

- Place of publication index

Under each place of publication, one finds references to items described. There is one hypothesis to check: if the city of Québec published 78% of all the production between 1764 and 1820 it seems that the centre of publication moved to Montréal between 1821 and 1967. We still have to check around what year and by what percentage.

- Onomastical subject index

We hesitated between the PRECIS system and the subject headings arrangement. Neither of these analytical systems was accepted. The onomastical index chosen is complementary to the methodical arrangement of items. It provides access to proper names used as subject headings; personal, corporate and place names.

Conclusion

In conclusion, I would like to remind you that these two projects represent an original and special contribution to the inventory of the literary heritage of Québec. They provide research tools for researchers who want to elaborate new hypotheses. And with automation, an essential aid these days for document data, we can make hitherto unimaginable cross-checks. For about ten years, many studies on the history of publishing in Québec came from university and research circles. We would like to mention the Groupe de recherche en histoire de l'imprimé au Québec (GRHIQ) and the Institut québecois de recherche sur la culture (IQRC). But it is only gradually that researchers will write a true history of publishing in Québec.

On a long term basis these two projects (the collective catalogue and the retrospective bibliography) will make available all the lesser known, unlocated, uncatalogued documentation, often lovingly preserved in attics, in dusty archives, in private collections of schoolbooks, brochures, history books or serial literature, in Québec as much as in Canada or Europe. Quebecers have a reputation of being thrifty but they are also protectors, guardians of this heritage whose extent we have yet to discover.

References

1 Hare, John et Wallot, Jean-Pierre. *Les Imprimés au Québec (1760–1820)*. In: Lamonde, Yvan éd. *L'Imprimé au Québec, aspects historiques (18e–20e siècles)*. Québec, Institut québécois de recherche sur la culture, 1983 (Collection: culture savante no 2). p.83
2 Hare, *op. cit.*, p.2
3 See also the article by Vlach, Milada. *Catalogue collectif des impressions québécoises antérieures à 1821*. Bulletin de la Bibliothèque nationale du Québec. Vol. 16, no 1, mars 1982, pp.15–17
4 Robert, Lucie. *Prolégomènes à une étude sur les transformations du marché du livre au Québec (1900–1940)*. In: Lamonde, Yvan, éd. *L'Imprimé au Québec, aspects historiques (18e–20e siècles)*. Québec, Institut québécois de recherche sur la culture, 1983. (Collection: culture savante no 2). pp.225–242

[Modified version of the English translation provided by Mme Filion: complete French text available from the French Section, British Library Reference Division.]

Patricia L Fleming

A Descriptive Bibliography of Upper Canada Imprints, 1801–1841

This progress report is appropriate for a British Library Colloquium since the study was initiated under the direction of the late Howard M Nixon using nineteenth-century Canadian imprints in the British Library.

I will begin with a definition of scope, then outline methodology and conclude with some observations about printing in Upper Canada (now Ontario).

The first eight years of the press are already recorded in Marie Tremaine's *A Bibliography of Canadian Imprints, 1751–1800*.[1] A handful of items not identified or located in Tremaine will form a preliminary section of my sequel to her work. 1841, the closing date, marks the Act of Union which reunited Upper and Lower Canada (Québec) to create the Province of Canada.

Scope has been expanded from an original limit of books, pamphlets, and serials to include broadsides and broadsheets. Many of the examples which have survived are too important as research materials and as evidence about printing to exclude or to separate from related items in a different format.

The printed sources most useful for identifying and locating imprints are the published catalogues of three outstanding collections: *A Bibliography of Canadiana* now in the Metropolitan Toronto Central Library[2]; the catalogues of the Library of the Public Archives of Canada in Ottawa[3]; and *The Lawrence Lande Collection of Canadiana in the Redpath Library of McGill University* in Montréal[4].

Access to other collections of Canadiana varies from the bibliographer's ideal library with its file of Canadian imprints arranged chronologically, to the splendid chaos of collections grouped only by broad subject with tantalizingly brief short-title lists. And of course the search for imprints must go beyond libraries to museums, historical societies, and archives of every size, from individual churches to provincial and national collections.

The importance of informal networks in scholarly communication is already recognized; I will only note that mine is working well. Librarians, archivists, and other colleagues have been notifying me of new acquisitions and suggesting other collections to visit. This summer (1983) the Canadian Institute for Historical Microreproductions is searching selected manuscript groups in the Public Archives of Canada to locate pre-Confederation printed items for filming. The Director, Ernie Ingles, has given me access to his file which appears to contain a significant number of previously unseen imprints.

Carrying the hunt for imprints back to contemporary printed sources has confirmed the value of newspapers. Literally hundreds of books were proposed or offered for sale, noted, praised or denounced in the weekly press and once a title is identified there it can be searched in a catalogue or union list. Unique imprints first noted in newspapers have been traced to the Library of Congress, Harvard and Brown Universities, the Universities of Chicago and Maryland, and the Presbyterian Historical Society in Philadelphia as well as to collections in Canada.

Newspapers are also providing evidence about other, unrecorded, newspapers. The editors tended to comment on new ventures in journalism in their districts, often naming the printer, remarking on his politics, and commending paper and typography. There was also a good deal of borrowing and quoting by editors, a practice which documents for modern researchers the existence of a particular journal. To date more than thirty Upper Canadian newspapers not recorded in the *Union List of Canadian Newspapers Held by Canadian Libraries*[5] have been firmly identified and a third of them examined. A directory of all the papers will form an appendix to the bibliography. A second appendix, a biographical directory of the printing trade, is also based in part on a thorough search of the newspapers.[6] Editorials, the annual newsboy's address, obituaries, marriage and birth announcements are all sources of information about the activities of members of the trade.

At this stage in the project I have described approximately one thousand books, pamphlets, and serials and I do not expect to discover any more than a hundred additional imprints for the final total. However I am still trying to see, within fiscal and geographic reason, all available copies of each title. The rewards of dedication to the principles of descriptive bibliography are not startling but they are real. My sixth copy of Toronto's first directory is rebound, as are the others, but rebound retaining wrappers printed with 'Errata and Additions Since the Alphabetical List Went to Press'. This is the copy for CIHM to film since it is the most complete.

For the coming year, 1983–4, the emphasis is on broadsides, again with the support of the Social Sciences and Humanities Research Council of Canada for travel, research, and technical assistance. A cautious estimate of the total of surviving broadsides is five hundred, the majority unique.

To turn from the methodology of the search to results is to offer some preliminary notes for a publishing history of Upper Canada. The thousand imprints mentioned earlier come from more than a hundred printing offices in thirty towns in Upper Canada. Virtually all were newspaper presses where the proprietor, who was often editor and printer as well, supplied his community with a weekly paper, handbills, notices, and a few pamphlets or books such as an almanac, a particularly well-received local sermon, or a standard reader or primer. The output of certain short-lived pioneer presses appears to have been limited to one or two such titles while, in the capital, Robert Stanton, government printer from 1826 to 1841, published more than one hundred and fifty imprints, many not connected with his official duties.

In Upper Canada the press was not licensed nor was there a tax on knowledge in the form of stamp duty. Printers were governed only by the harsh demands of the market which shortened many careers, and the laws of libel which interrupted others. An example of the latter is Bartimus Ferguson, a native of Vermont. At Niagara in 1819 he was fined, sentenced to eighteen months in jail and the pillory for printing seditious libel by Robert Fleming Gourlay, a Scottish reformer jailed and banished from Upper Canada that same year. Ferguson, who was spared the pillory and served a reduced sentence, later resumed his career in Niagara, worked as a foreman in Toronto, and started a paper in nearby Hamilton.

At Toronto a decade later Francis Collins, an Irish editor and printer, who libelled the Attorney General while reporting his own libel trial was fined and jailed for forty-five weeks. He continued his paper, the *Canadian Freeman*, from his cell and also fulfilled a contract with the government as recorded in a later investigation of printing for the House of Assembly: 'In 1829 Mr Collins, then in jail, did the body of the journal.'[7]

William Lyon Mackenzie, a contemporary of Collins, was never imprisoned in Upper Canada although he fled the province in 1837 with a hefty price on his head. Mackenzie had founded the *Colonial Advocate* in 1824 to criticize the government, and seldom wavered from this commitment even as a member of the House of Assembly and particularly when he was four times expelled by the Tory majority to be re-elected each time by the voters of York. He was the first mayor of Toronto following incorporation in 1834 and then became leader of the unsuccessful rebellion of 1837. Following amnesty Mackenzie returned to Toronto in 1850 and was elected to parliament defeating another Scottish journalist, George Brown, founder of the *Globe*.

In comparison with their flamboyant publishers the products of the Upper Canadian press are somewhat staid; more than half deal with God and government. The first representative of the latter, John Graves Simcoe, recruited a printer in Québec on the way to his new capital at Niagara-on-the-Lake; the earliest broadside printed there in 1793 launched a steady stream of official proclamations, sessional laws and, later, journals of the elected House of Assembly and the appointed Legislative Council. There were committee reports as well, dealing at first with trade and serious matters such as the importation of tea, but gradually reflecting the rise of the reform movement in the late 1820s. Its landmark publication is the report known as 'Seventh Grievances' printed in an edition of two thousand in 1835.[8] Sir Francis Bond Head, the lieutenant-governor, wrote of it: 'a large octavo grievance volume, in boards, containing 553 closely-printed pages; and it has been calculated (I believe accurately) that there exist in this book more than three times as many gross falsehoods as pages.'[9] William Lyon Mackenzie who chaired the committee and is generally regarded as the author of the report was selling copies at five shillings and describing it as 'nearly as big as the Bible'.[10]

Moving from government to God we do not find many bibles with an Upper Canadian imprint although Mackenzie himself printed a New Testament from American stereotype plates in 1837.[11] The staples of religious publishing were church administration, sermons and religious controversy. A protagonist in many disputes was a political priest, John Strachan or John Toronto as he was known after he was finally appointed bishop. Upper Canada did not have an established church but Strachan's links with the ruling Family Compact and his seat on the Legislative Council ensured a privileged place for the Church of England. One of the most persistent issues was the disposition of revenues from the Clergy Reserves, comprising one-seventh of all lands in the province, which had been set aside in 1791 for the support of a Protestant clergy, interpreted as meaning the Church of England. Both the Methodists and the Presbyterians protested in print and at length. Strachan and Egerton Ryerson, his Methodist counterpart in ability and influence, are represented in the British Library's collection.

Imprints reflecting the presence of minority religions are less numerous, but Baptists, Mennonites and Catholics all made use of the press, as did the American Quakers living north of Toronto. The British Library has copies of two works by David Willson who, following his expulsion from the Quaker's Yonge Street Meeting, founded the Children of Peace, a communal sect noted for its musical worship.[12]

Missionary work with the natives of Upper Canada required imprints in their languages, such as Mohawk primers, hymns, and psalms, and in Chippewa, a speller, a collection of hymns, two editions of Genesis, and the Gospel of Matthew which the British Library has in the original cloth binding.[13] Mennonites in Waterloo county began publishing prayer and hymn books for their community in German in the 1830s while the Scots of Toronto had a Gaelic catechism in 1835.[14]

Imprints answering the needs of daily life in Upper Canada include almanacs and school books where editions of British authors like Lindley Murray and William Mavor outnumber Americans such as Noah Webster. Notable among the textbooks produced by local educators is *An Introduction to Greek Declension & Conjugation* lithographed by Samuel Tazewell who introduced that art to the province.[15]

On the medical side there were three editions of Samuel Thomson's *New Guide to Health: or, Botanic Family Physician* in the early 1830s as well as a manual on the care of the teeth. The cholera epidemics of 1832 and 1834 which killed hundreds of immigrants and Upper Canadians, including the printer Francis Collins, are commemorated by two books about the disease published in 1832 and 1835.

Although the almanacs mentioned earlier contained practical advice for farmers and hints and recipes for housekeepers, two separate cookbooks were published as well. The first was an edition of an American work, *The Cook Not Mad*;[16] the second was original, *The Frugal Housewife's Manual*.[17] For the farmer there was a pamphlet on growing tobacco in the province and two catalogues of nursery stock, consulted now by researchers planning gardens for historical sites.

Social organizations, judged from the evidence of surviving imprints, appear at first to have developed from religious and charitable activities with the establishment in the 1820s of bible and missionary societies and the SPCK. Toronto also had a Society for the Relief of Strangers in Distress and another for Poor Women in Childbirth. In the 1830s political, national, agricultural, and literary organizations had their rules and proceedings printed while the Society of Artists and Amateurs published a catalogue of its first exhibition in 1834. The parallel development of financial institutions can also be traced through publications such as the reports of banks and stock companies. Evidence of Canada's well-founded preoccupation with transportation is apparent in imprints dealing with steam navigation, construction of the Welland and Rideau Canals, techniques of road making, and the beginning of the railway boom in the mid-1830s.

Original works of literature are outnumbered by many other subjects, but the foundations of a Canadian literary tradition are apparent. The first novel, Julia Beckwith Hart's *St Ursula's Convent, or The Nun of Canada*, was published in 1824.[18] Mrs Hart, who kept a school in Kingston where her husband worked as a bookbinder, included in the preliminaries a list of 165 subscriptions to the work. The following year *Wonders of the West, or A Day at the Falls of Niagara*, the first book of verse, was published, like the first novel, anonymously.[19] Between 1831 and 1833 four literary magazines were started, two in Toronto and two in Hamilton, but none survived longer than two years. Only one gift annual was ventured before 1841, *The Canadian Forget Me Not* of 1837.[20] The tradition of street literature was better observed with publication in both broadside and pamphlet form of dying confessions by several repentant murderers, including one young Toronto printer.

My final category, biography, is one of the smallest; the example I am citing may well have discouraged every such enterprise in Upper Canada for the next decade. In 1831 Henry Chapman of Niagara announced the publication by subscription of the Family Library combining in one extra gilt octavo four volumes of Murray's Family Library series: the lives of Alexander the Great, Mohammed, Lord Nelson, and Lord Byron. He reminded readers that this edition at two dollars fifty cost one dollar less than its American counterpart. The project, commended by editors in the province for its benefit to the community, was completed in November of 1831. One year later a Niagara newspaper announced that copies of the Family Library were to be sold at auction; they had been assigned to Thomas Sewell, the binder, in security for debt. There remained 800 copies in sheets, 174 in boards, and 216 sewed, indicating a print run of at least 1,190 copies for a scattered, largely rural population of fewer than 240,000 in all of Upper Canada.

The publisher Henry Chapman is unlikely to find a place in an economic history of Upper Canada but he will be a superstar in the printing history which is waiting to be written.

References

1. Marie Tremaine, *A Bibliography of Canadian Imprints, 1751–1800* (Toronto: University of Toronto Press, 1952)
2. Toronto Public Library, *A Bibliography of Canadiana* (Toronto: Public Library, 1934); *First Supplement* (Toronto: Public Library, 1959)
3. Public Archives of Canada. Library, *Catalogue of the Public Archives Library*, 12 vols. (Boston: G K Hall, 1979): *Catalogue of Pamphlets in the Public Archives of Canada*, 2 vols. (Ottawa: King's Printer, 1931–32)
4. *The Lawrence Lande Collection of Canadiana in the Redpath Library of McGill University* (Montreal: Lawrence Lande Foundation for Canadian Historical Research, 1965)
5. *Union List of Canadian Newspapers Held by Canadian Libraries* (Ottawa: National Library of Canada, 1977)
6. The style will be consistent with Elizabeth Hulse's *A Dictionary of Toronto Printers, Publishers, Booksellers and the Allied Trades, 1798–1900* (Toronto: Anson-Cartwright, 1982)
7. Upper Canada. Parliament (11th, 1st session: 1831). House of Assembly, *Journal* (York: John Carey, 1831), p.87
8. Upper Canada. House of Assembly. Select Committee on Grievances, *The Seventh Report* (Toronto: M Reynolds, 1835)
9. Francis Bond Head, *A Narrative* (London: John Murray; Toronto: Robert Stanton, 1839), p.7
10. *Correspondent and Advocate*, 3 December 1835; 3 March 1836
11. *The Productions of the Evangelists and Apostles* (Toronto: William Lyon Mackenzie, 1837)
12. David Willson, *The Impressions of the Mind* (Toronto: 1835); *Letters to the Jews* (Toronto: W J Coates, 1835)
13. Bible. N T Matthew. Chippeway, *Mesah Oowh Menwahjemoowin, Kahenahjemood owh St Matthew* (York: Colonial Advocate, 1831)
14. Westminster Assembly. Shorter Catechism. Gaelic, *Leabhar Aithghearr A'Cheasnachaidh* (Toronto: 1835)
15. *An Introduction to Greek Declension & Conjugation* (Toronto: S O Tazewell, 1833)
16. *The Cook Not Mad* (Kingston: James Macfarlane, 1831)
17. A B of Grimsby, *The Frugal Housewife's Manual* (Toronto: J H Lawrence, 1840)
18. Julia Beckwith Hart, *St Ursula's Convent, or The Nun of Canada* (Kingston: Hugh C Thomson, 1824)
19. James Lynne Alexander, *Wonders of the West, or A Day at the Falls of Niagara* (York: Charles Fothergill, 1825)
20. *The Canadian Forget Me Not* (Niagara: Thomas Sewell, 1837)

Ernest B Ingles

Canada's printed heritage – a microfiche collection and preservation project: the work of the Canadian Institute for Historical Microreproductions

In December last I had the privilege of meeting Alex Wilson and outlining for him the work of the Canadian Institute for Historical Microreproductions (CIHM). During our discussions he informed me of the British Library's intention of sponsoring a Colloquium to consider the role of the Library in terms of its support for Canadian Studies. Part of the programme, he suggested, would be devoted to Canadian projects which could demand considerable involvement by the whole of the British library community as well as by his own institution. The Institute, he felt, represented just such a project. He was, of course, correct and I am honoured for the invitation to speak to you about our work.

To understand the need for the services offered by the Institute and to understand its need for your assistance is to appreciate the historical bibliography of nineteenth-century Canada as well as the development and growth of Canadiana collections in the nation's libraries and archives. To understand the particular influences which converged to recommend in 1978 the establishment of the Institute is to appreciate: firstly, the constituted regional shape of the Canadian library network; secondly, the physical impermanence of the Canadian retrospective printed heritage; and thirdly, the impact of the argument, eloquently presented by Professor Thomas Symons in the *Report of the Commission on Canadian Studies*, that 'if a Canadian is to seek the self-knowledge that is essential for both health and wisdom, he must have access to a wider self-knowledge of his historical community . . . '[1]. Since time and circumstances prevent a full treatment of these themes today, the following synopsis will attempt to provide such explanation as is necessary to present the context of the Institute's project and its need for the cooperation, involvement and indulgence of British libraries and librarians.

On face value, the work of the Institute is only tangentially related to the history of printing and book publishing in Canada in the period before 1900. The identification and description of those end-products of publishing, whether at home or abroad, which have Canadian imprints, authors or subject matter is the Institute's concern. But, cursory examination of the early book trade does reveal the existence of a number of structural constraints which were to become institutionalized in the cultural agencies of the Dominion and which, in turn, came to complicate the work of the Institute.

Printing and publishing began in Canada in the year 1751/52 with the establishment of the first press at Halifax in the colony of Nova Scotia. The spread of printing was slow. It was not until late in the nineteenth century that all of those jurisdictions, which today we call provinces, could boast a productive press.[2] Moreover, as H Pearson Gundy pointed out in his study *Book Publishing and Publishers in Canada Before 1900*, 'no valid distinction could be made between Canadian printer and Canadian publisher'[3] for much of the period. The staple products of the early colonial printer/publisher were newsheets, business and legal forms, legislative materials, handbills and broadsides, almanacs, school primers, religious publications as well as light tracts on various practical subjects. Larger works of imagination, thought or research either by Canadians or on Canadian topics were published in Canada but their numbers were few. Most were imported from England or the United States. On those few occasions when a work published in Canada achieved international recognition, the Canadian publisher was not equipped to meet the demand. Subsequent editions or works by the same author were usually published elsewhere. The books of Thomas Chandler Haliburton can be cited as examples. In addition, better financial terms lured Canadian writers to publishers abroad. As James Douglas Jr told the Literary and Historical Society of Québec in 1875:

A Colonial publisher knows his own interest too well to give anything worth while for a manuscript which, if he publish it, will be likely not to meet with sale enough to cover cost of printing . . . A Canadian book is sure, with the stigma of a colonial imprimatur upon it, not to circulate beyond the confines of the Dominion and, therefore, when a Canadian writes a meritorious book . . . he seeks a publisher abroad.[4]

Commercial pragmatism was not the only impediment to the growth of the book trade in Canada. Development was hampered by a surplus of geography, a forbidding topography and the psychological and mercantile colonialism of the population. Progress toward an indigenous publishing industry was further repressed by the Imperial Copyright Acts of 1842 and 1847. By denying compensation to Canadian authors or publishers for books reprinted in the United States, by facilitating the American manufacture of British books in cheap editions for export to Canada and by permitting, under certain circumstances, the forfeiture of a Canadian writer's copyright in Great Britain, the Acts measurably affected the health of the trade in the colony. Speaking to the Royal Society of Canada in 1884, William Kirby said:

Those great American publishing houses control the book trade of the continent – they are gradually rooting out the last remnant of bookmaking and book-publishing in

Canada. Pressed on the one side by the English copyright law and on the other by American piracy of English books, reprints of which now fill our Dominion book shops, Canadian book publishing has become almost a lost industry among us, and with it Canadian authorship fails likewise, for authorship without publishers is like the voice of one crying in the wilderness.'[5]

Kirby's criticism was unnecessarily harsh. The publishing industry was expanding in the last quarter of the century. Publishers such as Graeme Mercer Adam, John Lovell, William Briggs, Robert Hunter, George Ross, George Desbarats, Charles Beauchemin and Augustin Coté had made significant contributions. However, quantitative imprint analysis of 65,000 monographic titles printed before 1901 and defined in standard fashion as 'Canadiana' shows that only 59% of the publications carried a Canadian imprint, 16% were published in Great Britain, 18% in the United States, 3% in France and 4% elsewhere. And, even though the percentage of documents published in Canada was increasing as the century came to a close, the character of the trade and its publications remained constant. Qualitative analysis, necessarily subjective in nature, reaffirms the regionalism inherent in the industry and the utilitarian nature of the publications.

The forces which contributed to the regionalism of Canadian publishing in the nineteenth century, ie distance, population density, and cultural duality, also contributed to the strong regional base of the Canadian library network. This, in turn, gave rise to regional collections of nineteenth-century Canadiana and not to a single national collection of overwhelming size or importance on the scale of the British Library or the Library of Congress. Even so, the local collections today are disconcertingly uneven. Their holdings reflect a history of inspired attention or benign neglect. Periods of energetic collecting activity can be attributed to personal initiatives. As various forces and influences came together to shape the Canadian library movement in the nineteenth and early twentieth centuries, it was the inspired public official or private collector who salvaged for posterity the often-ravaged collections of the disbanding rural reading rooms, historical societies, athenaeums and mechanics' institutes. From such sources came the core titles and regional collecting impetus for institutions like the Nova Scotia Legislative Library, the Fraser-Hickson Institute and numerous major metropolitan public libraries.

Many local Canadiana collections had their origins as private libraries. The Library of the Public Archives of British Columbia is a good example. It was started in the late nineteenth century by Archer Martin, a judge of the British Columbia Supreme Court and descendant of 'Humanity Dick' Martin, the Regency beau and founder of the Royal Society for the Prevention of Cruelty to Animals. Subsequent enlightened curators have created an outstanding library of the Pacific North-West. Similarly, we might look at the Library of the New Brunswick Museum. In the Museum's division of printed books the bibliophilic identity of two collectors of maritime materials, W F Ganong and J C Webster, has been preserved. In addition, the division boasts a collection of nineteenth-century New Brunswick printed documents which, in terms of its size, is the finest in the country. Regrettably, fifty years of inadequate financial support, precipitated by a stagnant provincial economy, is responsible for such physical deterioration of the collection as makes unlikely its usefulness for research even in the short term.

There are numerous other examples of good regional collections of retrospective Canadiana. Notable among these might be: the Library and Archives of the Glenbow Institute; the Shortt Collection of the University of Saskatchewan; the Regional History Room of the University of Western Ontario; the Dennis Collection at Acadia University; and the Centre for Newfoundland Studies at Memorial University. All these collections are under considerable user-pressure with predictable consequences on the physical condition of the materials.

The holdings of these and like repositories account for much of the Canadian printed record. But, it would be an act of presumption, if not folly, to suggest that there are no collections of Canadiana in the country which are national in scope. A substantial collection exists at the University of Toronto, split between the main John P Robarts Research Library, the Thomas Fisher Rare Book Room and several of the University's affiliated colleges. A few short blocks away stands the cavernous Toronto Metropolitan Central Library with its acclaimed collection of pre-Confederation Canadiana. The collections of McGill University libraries might be similarly classed with those of the University of Toronto although the holdings are neither as extensive nor as representative of the outlying regions of the country.

Several broadly-based collections of pre-1900 Canadiana belong to or originated in religious orders or ecclesiastical foundations. Truly outstanding is the Canadian collection in the library of the Séminaire de Québec. The Séminaire was founded in 1663 by Bishop François de Laval. The venerable library can date its bibliographic lineage at least thirty years earlier to the foundation in 1635 of the Collège des Jésuites. This was one year before the establishment of Harvard University. The present day Bibliothèque nationale du Québec can trace its origins back through a number of name changes and institutional transformations to the Sulpician œuvre des bons livres of 1844. The Library's direct antecedent, the Bibliothèque Saint-Sulpice, acquired a number of private collections and absorbed the libraries of several Montreal-based institutions, thus building its Canadiana collection. In 1961 the Bibliothèque came under the jurisdiction of the Ministère des affaires culturelles of the Québec provincial government. Since that time, under the able stewardship of its librarians, the Library has strengthened its collections giving special attention to the acquisition of printed documentation relating to French Canada.

Finally, as inadequate as this survey is of retrospective Canadiana resources, it would be incomplete without recognition of the collections at the National Library of Canada and the Public Archives of Canada. The National Library was officially created in January, 1953. The story of its development is best told by Sister Francis Dolores Donnelly in her book, *The National Library of Canada, A Historical Analysis* . . .[6] For our purpose it is important to know that upon its creation the Library was not heir to a substantive retrospective Canadiana collection. While it received and accessioned more than 250,000 volumes transferred from the Library of Parliament, most of these were not pre-1900 Canadiana titles. The Library of Parliament, while maintaining respectable Canadiana holdings particularly in its pamphlet collection did not itself fully meet expectation, given the continuity of its development from the first establishment of the Legislative Libraries of Upper and Lower Canada in 1791–1792, through the amalgamation of these Libraries in 1841 and finally to the constitution of the present Library in 1871. This could be attributed either to our forefathers' regrettable habit of regularly burning the Library in fits of political pique; or alternatively sinking it in the frigid waters of the St Lawrence or Ottawa Rivers as it followed the itinerant government to Kingston, Toronto, Montreal, Québec, and finally Ottawa. Possibly, the superficiality of holdings might relate to the inexplicable but clearly negligent handling by early government officials of our deposit collection of copyrighted materials as recently outlined by my countrymen Patrick O'Neill and John Ettlinger.[7] Whatever the reason, the National Library has had to rely on the uncertainties of the antiquarian marketplace to create over the past twenty-five years its Canadiana collection. Given the consequent limitations, the Library's present holdings, augmented as they are by the superb collection of pamphlets in the Library of the Public Archives of Canada, represent an admirable achievement.

What about the question of the deterioration of all these collections? Little need be said to this audience. The past fifteen years have seen a growing awareness of the problem. The professional literature is burgeoning with informative articles, with reports of preservation assessments and with notices of curatorial workshops.[8] Even the popular press has recognized the significance of the issue. Articles and headlines such as: 'From Rags to Ruin' in the *Atlantic Monthly*; 'Acid in paper eating all books at libraries' in the Toronto *Globe and Mail*; and 'Millions of books disintegrating in nation's libraries' in the unlikely tabloid, the *National Enquirer*, all attest to the growing concern over the issue. National libraries and international library organizations have also responded to the problem. As an example, the Advisory Board of the National Library of Canada endorsed a National Preservation Programme in April 1979.[9] This was a response to the negative findings of its own national investigation of a year earlier.[10]

To recapitulate, the pre-1900 Canadian printed record was substantial in size; it was larger, in fact, than many people have supposed. But a disproportionately high percentage of that record was published abroad. Today, many of these publications cannot be located in the country. Those titles which carry a Canadian imprint were functional in purpose. They were generally used and cast aside. If they have survived at all, they are usually scarce and in a fragile condition. Indeed, most Canadiana, whether printed at home or abroad, is now endangered for it was produced well within the era of wood-pulp book papers noted for high levels of alum-rosin size.

That which presently exists of this record in Canada can be found in a network of regional repositories. Between regions the collections tend to be mutually exclusive. Those few collections which are broader in scope and depth contain only a segment of the total record. Even these tend to be regional in the sense that they focus on central Canada. As such, they also overlap one with the other. Their concentration in the industrial heartland of the country further diminishes their usefulness for research.

It was these realities which prompted the Consultative Group on University Research Libraries to issue two warnings to the Canada Council in 1977. They stated:

One striking and, to us, important characteristic of research collections . . . was their weakness in Canadian materials. Collections of Canadiana are poor at most libraries and incomplete overall. A great deal of Canadiana is not preserved anywhere within the country.[11]

They went on to say:

. . . Not only is it difficult to obtain access to Canadiana, but books are rapidly deteriorating . . . We are faced with the alarming prospect that students in future generations will have very little early Canadian material to study, unless some large and constructive measures are taken immediately.[12]

The Council, perhaps more than any agency save the Commission on Canadian Studies, realized the interest in contemporary and retrospective research on Canadian topics. Students and researchers were turning in increasing numbers to the study of Canada's social, political, economic, literary and scientific past. This growing interest was reflected at the university and college level by increased enrolment in Canadian courses and by the establishment of formal Canadian studies programmes.[13] The heightened interest of the general public was recognized by their increased use of regional archives and libraries. But the message which the Council received from the library community, through the Consultative Group, was that they were poorly equipped to support this study and research, especially with regard to retrospective materials. If they were to assist in the pursuit of 'self-knowledge', particularly as that pursuit entailed 'a constant effort to recapture the past through historical recollection'[14] they were in a desperate state. As one west-coast librarian has said: 'far-reaching programmes . . . [were needed in order] . . . that our students and researchers [would] have [even] reasonable opportunities to obtain access to the materials they require'.[15] It seemed commonsense that all universities would be able to support a markedly wider range of teaching and research if they were given access to the corpus of the national literature. It was presumed as a corollary that no serious desire for 'self-knowledge' could permit indefinitely the continued over-use of fragile and embrittled historical documents without jeopardizing this heritage for future generations of researchers.

To these arguments the Council responded quickly and decisively. On 17 January 1978 it created the Institute with a mandate:

- To ensure the preservation in Canada and elsewhere of written material by Canadians or about Canada or Canadians;
- to collect, store and distribute such material in microreproduction;
- to make such material already in the country more easily available to all Canadians; and specifically, to facilitate access to such material by the compiling of appropriate catalogues;
- to make such material not now in Canada available to Canadian libraries;
- to make such material as is rare or scarce more widely available;
- to bring together fragmented collections of such material.

In the five years since its establishment the Institute believes it has made progress towards the objectives set by the Council. Individuals with diverse specialties, ranging from bibliographic expertise to micrographic expertise, have been assembled into a unique team. Researchers, borrowing heavily and gratefully from the methodologies for retrospective bibliographic research developed by the ESTC project, have investigated over 200 repositories which hold materials of interest to the project. Over 65,000 monographic titles have been identified, located and described. Permissions have been negotiated with these same institutions for the filming of titles in their collections. Filming centres have been established across the country and in the United States. By the end of 1983 over 30,000 titles will have been filmed. These titles will be fully catalogued and subject analysed. In bibliographic support of the collection the Institute publishes an annually cumulating catalogue, entitled *Canada: The Printed Record: A Bibliographic Register with Indexes – Catalogue d'imprimés canadiens: Répertoire bibliographique avec index.* This tool provides unprecedented access to the collection. Machine-readable bibliographic data is also made available in CAN/MARC format from the Institute or through the bibliographic utilities UTLAS and OCLC. All titles in the catalogue have been distributed to libraries, archives and researchers in Canada. Outside Canada the collection is distributed by University Microfilms International and Information Publications International.

Whether or not our achievements will meet the initial expectation must await the project's completion and the critical review of the research community. We have, however, had some response on our contribution to date. An objective of the project was to make mutually accessible the literatures of our vibrant regional traditions: to give the Nova Scotian access to the printed heritage of British Columbia and *vice versa*. This we have done.

But the reverse has also been the case. We were able to supply a local historian in Victoria, British Columbia, with printed documents issued by that province's first printer/publisher and available only in a library in New Brunswick. Similarly, the historian working on the Riel rebellions acquired materials available previously only in the Michigan State University Libraries. The researcher studying nineteenth-century German emigration to Canada at the J F Kennedy Institut in Berlin easily accessed *Briefe an die Mennonisten Gemeine in Ober Canada* (1840) published in Berlin, Upper Canada. The academician writing a new biography of the nineteenth-century politician Edward Blake was able to obtain copies of all of Blake's published works. Previously, the holdings of seventeen libraries would have needed to be consulted.

These examples, among many, have encouraged us in our work. Perhaps they might best be summarized by quoting a recent letter from noted art historian Professor François-Marc Gagnon of the Université de Montréal. Professor Gagnon turned to the Institute for assistance in his work on 'le "mythe" du Saguenay dans la première littérature de voyages au Canada'. The documents he needed were scarce and they were scattered both in the country and outside. In thanking the Institute for its assistance, Professor Gagnon wrote:

Up to now I had heard of the kind of services the Institute was able to provide but now I know they are incredibly good and important. They should have a profound impact on the development of the history of Canada and on Canadian history. The access to primary sources makes all the difference. It is the possibility to have in a file box the equivalent of a whole library, and of a library undreamed of before in Canada. I used to say after visiting the great American Libraries (The John Carter Brown, the Huntington Library, the Library of Congress, etc) and Libraries like the Bibliothèque nationale in Paris, that we lived in Timbouktou in terms of research. But it seems to me that due to your Institute this is no longer the case.[16]

What might be the contribution of British libraries to this work of the Institute? The answer is simple and straightforward. A significant number of titles which we have identified and which we consider important to the imaginative reconstruction of our past were not published in Canada. Many cannot now be located in the country. Moreover, some 30% of our entire printed record cannot be found within Canada's borders and we can only speculate as to the number and situation of publications not yet identified. All these works are part of a cultural heritage, which we share with Great Britain. However, many of the publications are your country's unique cultural property. We ask that you will, over time, work with us and help us to identify and to locate these titles within your libraries. We request, respectfully, a sympathetic hearing when we beg leave to copy or have copied these works for return to Canada and inclusion in the national microfiche collection. We hope for a similar reception when we seek to identify and to microfilm titles that carry a Canadian imprint despite the fact that historically we had neither the will nor perhaps the opportunity to secure and to preserve copies upon publication. And finally, we request that you continue to give these publications, which we now hold dearly as works of our culture and as our contribution to the cultural heritage of all mankind, the same level of conservatorial care which you would afford your own printed heritage.

References

1 T H B Symons, *To Know Ourselves: The Report of the Commission on Canadian Studies* (Ottawa: Association of Universities and Colleges of Canada, 1975), p. 14
2 See Bertha Bassam. *The First Printers and Newspapers in Canada* (Toronto: University of Toronto School of Library Science, 1968); *Canadian Book of Printing: How Printing Came to Canada and the Story of the Graphic Arts* . . . (Toronto: Toronto Public Libraries, 1940); Aegidius Fauteux, *The introduction of Printing Into Canada* (Montreal: Rolland Paper Company Ltd, 1930); H Pearson Gundy *Early Printers and Printing in the Canadas* (Toronto: Bibliographical Society of Canada, 1964) Eric Hawarth, *Imprint of a Nation* (Toronto: Baxter Publishing, 1969)
3 H Pearson Gundy, *Book Publishing and Publishers in Canada Before 1900*. (Toronto: The Bibliographical Society of Canada, 1965), p. 1
4 H Pearson Gundy, 'The Development of Trade Book Publishing in Canada,' in *Ontario Royal Commission on Book Publishing: Background Papers* (Toronto: Queen's Printer and Publisher, 1972). pp. 4–5
5 Gundy, *Book Publishing* . . . , p. 22
6 F Dolores Donnelly, *The National Library of Canada: A Historical Analysis of the Forces which contributed to its Establishment and to the Identification of its Role and Responsibilities* (Ottawa: Canadian Library Association, 1973)
7 Patrick O'Neill and John R T Ettlinger, 'Copyright Canada 1895–1924', *Canadian Library Journal* 40 (June, 1983), pp. 143–145
8 An excellent compilation collecting many of the significant articles on preservation/conservation is *Library Conservation: Preservation in Perspective*, by John P Baker and Marguerite C Soroka (Stroudsburg, Pa: Dowden, Hutchinson & Ross, 1978)
9 M Hillman, 'A National Preservation Program for Library Materials in Canada', Ottawa, National Library of Canada, 1980
10 Joyce M Banks, 'Some Notes on Conservation in Canada,' Ottawa, National Library of Canada, 1979 (Mimeographed)
11 *University Research Libraries: Report of the Consultative Group on University Research Libraries* (Ottawa: The Canada Council, 1978), p. 1
12 *Ibid.*, p. 25
13 James E Page noted in 1980 that 29 Canadian universities had Canadian studies programmes. He pointed out, moreover, that the number would be larger if the federated colleges and universities were included in the count. For example in his figures the University of Toronto appears only once, even though there are seven different Canadian studies programmes at various colleges. See James E Page, *Reflections on the Symons Report: The State of Canadian Studies in 1980*. (Ottawa: Minister of Supply and Services, 1981), p. 128
14 Symons, *To Know Ourselves* . . . , p. 15
15 Letter, D W Halliwell to William Taylor, 4 July 1983
16 Letter, François-Marc Gagnon to Ernest B Ingles, 4 February 1983

Note on the Eighteenth-Century Short-Title Catalogue

Dr Robin Alston, Editor-in-Chief of the Eighteenth-Century Short-Title Catalogue, also spoke in this session. He said that Canada in the eighteenth century could not be studied in isolation but that the ESTC would provide a resource for students and scholars of Canadian Studies. He spoke of the contributions made to the ESTC by over 400 libraries in Canada and in the USA and by libraries in the UK, with particular reference to the Canadian material located in the Public Record Office and in the British Library Reference Division, Department of Manuscripts. He emphasized the collaborative nature of this work. The first phase of the project would culminate with the publication at the end of 1983 of *The ESTC: the British Library collections*, containing 150,000 records of BL eighteenth-century printed items, including at least 20,000 items not listed separately in the BL's General Catalogue of Printed Books.

Dr Alston provided copies of brochures and other illustrative material, including a facsimile which he had printed himself of one of the eighteenth-century printed items located in the Haldimand Papers held in the Department of Manuscripts (see PLATE SECTION.)

John M Robson

The Centre for Editing Early Canadian Texts and other projects, actual and ideal

While admitting initially that Canadian Studies is not my primary field of research, I welcome the opportunity so kindly provided by the organizers of this Colloquium to say a few words about one major project and then make some comments on other projects, in progress and potential, that have important implications for research collections in the UK.

Among the projects funded by the Social Sciences and Humanities Research Council of Canada (SSHRCC, pronounced variously 'Shirk', 'Shriek', and 'Shark', in different parts of Canada), one of particular interest to participants in this Colloquium is the Centre for the Editing of Early Canadian Texts (CEECT, pronounced 'Seekt'). With its headquarters at Carleton University in Ottawa, it is under the guidance of Professor Mary Jane Edwards (English, Carleton), as General Editor, and draws on the knowledge and talent of scholars from across the country.

The initial mandate, under a five-year grant, is to prepare an editorial manual, to hold a conference on editorial principles and procedures, and to prepare for publication a series of literary texts. The conference (to which I was pleased to contribute a talk on collating) was held in May 1983 at Carleton, and made considerable progress in raising and even settling the outstanding questions, which ranged from the minutiae of footnoting to major decisions about computer-set texts. The first group of works being prepared for publication includes Frances Brooke's *The History of Emily Montague* (1769), edited by M J Edwards (Carleton); James De Mille's *A Strange Manuscript Found in a Copper Cylinder* (1888), edited by Malcolm Parks (Dalhousie); Thomas McCulloch's *Letters of Mephibosheth Stepsure* (1821–23), edited by Douglas Lochhead (Mount Allison, but in 1983–84 Visiting Professor of Canadian Studies at Edinburgh); Susanna Moodie's *Roughing It in the Bush* (1852), edited by Carl Ballstadt (McMaster); John Richardson's *Wacousta* (1832), edited by Douglas Cronk (Vancouver); and Catharine Parr Traill's *Canadian Crusoes* (1852), edited by Rupert Schieder (Toronto).

What will be immediately evident as appropriate to our concerns at this Colloquium is that the scholarly editing of these works entails continuous and thorough use of resources in the UK. I need hardly elaborate for this audience, beyond the simple reminders that the collation of all relevant editions means finding the editions and filming or photocopying them (and then checking the actual copies, usually *in situ*), and that the biographical and other information needed for introductions and notes is more often than not to be found in British manuscript and book collections.

It will be noted that all but one of the texts in the initial group was first published in the nineteenth century, the richest in British influence in Canada. Though this is not the place for a discussion of the differences, it is appropriate just to signal that the other major contributors to Canadian life and culture, France and the United States, have had their greatest effects in other periods, and in other ways; if one were to hold similar colloquia in those countries on resources for Canadian Studies, quite markedly different issues would arise, and I would argue (here merely assert) that particularly in the case of the United States, there is less hope of finding as well as less need to find research materials south of the border. But Canada's relations with Britain, particularly in the nineteenth century, make it mandatory to follow the arrow back to the bow. There are several reasons: generally (and ideologically) one can talk of governmental benign neglect or malign attention (and too often it is forgotten that there is benign attention – as well as malign neglect), making it obligatory to look at public documents and private archives; more specifically one can discuss the emigration of people and ideas, transferred and adapted institutions, trade and armies, and all the other historical facts that demonstrate the essentiality of continuous cross-Atlantic reference.

Let me spend just a moment on the implications of this observation. Earlier in one of our discussions Dr Ged Martin mentioned that, in our concentration on Canadian *Studies*, we should not forget Canadian *studies* with a small 's'. I agree, and would go further – indeed in another context I have argued strongly that the best sense of the term encompasses all studies engaged in by Canadian scholars, and the resulting scholarship, with its strengths, weaknesses, and characteristic marks. Let me give four examples of different kinds: first, Mr Ian Willison paid rich tribute in his paper to my colleague Northrop Frye, who has had a demonstrably significant influence on the development of Canadian Studies. But he himself is a Canadian Study, and his growth into a living monument would be charted internationally – and properly – by his scholarly work on William Blake, literary theory, and the Bible, to mention only the most significant of what could hardly be less Canadian in material, formal, or final causes, though certainly Canadian in efficient cause.

Second, SSHRCC funds a team, centred in Toronto, gathering, studying, and publishing the Royal Inscriptions of Mesopotamia. This represents Canadian scholarship, linguistic and archaeological, at its very best, and while I prefer not to look at it in a narrow nationalistic way – this project could not exist if civilization in West Asia had not flourished – I am troubled when it is hinted that Canadian scholars should concentrate on native materials, and that nothing else has national significance.

Third, another colleague of mine, Professor Ian Drummond, is currently doing research at the Public Record Office on the tri-lateral trade negotiations carried on in 1937–38 among Britain, the United States, and Canada. He needs to consult, *inter alia*, papers of the Dominions Office, the Board of Trade, the Cabinet, and the Foreign Office. His work as an economic historian has focused on both Canada and the UK, but is necessarily international in its back-, middle-, and even foreground. He is a *bona fide* Canadianist (having been a visitor at the Centre in Edinburgh), but to be a *good* Canadianist he must be more, and that more includes being a researcher in Britain.

Fourth and finally, SSHRCC some years ago began funding major editorial projects in a far-sighted and generous way that has created undisguised envy in scholars elsewhere. Two of these projects are CEECT, with which I began, and the great DCB/DBC, outlined and explained in Dr Francess Halpenny's paper, both of which are Canadian in everyone's eyes; others, however, include the Records of Early English Drama (REED), the Works of Erasmus in English, the Letters of Benjamin Disraeli, the Collected Papers of Bertrand Russell (the first volume of which will have appeared by the end of 1983), and my own major labour, the Collected Works of John Stuart Mill (nineteen volumes to date, with two more in the press). It seems to me that any definition of Canadian Studies that rules out such scholarship is, at best, narrow. And, to make my practical point, research in the UK is mandatory for all these projects; my own work on Mill would be impossible without the British Library, the British Library of Political and Economic Science, the Somerville College Library, etc, etc.

I must not pursue this line of argument further, not least because attempts to define Canadian Studies have a greater tendency to anger than to enlighten. Let me instead simply mention some important areas of study that will be less contentious, as having a central and obvious focus on Canadian materials. I omit those that have been discussed during the Colloquium and those whose manifestations will be familiar to all who have attended to recent major developments. Still there is much left of great potential interest, on which little has yet been done, and on behalf of which I make a plea for the preservation, recording, and making accessible of books, manuscripts, recordings, film, and ephemera, in public and private collections alike. My list (in chance order) includes the history of the book and of publishing, the history of institutions (libraries, academies, universities, churches, and so on), law, the fine and performing arts (including cinema), architecture, folk lore, place names, communications (including radio and television), recreation, technology and science, maritime history, and – certainly not least in my mind – the history of ideas and scholarship. About each and all of these much needs to be said specifically and in general, but I have already exceeded my brief. My point is a simple one: 'the two founding nations' is a commonplace in Canadian discourse; in the context of this Colloquium we are justified in saying less about French resources (and almost nothing about the other sources of our population and culture; a second dominant commonplace in Canada is 'multi-culturalism'). But virtually all work in Canadian Studies done in English and on English-language materials is trivial without reference to sources in Britain, the home of our other 'founding nation'. No statement could emphasize more strongly the importance of the results of this Colloquium.

Richard Landon

The history of the book in Canada and British research resources

It is generally agreed that Canada has lacked many of the basic bibliographical compilations for its literature and history, although a determined effort is being made by a number of scholars to fill these lacunae. Indeed, a number of the papers presented at this Colloquium indicate the kind of scholarly enthusiasm directed towards Canadian bibliography. There is still, however, almost a total absence of adequate general works on the history of the book in Canada, including histories of printing, publishing and bookselling. One of the reasons for the neglect of these areas has been the lack of sources of precise and detailed information concerning the book trades in Canada. Fire and neglect have resulted in the destruction of most printers' and publishers' archives and most of the information concerning trade activities has to be extrapolated from the books themselves and from published bibliographies like Elizabeth Hulse's splendid *A Dictionary of Toronto Printers, Publishers, Booksellers and the Allied Trades 1798–1900* (Toronto, Anson-Cartwright Edition, 1982). The paucity of documentary records in Canada means that scholars must look elsewhere.

As this Colloquium is concerned, in part, with the examination of resources in the United Kingdom for advanced research in Canadian Studies it seems natural to ask whether records concerning the book trades in Canada exist in British archives and libraries. The answer to this general question must cetainly be a qualified 'yes', if only because of what we know about the complex arrangements between British publishers during the nineteenth and twentieth centuries and their Canadian counterparts. Many British publishers maintained Canadian branches or evolved a close relationship with a Canadian firm for the distribution of books. We know, for instance, of the curious history of the Canadian edition of Disraeli's *Endymion*, published by Dawson Bros of Montreal on 26 Nov 1880, the same day as both the British and American editions appeared.[1] The reason that Longmans had made an arrangement for simultaneous publication in Canada, apart from the expectation of some sales of the book, was a vain attempt to forestall the sale of American pirated editions in Canada. Dawsons even stationed a private detective at Windsor to uphold the recently passed Canadian law which guaranteed British authors protection against the importation of unauthorized editions of their works. The information regarding this fascinating segment of

Canadian publishing history is contained in the correpondence files of the Longman Archive and, no doubt, these files contain much else of interest to Canadian bibliographers and historians.

Another example, well known in general to interested scholars but not yet fully explored, is the Thomas Nelson & Sons Archive at the University of Edinburgh. The Methodist Book & Publishing House (later Ryerson Press) acted as the Canadian agents for Nelsons and the records of that relationship are presumably in the Nelson Archive. A detailed study of this firm, which could not be wholly conducted from Canadian sources, would provide at least an example of a typical colonial relationship and, by analogy, reveal something of this aspect of Canadian publishing history in general.

More specific questions of book trade history which arise from research in other fields might also be answered from British archival resources. I have often wondered, for instance, why there were no Canadian editions of any of the works of Charles Darwin. British editions of his books were published by John Murray and the US editions by Appletons. The Murray Archives are extensive and extant and perhaps the answer to the question might be revealed through examination of them.

I would like, in conclusion, to suggest to the members of this Colloquium that there are probably a whole series of untapped sources for the history of the book in Canada residing in the institutions of the United Kingdom. The discovery, description and exploitation of these resources promises to be exciting and important. It also adds another dimension to what we traditionally refer to as Canadian Studies.

Reference

1 Jones, Annabel. 'Disracli's *Endymion*: A Case Study' in *Essays in the History of Publishing* ed. by Asa Briggs, London, Longman, 1974, pp. 161–5

Guy Sylvestre

Concluding remarks and proposals for future cooperation

I am most happy indeed to have attended this interesting Colloquium which my friend and colleague Alex Wilson has organized and which has generated so many good papers which, in turn, have engendered such good discussion and suggestions. As a Canadian official, I am naturally grateful to the British Library for having sponsored this initiative and I trust that the role of the British Library in supporting advanced research in Canadian studies will be enhanced as a result of this exchange of views and information. The fact is that papers, suggestions and proposals should also contribute to improving Canadian studies in a number of other institutions, both Canadian and British.

As National Librarian, I am concerned with the preservation, promotion and availability of the country's library resources and services at home, but also with the promotion and diffusion of Canadian publications abroad, for national libraries, at least those which have reached a high level of development, are not only national institutions, they are also international information providers in a shrinking world where they grow increasingly interdependent in fulfilling their role.

The British Library and the National Library of Canada enjoy very close and, I feel, fruitful relations. This is not surprising between institutions from countries which have such close historical and cultural ties. I must say, however, that for generations, official cultural exchanges between our two countries were not developed enough for the simple reason that we took one another for granted. There were so many family and other unofficial ties between such large segments of our peoples that the need to institutionalize our relations was not felt on either side of the Atlantic. These ties remain and should remain strong, but our respective governments have now developed institutions and programmes in support of cultural promotion in the other country. We have heard about such initiatives during these two days. I have authority to speak on behalf of External Affairs regarding initiatives they may take with a view to promoting and expanding Canadian studies in Britain, or indeed pursuing their present programme. We have also heard interesting and encouraging reports on plans aiming to develop more comprehensive and detailed inventories of the substantial archival collections in both public and private hands in the United Kingdom relating to Canada. We all know that the Public Archives of Canada have brought home through copying methods, at first manual, now photographic, hundreds of thousands of documents related to Canada's colonial period, which is the Canadian way of resolving the so-called displaced archives problem which you, Mr Wilson, and I, have had occasion to debate in international fora. The National Library of Canada would like to pursue a similar approach related to published material.

This leads me to observe that the National Library of Canada's and the British Library's close relations to which I referred earlier are in no way restricted to English, and Scottish, studies in Canada, or to Canadian studies in the United Kingdom. They encompass almost the whole spectrum of library services, regarding which we have had useful exchanges of views for several years on a bilateral basis and which we have also contributed to improve through our parallel or concerted action at the multilateral level, both governmental and non-governmental. We are internationalists, for our respective populations include scholars, scientists and others who are interested in every discipline, in all regions of the world. This calls for encyclopaedic collections at home and for effective international information exchange mechanisms. Of course, as a result of the gradual improvement of policies, programmes and techniques, special programmes can be developed more efficiently, such as ESTC, or programmes aimed at improving specifically the acquisition, cataloguing, preservation and diffusion of Canadian materials. We now have better techniques than ever to preserve library materials either in the original or in microreproduction, to store and transmit either information about documents or the documents themselves, but we still have a long way to go before we have all items in our respective collections fully catalogued for retrieval or preserved for future generations. Library processes are labour-intensive, and there are never enough people available to do everything that could be done to satisfy increasingly numerous, sophisticated and demanding readers. But we are making progress, as was emphasized by Professor Symons, Professor Piternick and others in their papers. The fact is that we have colloquia *in Canada also* where we discuss ways and means of improving Canadian studies at home, let alone abroad. Several of you attended the conference in Halifax two years ago, where achievements and shortcomings were reviewed and discussed, and I was struck by the dedication to the development of Canadian studies abroad shown by the participants, especially those from the United Kingdom, an impression confirmed here.

In a way, this is not too surprising when one considers the wealth of Canadian resources in the United Kingdom, as recorded in Mrs Bloomfield's survey. It is gratifying to know that her excellent guide has been updated and enlarged and that the 2nd edition will be available soon. It is also gratifying to know that Dr O'Neill and Professor Ettlinger will contribute so much to the inventory of Canadian publications of diverse categories in the British Library collections, which will add to the first phase, and to later phases of the programme of the Canadian Institute for Historical Microreproductions. As pointed out by Dr O'Neill, many of the Canadian items deposited with the

British Museum Library prior to 1924 cannot be found in Canada where the copyright collection, after several peregrinations, was dispersed in 1938. Canadian publications were deposited from 1895 to 1924 with the British Museum Library. In introducing an amendment to that effect to the Copyright Act, Sir Charles Tupper made a very short statement (that was on 9 July 1895). He said: 'The amendment to the bill is simply to provide for a copy to be deposited with the British Museum in compliance with the desire of the Imperial authorities'. The record has it that several members opposed this amendment when the bill was discussed in committee, but the nationalists' views did not prevail, the amendment passed and what was considered by many at the time as a controversial provision appears in retrospect to have been a very happy one indeed, when one considers the unhappy fate of the Canadian copyright collection as a result of the carelessness and ineptitude of those responsible for it – before World War II.

Deposited at the time were also Canadian newspapers and the British Library has microfilmed several titles which have not been filmed in Canada. The National Library is buying copies, at the moment some 1,700 reels, which will enrich its collection of Canadian newspapers, the most extensive in Canada. We try to acquire as a first priority anything Canadian which is published or reprinted abroad, to complement our legal deposit collection of monographs, periodicals, sound recordings and educational kits. As indicated in Professor Piternick's paper, legal deposit has not been extended to newspapers, maps and microforms, although we buy most of the latter and we are promoting a decentralized plan for the preservation of Canadian newspapers in cooperation with provincial institutions.

There is no need for me to elaborate further on the excellent papers we have heard on the achievements and shortcomings of our domestic programmes; as to many of the shortcomings mentioned by Professor Piternick and others, we agree that something ought to be done about them, but in most cases action is postponed owing to lack of staff. Many good suggestions, I am afraid, are not likely to be acted upon until the economic situation improves, although continued pressure is to be expected from many quarters, including Professor Piternick and her committee.

I do not want to be too long, and I wish to make a few concrete suggestions regarding possible additional areas of cooperation between the British Library and the National Library of Canada especially. Before doing so, may I be allowed to correct a statement I found in one of the documents circulated to us, in which I read that Canadian theses had to be obtained from Canadian universities. This is not true, because there is a collection of Canadian dissertations at BLLD at Boston Spa, and a much more complete one at the National Library of Canada in Ottawa, from which they can be purchased on microfilm or microfiche, or even borrowed on interlibrary loan. While I am on the subject of theses, I should mention that we will publish very shortly a substantial inventory by Professor Dossick of theses on Canadian subjects accepted by British, American and Canadian universities.

It is not for me to say what UK universities, colleges and other research institutions should do with a view to improving their own programmes of Canadian studies, or their resources to support them. I am sure that they can determine their own approach, their own priorities by themselves; I am also sure that the Canadian Department of External Affairs and the granting councils will do everything in their power, and within their resources, to support these initiatives. I shall limit my observations to cooperation between the British Library and the National Library of Canada – because there is a strong tradition of cooperation between them and because it is entirely proper for national libraries to discuss cooperative schemes with their counterparts in other countries, and to attempt to achieve, whenever possible, in these cooperative schemes, as much reciprocity as possible. Although, I must say, between friendly institutions like the British Library and the National Library of Canada, we have not insisted on arrangements being always on a *quid pro quo* basis.

Here are some suggestions aiming at improving further the library support for Canadian studies in the UK. I shall refer to them under the following headings: (a) collection development, (b) lending and reference services, (c) bibliographic support, (d) conservation.

COLLECTION DEVELOPMENT

Under collection development, I would suggest, Mr Wilson, that the British Library examine the possibility of acquiring more Canadian theses, especially doctoral dissertations. I am told you buy annually some 200 out of some 3,500.

Considering that the British Library's collection of Canadian newspapers is very large for the nineteenth and early twentieth centuries, but rather small for recent and current newspapers, I would welcome discussion on the merits of exchanging microfilm copies of other important Canadian newspapers not available in the UK against UK materials, thus enriching both national collections.

There are 11 selective depository libraries for Canadian official publications, and the British Library is a full depository for federal documents. External Affairs and I have reviewed the list of selective depositories abroad and I am optimistic about the possibility of reinstating depository status to libraries which regretfully lost it at the time when the budget of the Publishing Centre was cut by more than £1,000,000 five years ago.*

We would also like to examine the possibility of obtaining copies of recordings from the National Sound Archive's collection, of Canadian material not available in Canada – such as, for instance, the Atwood readings and lectures referred to this morning. This would not contribute to improving

*Mr Hellyer of Canada House then announced that this has been done.

Canadian resources here, unless the National Sound Archive would like to obtain some Canadian material in payment, rather than hard cash.

Finally, we know that the British Library is acquiring the Canadian Institute for Historical Microreproductions file, so that it is available in the UK. Owing to the fact that it is inexpensive and easy of access due to the accompanying catalogue, we hope that this important collection of early publications would be acquired also by other libraries, especially in universities where there are significant Canadian studies programmes, if not *in toto*, at least some segments – it is available in segments – directly related to the subjects taught.

LENDING AND REFERENCE SERVICES

I have asked Hope Clement to discuss with Alex Wilson ways in which we could cooperate effectively in handling difficult reference questions related to the UK and to Canada respectively, that is, having some kind of referral policy as appropriate.

BIBLIOGRAPHIC SUPPORT

Now, as to bibliographic tools, may I suggest that the British Library look into the desirability of mounting the CANMARC tapes on BLAISE, which would be advantageous to many in selecting, cataloguing and using Canadian materials, as the UK bibliographic network develops and the data base can be queried on line. We have the UK MARC tapes, we use them and we make the British Library records available to Canadian libraries on demand. A similar programme in the UK would, it seems, be a significant enhancement of bibliographic support for Canadian studies. I also feel that, for the same reasons, the British Library may wish to investigate mounting the CIHM records, as well as the National Library's RETRO files. Conversely, we participate in ESTC, and this includes Canadian titles too.

CONSERVATION

Finally, in the area of conservation, CIHM is an important contribution to the conservation and availability of pre-1900 Canadian books and pamphlets – that is Phase 1 – and we hope that the next phases will be financially supported also and cover pre-1900 periodicals, and then post-1900 materials. I know that Mr Ingles will be discussing with the British Library the filming of those items located by Dr O'Neill and Professor Ettlinger – whose contribution is indeed a major one – which fall within the parameters of the collection, as well as other items preceding the deposit collection. I am sure that the cooperation of the British Library will be forthcoming in support of this important Canadian initiative. I wish to add that the National Library of Canada is also interested in having the British Library film those items – and there are a great many – which would not fall within the CIHM programme. Once filmed, this material would be more readily available on both sides of the pond.

There may be other suggestions regarding cooperative initiatives in support of Canadian studies in the United Kingdom and my Canadian colleagues and I would be happy to hear them from the floor.

Dr O'Neill gave us this morning a rather devastating account of the way in which we mismanaged the copyright collection in Canada, and it is a blessing that so much that we neglected to keep should still be available thanks to the enlightened attitude of the British Museum Library staff.

Of course, we think that we are better today and the material received under legal deposit is kept by the National Library of Canada. That we should have made so much progress in so little time with respect to our attitude towards books is evidenced by the fact that, when Canada celebrated the centenary of the Confederation in 1967 and was asked by the British authorities what she would like to receive as a birthday gift, the answer was: a collection of books for the National Library of Canada which would be moving into its own building that year. This is what we still refer to as the British Book Gift – worth at the time £100,000 and supplemented by Henry Moore's *Three Way Piece* which is the principal ornament of the main foyer. We owe much indeed to British generosity.

* * *

In concluding, let me say once again how happy my Canadian colleagues and I are at this British Library initiative which, from our point of view, is a success indeed. We learned a good deal about Canadian studies here, about Canadian library and archival resources at the British Library and elsewhere, and I trust that the suggestions made by both scholars and librarians will be given every attention on both sides of the ocean and that we can look forward to even better and closer cooperation in the years ahead than the high degree already achieved of which this Colloquium is an eloquent manifestation.

List of British Library items exhibited: books

HENRY STEVENS (1819–1886)
Catalogue of Canadian Books in the Library of the British Museum Christmas 1856 . . . by Henry Stevens. London: Printed by Charles Whittingham for Henry Stevens, 1859. 11903. dd. 9(2).

Henry Stevens, who described himself as 'a bibliographer and lover of books', was employed by Panizzi as the Library's agent for North American material. This is the first catalogue of the Library's holdings of Canadian material.

JACQUES CARTIER (1491–1557)
Brief recit, & succincte narration, de la navigation faicte es ysles de Canada . . . Paris: P Roffet and A. Le Clerc, 1545. Grenville 7082.

Cartier reached Newfoundland, the coasts of Labrador and the St Lawrence river in 1534. He made two more expeditions, the last being in 1541. This book was possibly written by Jehan Poullet rather than by Cartier himself.

One of only three copies known. Sabin 11138. Alden 545/8.

SAMUEL DE CHAMPLAIN (1567–1635)
Des Sauvages, ou, Voyage . . . fait en la France nouvelle, l'an mil six cens trois. Paris: C. De Monstr'oeil [1603]. Grenville 7268.

Champlain made his first voyage to Canada in 1603. He founded Quebec in 1608 and subsequently became the first Governor of French Canada.

The first and last leaves of this book were stolen in July 1972 and subsequently recovered by the police. Sabin 11834. Alden 603/23.

ROBERT HAYMAN (1575–1629)
Quodlibets, lately come over from New Britaniola, old Newfoundland . . . London: Elizabeth Allde, for R Michell, 1628. C34.f.15.

'Probably the first book of original English verse written on the North American continent' (Klinck) Sabin 31036–37. Alden 628/55.

The Order for Morning and Evening Prayer, and Administration of the Sacraments . . ./ Ne Yakawea Niyadewighniserage Yondereanayendakhkwa Orhoenkéne neoni Yogarask-ha Oghseragwegouh . . . The Third Edition . . . published by order of His Excellency Frederick Haldimand . . . revised with corrections and additions by Daniel Claus. 1780. 3408.bb.23.

This was printed at Quebec by William Brown. It was prepared for the Mohawks who had moved from upper New York into Canada during the American Revolution, and, together with Claus' primer, succeeded in strengthening English influence among the Indians. Sabin 57489. Tremaine 335.

DANIEL CLAUS (1727–1787)
A Primer for the use of the Mohawk Children . . ./Waerighwaghsawe Iksaongoenwa Tsiwaondad – derighhonny Kaghyadoghsera . . . Montreal: printed at Fleury Mesplets, 1781. Grenville 16708.

14

The text was supervised by Daniel Claus, deputy superintendent of Indians in Canada, 1760–1787. The book was printed in Mesplet's shop but not under his personal supervision. Sabin 65547. Tremaine 355.

SIR FREDERICK HALDIMAND (1718–1791) Governor of Quebec 1778–1786.
These four items are from a volume of the Collection of Haldimand Papers held in the Department of Manuscripts (BL Add. MS 21880).
(a) ff. 178–9: a proclamation to the Calumet signed by Sir Frederick Haldimand, August 1778. Not in Tremaine.
(b) ff. 185–6: *Quebec, February 3, 1779. Every able-bodied Seaman/Quebec, ce 3 Febrier 1779. Tous bon Matelots*... Probably printed at Quebec by William Brown, 1779. Tremaine 327.
(c) ff. 189–90: *Instructions pour les voyageurs*... Printed at Quebec by William Brown, 1779. This sets out the Government's regulations for fur-traders. Tremaine 321.
(d) ff. 197–8: *A translation of His Excellency General Haldimand's speech to the Oneida Indians in the rebel interest, as delivered to them in the Iroquois Language / Goragh Asharegowa Raoweana tekawenadennion Tyoghtyaky nonwe yeghsagodadigh Oneayotronon.*
Printed at Quebec by William Brown, 1779. The Oneidas, alone of the six Iroquois nations, 'deserted the King's Cause' and supported the rebel American colonists in the American Revolution. Haldimand reiterates the advantages of the King's Bounty and urges the Oneidas to repent for their past 'vile actions'. Tremaine 325.

FRANCES BROOKE (née Moore) (1724–1789)
The History of Emily Montague. London: printed for J Dodsley, 1769. 4 volumes. 12614.ee.6.
Emily Montague may truly claim to be 'the earliest Canadian novel – and, indeed, the earliest novel emanating from the North American continent' – (Klinck). Although published in England, it was written in Canada and most of its action takes place in a Canadian setting. The novel is dedicated to His Excellency Guy Carleton, Governor and Commander in Chief of the Province of Quebec.

CHARLES TAYLOR (–1816), Secretary to the Society for the encouragement of Arts, 1800–1816.
Remarks on the culture and preparation of hemp, in Canada... by Charles Taylor/Remarques sur la culture et la preparation du chanvre en Canada...
Quebec: printed by John Neilson, 1806. 7075.c.51.
Hemp was required for ropemaking and other purposes in the important Canadian ship-building industry; if it could be successfully cultivated within the country according to the guidelines set out in this book, this would obviate the need to import it and could also lead to a flourishing export trade from Canada to England.
Not in Bibliography of Canadiana. Not in NUC. Not in Sabin.

JOHN RICHARDSON (1796–1852)
Kensington Gardens in 1830 ...by the author of Écarté. London: Marsh and Miller, 1830. 11601. dd 7(6).
This was published two years before Richardson's masterpiece *Wacousta*, and is one of the rarest of all Canadiana. This is the only copy located in W F E Morley's bibliography of Richardson.

SARA JEANNETTE DUNCAN (Mrs Everard Cotes) (1862–1922).
His Honor and a Lady. London & New York: Macmillan & Co, 1896. 012627. h.50.

His Honour, and a Lady. Toronto: G M Rose & Sons, 1896. 012624.de.3.
Two editions of the same work, one published in London and New York and received in May 1896 by copyright deposit and the other published in Toronto and received in September 1896 by colonial copyright. There are some textual variants and differing numbers of illustrations.

Journals of the Legislative Assembly of the Province of Canada . . . 1841. Volume 1. [Kingston: printed by Desbarats & Cary, 1842]. C.S.E. 42.
This records the first session of the first Provincial Parliament of Canada. Following the recommendations made by Lord Durham in his Report of 1839, the Provinces of Upper and Lower Canada were united by an Act passed in July 1840. This Act came into effect in the following year and the Parliament first met at Kingston, Ontario on 14 June 1841, with members from 81 constituencies under the Premiership of John A MacDonald.

Census of the Three Provisional Districts of the North-West Territories 1884–5. Ottawa: printed by Maclean, Roger & Co, 1886. C.S.E. 9/16
The three districts surveyed were Assiniboia, Saskatchewan and Alberta. There were five enumeration schedules:
I. *Nominal return of the living.* 19 columns for the insertion of answers on such subjects as name, residence, profession, religion and so forth
II. *Public Institutions and Industrial Establishments.* 20 columns
III. *Cultivated Lands, Field Products.* 26 columns
IV. *Live Stock, Animal Products, Fur-bearing Animals and Pelts.* 30 columns
V. *Fisheries, Products of the Forest, Minerals and Prairie Lands.* 25 columns

Official Programme of the 300th Anniversary of the Founding of Quebec by Champlain, July 20th to July 31st 1908. Issued under the direction of the National Battlefields Commission by the Cambridge Corporation, Ltd, Montreal. 010470.i.12.

The King's Book of Quebec. 2 volumes. Ottawa: The Mortimer Co Ltd, 1911. 10470.p.7.
This book was dedicated 'to his most gracious Majesty King George V who as Prince of Wales crossed the Ocean to render homage to the memory of the Founder of Quebec'.
The text shown describes the pageant in the panoramic photograph displayed.

EDWIN JOHN PRATT (1883–1964)
Of these first five commercially published books of Pratt's verse, the last three illustrate the 'North Atlantic publishing triangle'. Published by Macmillan in London, Toronto and New York respectively, they were all three received by copyright deposit.
Newfoundland Verse. Toronto: Ryerson Press, [1923]. 011686.e.75. Received by colonial copyright June 1923
The Witches' Brew. London: Selwyn & Blount, [1925]. 011645.g.72. Received by copyright February 1926
Titans. London: Macmillan & Co Ltd, 1926. 011645.h.80. Received by copyright December 1926
The Iron Door. Toronto: The Macmillan Company of Canada Limited, 1927. 011686.aa.13. Received by copyright December 1927

The Roosevelt and the Antinoe. New York: The Macmillan Company, 1930. 011686.cc.4. Received by copyright June 1930

GABRIELLE ROY (Mme Marcel Carbotte) (1909–1983)
Bonheur d'occasion. Montréal: Société des Editions Pascal, 1945. 2 tom. X.908/11252.

The first work of this major Quebec novelist, who died recently. This was among the items donated by the Quebec Delegation in Paris.

Whale Sound: an anthology of poems about whales and dolphins. Edited by Greg Gatenby. Toronto: Dreadnaught Press, 1977. Cup. 407.mm.25.

One of a limited edition of 100 copies, on hand-made paper, this is an impressive work, distinguished by the splendour of its conception and the excellence of its execution and presentation. Most of the 56 poets represented here wrote their contributions especially for this anthology. The text shown features two well-known Canadian poets, the prolific Irving Layton (1912–), originally associated with the Montreal movement of the 1940s and Jay Macpherson (1931–) a master of intricate styles. The illustration on the left is by Ken Danby; the coin shown on the right is a silver didrachm of Tarentum in southern Italy of the third century BC, depicting the eponymous Taras, son of Poseidon, riding his father's dolphin.

List of British Library items exhibited: maps

1 MAP OF CANADA 1592
Nova Francia, alio nomine dicta Terra Nova, anno 1504 a Britonibus primum detecta . . . [Amsterdam, Cornelius Claesz, c 1592.]. Maps C.2.a.3.
   By the Dutch cartographer Peter Plancius; engraved by Johannes van Doetechum.
   A rare map showing Canada, Labrador, Greenland and the western coasts of Europe; and marking the discoveries of Martina Frobisher (1576–78) and John Davis (1585–87) made in search of the North-west Passage to Asia. An inset depicts the whale fisheries off the coasts of Canada.
   A facsimile was published in 1928 in *Six Early Printed Maps selected from those exhibited at the British Museum on the occasion of the International Geographical Congress 1928*. London, British Museum, 1928.

2 MAP OF NOVA SCOTIA AND CAPE BRITAIN 1735
A New Map of Nova Scotia, and Cape Britain, with the adjacent parts of New England and Canada, Composed from a great number of actual surveys . . . with An Explanation.
   May 1755. Published according to Act of Parliament by Thos. Jefferys Geographer to His Royal Highness the Prince of Wales at the Corner of St Martins Lane, Charing Cross, London. Maps 184.i.3.(8.).
   A label pasted on the map reports on the 'French Incroachments and extensive Claims', which are coloured yellow.
   The author of the map and accompanying *Explanations* has been identified as the geographer John Green (previously Bradock Mead). This is the first state of the map which in this particular copy illustrates the claims made by the French Commissioners negotiating with Great Britain over the boundaries of Nova Scotia. The map was reissued up to 1794 in a series of revised versions and with different territorial colourings. It ranks as one of the most important maps documenting the political vicissitudes of the region in the period covering the Seven Years War (the French and Indian War) and the American War of Independence.

Explanation for the New Map of Nova Scotia, London, 1755. Maps C.27.c.1.
   John Green sets out his sources in detail, comparing other maps with their various alleged shortcomings, and in conclusion discussing Great Britain's territorial claims.

3 PLAN OF QUEBEC, 1720
Plan de la Ville de Quebec. Designé d'après le Plan en Relief que Monsieur de Chaussegros de Leris, Ingéneur en Chef, envoya en France en l'année 1720 pour etre mis au Louvre avec les autres . . . fidellement copié. MS.K.Top.CXIX.32.
   King George III's Topographical Collection was presented to the British Museum in 1828. The four guard volumes of K.Top.CXIX, together with large plans on rolls and other items, cover the main part of what is now Canada. Other items are in K.Top.XCCI, classified as the 'State of New York'.

4 THE HARBOUR OF HALIFAX, 1759
A chart of the harbour of Halifax in Nova Scotia; with Jebucto Bay and Cape Sambrô
. . . Survey'd . . . By C Morris, Chief Surveyor, 1759. London: T Jefferys, 1759.
K.Mar.VII.18.

5 MAP OF UPPER CANADA c 1795
Sketch of Upper Canada. Pen and wash on birchbark. Drawn by Mrs Elizabeth
Posthuma Simcoe. K.Top.CXIX.15.A.2.

When John Graves Simcoe, appointed Lieutenant-Governor of Upper Canada in 1791, travelled round the new province in 1792–95 his wife Elizabeth (who claimed 'the picturesque eye') accompanied him and drew on birchbark sketches of the scenes observed. Her map of Upper Canada shows the proposed new towns and military roads.

6 BIRCHBARK INDIAN MAP c 1841
Annotated: 'Map drawn by Indians on birch-bark and attached to a tree to shew their route to others following them, found by Capt. Bainbrigge RL. Engineers at the 'ridge' between the Ottawa and Lake Huron May 1841.' Map Library RUSI Misc.1.

A redrawing is added below with a note that it is forwarded to the United Service Institution in the hope that it may be regarded as an example to young engineers in their early efforts at surveying.

7 PHOTOGRAPHIC VIEW OF TORONTO 1903
'Panorama of Toronto'. Entered according to Act of Parliament of Canada in the year 1903 by Mr T Freeland at the Department of Agriculture. Map Library 70646.(55). sh.1, 3, 4.

8 PHOTOGRAPHIC VIEWS OF TORONTO 1906
Toronto from the roof of the Traders Bank Building. Illustrations from photographs taken August 6 (Civic holiday) by the Globe's photographer through the courtesy of the president of the Traders Bank and for the exclusive use of the Globe Magazine. The Globe, Toronto, Saturday 18 August 1906. (Entered according to Act of Parliament at the Department of Agriculture, Ottawa, 1906, by the Globe Printing Company, Toronto.) Map Library 70646.(18.).

An example of the many photographic views of Canada deposited under Colonial Copyright between 1895 and 1924.

9 INSURANCE PLAN OF THE CITY OF TORONTO 1909
Insurance plan of the City of Toronto, Ontario, Canada. Chas E Goad, Civil Engineer. Toronto & Montreal & London Eng.
Volume One. March 1909. Maps 147.b.21.(1).
Scale of plans 50ft=1 inch.

Open at sheet 28, covering the area of City Hall south to Adelaide west. Deposited under Colonial Copyright. Charles E Goad, Civil Engineer of Montreal, was the British pioneer in Fire Insurance mapping. The firm was producing fire insurance plans in Canada from 1875 to 1917, when the rights for Canadian fire insurance plans were handed over to the Insurers Advisory Association. This firm ceased publication in 1975.

10 CANADA 1:50,000
Dunnville, Ontario.
Edition 5, Ottawa, Surveys and Mapping Branch, Department of Energy, Mines and Resources, 1977. Map Library 70615.(96.).

The Map Library has regularly received the official series mapping of Canada. Listed as a 'Partial Depository' up to 1969, we were re-scheduled as a 'Full Depository' in March 1969, receiving henceforward maps of the National Topographic System of Canada at all scales. In addition we receive all thematic maps for sale to the public, all atlas maps, all military city plans with indexes. Monthly lists of 'New and revised maps' are received, together with the map catalogue (on fiche) issued by the Surveys and Mapping Branch.

List of British Library items exhibited: philatelic material

All this material was from the Tapling and Fitzgerald Collections. It included: British Columbia: Vancouver Island: 1865 (19 Sept) Imperforate 5c rose, unused, two copies. Canada: a range of 'Pence Issues' including 1851 Imperforate, Laid paper, 12d black, an unused horizontal pair. New Brunswick: 1851 (5 Sept) blue paper, Imperforate, 1/- mauve, six unused copies, shewing shades. Newfoundland: 1857 (1 Jan) No Watermark, thick paper, Imperforate, 2d scarlet-vermilion, four copies, 6d scarlet-vermilion, an unused example, 1/- scarlet-vermilion, four unused copies; A selection of Airmails with 1919 (12 April) 3c brown, a copy on cover, carried by Mr Hawker on his Atlantic flight. Nova Scotia: 1851 (1 Sept)–57 Bluish paper, Imperforate, 1d red-brown, seven unused examples, 6d green, seven unused and two used; 1/- violet or purple, six unused and two used. Prince Edward Island: 1861 (1 Jan) Perforated 9, values to 6d, Rouletted 2d rose, an unused copy.

List of British Library items exhibited: photographs

The description of the photograph, the name of the photographer, the copyright number and the date and place of registration are taken from the British Museum Canadian Copyright Lists.

1 SHRINERS' EXCURSION TO KING SOLOMON'S DOME. AUG. 4, 1910
Erling Olav Ellingsen
19×23.5 cm
23019 30.9.1910 Dawson, Yukon Territory.

2 FROM AUSTRIA TO ALBERTA
Mariam Elstor
14×8.5 cm
23665 2.3.1911 Edmonton, Alberta

3 RUTHENIAN WOMAN IN BEST ATTIRE
Miriam Elstor
14×8.5 cm
23671 2.3.1911 Edmonton, Alberta

4 HAULING SPUD WEIGHING TWENTY-SEVEN TONS TO BEAR CREEK FOR THE CANADIAN KLONDIKE MINING COMPANY'S DREDGE, THE LARGEST IN THE WORLD
Erling Olav Ellingsen
18.5×23.5 cm
23020 30.9.1910 Dawson, Yukon Territory

5 THE DOUKHOBOR PILGRIMS CARRYING THEIR HELPLESS
Thomas Veitch Simpson
10×12.5 cm
13520 21.11.1902 Yorkton, Assiniboia

6 THE DOUKHOBORS REFUSE TO RETURN TO THEIR VILLAGES
Thomas Veitch Simpson
10×12.5 cm
13522 21.11.1902 Yorkton, Assiniboia

7 HOMESTEADERS TREKKING FROM MOOSE JAW, SASKATCHEWAN
Lewis Rice
16.5×22 cm
20797 10.4.1909 Moose Jaw, Saskatchewan

8 JOHN BARAN'S HOUSE
Howard Henry Allen
20.5×25.5 cm
26809 26.2.1913 Dauphin, Manitoba

9 PORCUPINE'S LADY PROSPECTOR
Henry Peters
15×20 cm
24373 15.9.1911 Golden City, Ontario

10 TYPICAL GALICIAN HOME, ALBERTA
Miriam Elstor
8×13.5 cm
23664 2.3.1911 Edmonton, Alberta

11 RUTHENIAN SETTLER BREAKING THE SOD IN ALBERTA
Miriam Elstor
8×13.5 cm
23669 2.3.1911 Edmonton, Alberta

12 THE HONOURABLE SIR WILFRID LAURIER
W J Topley
13.5×9.5 cm
16876 17.2.1906 Ottawa, Ontario

13 FLOATING CLOUD, A YORKTON INDIAN
Thomas Veitch Simpson
12.5×10.5 cm
14628 5.1.1904 Yorkton, Assiniboia

14 MARY PICKFORD
F G Goodenough
14.5×9.5 cm
40607 4.10.1922 Victoria, British Columbia

15 THE OLD VOYAGEUR
John W Bald
14×10 cm
12512 9.10.1901 Midland, Ontario

16 THE THREE CARDINALS
William Notman and Son
19.5×22.5 cm
23100 17.10.1910 Montréal, Québec

17 CHIEF DUCKHUNTER
A W Gelston
16×11 cm
27759 6.10.1913 Victoria, British Columbia

18 T. LONGBOAT, THE CANADIAN RUNNER
Charles A Aylett
14×10 cm
18314 22.4.1907 Toronto, Ontario

19 PRESENTING THE CALUMET TO THE GREAT SPIRIT BY CHIEF SKEET
William S Piper
12×18 cm
37728 18.8.1920 Fort William, Ontario

20 TSIMPSIAN TRIBE
Edwards Brothers
18×23.5 cm
11581   9.8.1900   Vancouver, British Columbia

21 LIEUT. SOUSA AND INDIANS
Howard Henry Allen
19×24 cm
36074   29.8.1919   Brandon, Manitoba

22 CHEF ET DES SOUS-CHEFS DE LA TRIBU HURONNE DE LORETTE
J Alphonse Boivin
9×15 cm
319F   12.10.1921   Loretteville, Québec

23 MEDICINE LODGES, BLACKFOOT INDIANS
The Consolidated Stationery Company, Limited
9.5×12.5 cm
18742   11.9.1907   Winnipeg, Manitoba

24 DRYING FISH
C G Linde
12×17 cm
26193   2.11.1912   Kenora, Ontario

25 GROUP OF ESKIMO WOMEN AND CHILDREN. FULLERTON, 1906
Geraldine Moodie
16×11.5 cm
18546   8.7.1907   Churchill, Hudson's Bay

26 A COLLECTION OF INDIANS AND ESKIMOS OF HUDSON'S BAY
A A Chesterfield
18.5×16 cm
17768   10.11.1906   Montréal, Québec

27 RAISING THE CENTRE POLE, SUNDANCE TENT
Geraldine Moodie
17×22.5 cm
10661   24.6.1899   Lakefield, Ontario

28 DAWSON BY THE LIGHT OF THE AURORA BOREALIS
Jerry Doody and M H Craig
18.5×24 cm
19199   23.1.1908   Dawson, Yukon Territory

29 LAKE ADOLPHUS
Byron Harmon
9×29 cm
24778   9.12.1911   Banff, Alberta

30 THE BEACH KELOWNA LOOKING TOWARDS THE GRANDSTAND AND AQUATIC BUILDING
G H E Hudson
19×24 cm
23409   28.12.1910   Kelowna, British Columbia

31 PRAIRIE VALLEY, SUMMERLAND, BRITISH COLUMBIA
G H E Hudson
24.5×15.5 cm
21793 29.12.1909 Kelowna, British Columbia

32 TRANSFERRING REAL ESTATE IN NOVA SCOTIA
William Herbert Perry
8.5×12.5 cm
27387 24.7.1913 Hebron, Nova Scotia

33 PREMIER FALLS
Byron Harmon
29×9 cm
24776 9.12.1911 Banff, Alberta

34 CATTLE ROUND UP, BIG VALLEY, NEAR STETTLER, ALBERTA
Reynolds and Unwin
22×15 cm
23715 14.3.1911 Stettler, Alberta

35 BREAKING NEAR MOOSE JAW, SASKATCHEWAN
Lewis Rice
16.5×22 cm
20796 10.4.1909 Moose Jaw, Saskatchewan

36 TOBOGGANING PARK SLIDE
William Notman and Son
18×24 cm
22084 4.3.1910 Montréal, Québec

37 OLD FRENCH HOUSE OWNED BY P CAMPBELL, SITUATED ON ST LOUIS STREET CITY OF QUÉBEC, AND SINCE DEMOLISHED, AND THE SITE OF THE PRESENT NUMBER 47 ST LOUIS STREET, QUÉBEC
Frederick Christian Wurtele
10×15.5 cm
12669 19.12.1901 Québec, Québec

38 SPARKS STREET SKY LINE, OTTAWA
William Thomson Freeland
1.5×11.5 cm
26849 7.3.1913 Toronto, Ontario

39 THE KNAPP ROLLER BOAT AND ITS INVENTOR
William Thomson Freeland
19×21 cm
9773 28.2.1898 Toronto, Ontario

40 MONSTERS OF THE DEEP. RIVER JOHN, 1918
Edwin Clay Blair
11.5×16.5 cm
34529 31.8.1918 Stewiacke, Nova Scotia

41 MONSTERS OF THE DEEP. CAST ASHORE AT RIVER JOHN, N.S., 1918
Edwin Clay Blair
11.5×16.5 cm
34530 31.8.1918 Stewiacke, Nova Scotia

42 AT RIVER JOHN, N.S., AUGUST 1918
Edwin Clay Blair
11×16.5 cm
34532 31.8.1918 Stewiacke, Nova Scotia

43 'SECOND PAGEANT: CHAMPLAIN RECEIVES HIS COMMISSION FROM HENRY IV, QUÉBEC'S TERCENTENARY, 1908'
H O Dodge
18×96 cm
19811 10.8.1908 Sydney, Nova Scotia

44 ICE CAVE ILLECILLEWAET GLACIER. (A) Stereoscopic Photos
Byron Harmon
8×15 cm
19328 11.3.1908 Banff, Alberta

45 ICE CAVE ILLECILLEWAET GLACIER. (B) Stereoscopic Photos
Byron Harmon
8×15 cm
19329 11.3.1908 Banff, Alberta

46 ICE CAVE ILLECILLEWAET GLACIER (C) Stereoscopic Photos
Byron Harmon
8×15 cm
19330 11.3.1908 Banff, Alberta

47 MR AND MRS TURTLEDOVE'S NEW FRENCH COOK. 'NOW DON'T BE SO SHY'. Stereoscopic Photos
Arthur Lawrence Merrill
8×16 cm
17212 18.5.1906 Toronto, Ontario

48 MR AND MRS TURTLEDOVE'S NEW FRENCH COOK. 'SH! SH! I HEAR MY WIFE COMING'.
Stereoscopic Photos
Arthur Lawrence Merrill
8×16 cm
17214 18.5.1906 Toronto, Ontario

49 MR AND MRS TURTLEDOVE'S NEW FRENCH COOK. 'HEAVENS! WHAT DOES SHE MEAN?'
Stereoscopic Photos
Arthur Lawrence Merrill
8×16 cm
17215 18.5.1906 Toronto, Ontario

50 MR AND MRS TURTLEDOVE'S NEW FRENCH COOK. 'WELL, I AM CAUGHT SURE ENOUGH'.
Stereoscopic Photos
Arthur Lawrence Merrill
8×16 cm
17216 18.5.1906 Toronto, Ontario

51 MUNITIONS WORKER MAKING SHELLS
Stone Limited
23×19 cm
30568 3.8.1915 Toronto, Ontario

52 INSPECTION BY THE KING (GEORGE V) OF THE CANADIAN TROOPS ON SALISBURY PLAIN
Goodwins, Limited
10.5×17 cm
32782 10.4.1917 Montréal, Québec